*To Sheila
With love & blessings
Patricia ♡*

# CARRIED
## *on*
# SPIRIT
# WINGS

*In memory of Andrew*

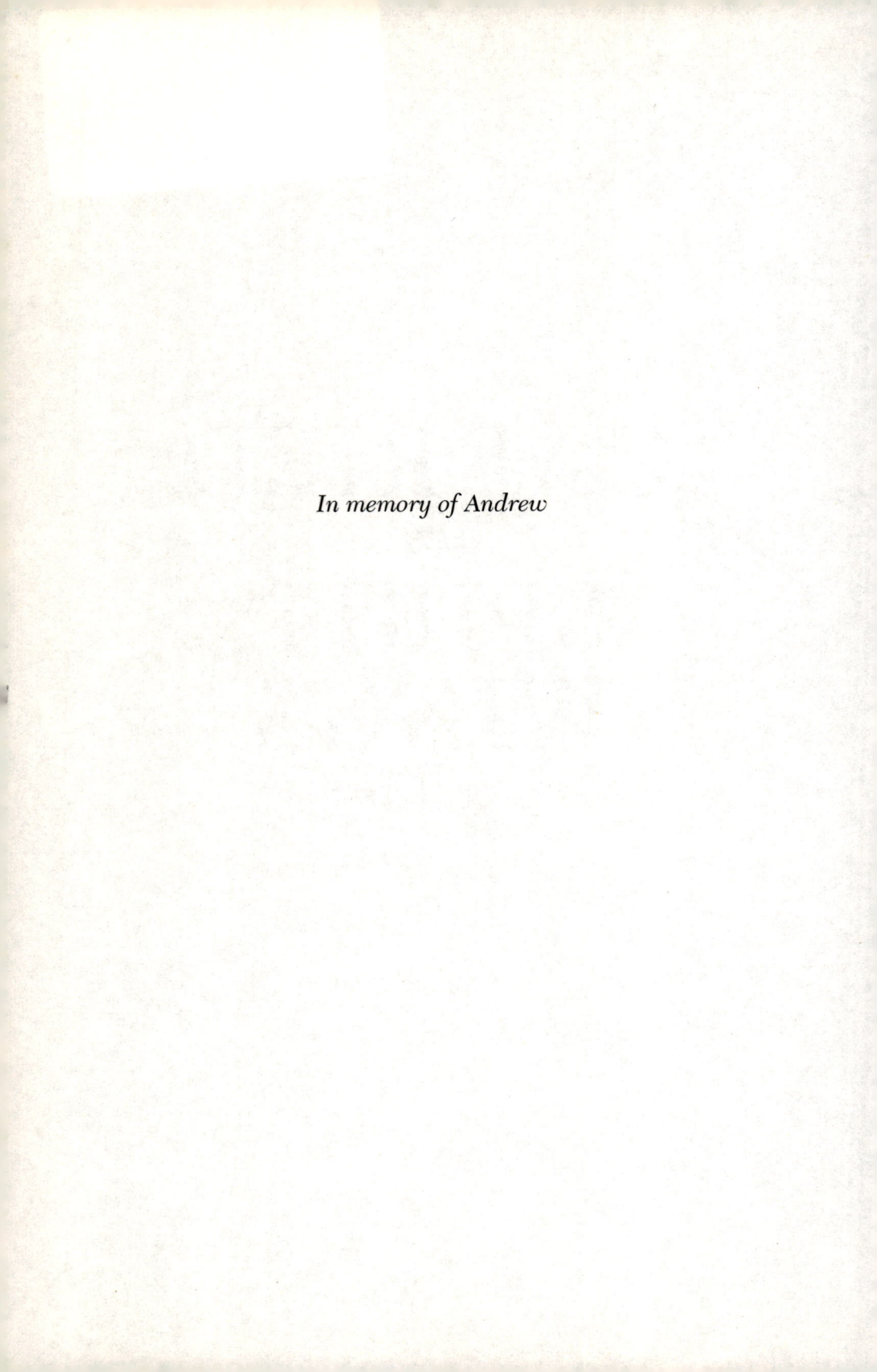

## ANN MARIA DUNNE

**A Journey Through Darkness to Light**

# CARRIED
*on*
# SPIRIT WINGS

First published in 2021 by
Ann Maria Dunne
Co. Wicklow
Ireland

Copyright © 2021 Ann Maria Dunne

| Paperback | ISBN: 978-1-78846-186-3 |
| Ebook – Mobi format | ISBN: 978-1-78846-188-7 |
| Ebook – ePub format | ISBN: 978-1-78846-187-0 |
| Amazon paperback | ISBN: 978-1-78846-189-4 |

All rights reserved. No part of this book may be reproduced or utilised in any form or by any means electronic or mechanical, including photocopying, filming, recording, video recording, photography, or by any information storage and retrieval system, nor shall by way of trade or otherwise be lent, resold or otherwise circulated in any form of binding or cover other than that in which it is published without prior permission in writing from the author.

The right of Ann Maria Dunne to be identified as the author of the work has been asserted by her in accordance with the Copyright, Designs and Patents Act 1988.

The publishers has made every reasonable effort to contact the copyright holders of poetry reproduced in this book. If any involuntary infringement of copyright has occurred, sincere apologies are offered and the owner of such copyright is requested to contact the publisher.

A CIP catalogue record for this book is
available from the British Library

We support sustainable forest management by printing this book on materials made from wood that comes from responsible sources and reclaimed material.

Produced by Kazoo Independent Publishing Services
222 Beech Park, Lucan, Co. Dublin
www.kazoopublishing.com

Kazoo Independent Publishing Services is not the publisher of this work. All rights and responsibilities pertaining to this work remain with Ann Maria Dunne.

Co-author and edited by Kathryn Rogers
Cover artwork by Emily Doyle
Cover design by Andrew Brown

Printed in the EU

# CONTENTS

| | |
|---|---|
| Prologue | ix |
| *Early Days* | 15 |
| *Growing Up* | 30 |
| *Andrew* | 42 |
| *Mother* | 50 |
| *Marriage* | 58 |
| *The Omen* | 68 |
| *Death* | 78 |
| *The Fog* | 89 |
| *The Quest* | 99 |
| *Poustinia* | 110 |
| *To Love Again* | 119 |
| *Mystical India* | 131 |
| *Awakening* | 142 |
| *Chrysalis* | 152 |
| *Healing Stories from Chrysalis* | 166 |
| *Peter* | 191 |
| *The Monk* | 200 |
| *Cancer* | 215 |

| | |
|---|---|
| *Endings* | 229 |
| *The Recurrence* | 244 |
| *The Wish List* | 252 |
| *Mindfulness* | 260 |
| *Death* | 267 |
| Acknowledgements | 278 |
| Author Biography | 281 |

# The True Meaning of Life

### The Dalai Lama

*We are visitors on this planet.
We are here for ninety or one hundred years at the very most.
During that period, we must try to do something good,
something useful with our lives.
If you contribute to other people's happiness,
you will find the true goal, the true meaning of life.*

# PROLOGUE

The little girl gripped a blue crayon in her chubby fist as she coloured in the outline of the sun. The tip of her tongue protruded between her lips as she carefully filled in the page of her colouring book. She was so absorbed that she barely heard her mother move about the kitchen, and outside the window, she missed the sight of her father pulling his black Ford sedan into the drive.

The child only raised her head from her task when she heard the click of the front door shutting and her father's footsteps in the hall. Her face lit up in a big smile as her father's hand curled around the door jamb, and he stood swaying slightly in the open doorway to the lounge.

'Dadda!' the child cried, lifting her hands and waving a crayon in excitement. The man's collar was tugged open, his navy tie askew, and he carried his suit jacket bundled over the briefcase in his hand.

His grey-tinged face softened at the sight of his golden-haired child, but his smile was faint. The little girl didn't see the salty droplets of sweat flowing down his face or the spreading map of dark perspiration on his white shirt as she clambered down from the dining room chair.

She didn't understand the grimace that passed over his face or his limping gait as he took a step into the room.

Before she could reach him, he dropped heavily to his knees, his jacket and briefcase careering to one side, a single rasping breath on his lips. Then she saw him keel forward onto the tufted carpet below.

The little girl was uneasy, but she took a hesitant step towards her father. She reached down and patted his wispy hair.

'Dadda?' she said, but the man didn't stir. 'Wake, Dadda!'

She tugged on the hem of her cotton dress and waited, but still, Dadda didn't move. She heard the clock ticking on the mantelpiece and strains of muted music from the wireless in the kitchen.

She grew anxious and glanced towards the door.

'Mamma?' she called, but all she heard was the clang of a pan on the stove, and music from the radio.

The child's chin wobbled, and her eyes filled with tears.

'Mamma!' she cried, more insistent, louder this time.

She stared at her father, desperate for any sign of movement, but he continued to lie before her, still and endlessly silent.

'MAMMA!' Her voice was a desperate plea now, her pitch higher and fearful.

Her mother rushed in, flustered, adjusting her spectacles before her eyes fell on the slumped form of her husband.

'Jesus Christ!' she said, rushing to her spouse and dropping to her knees beside him. The child stepped back. She knew now for sure something terrible had happened.

'Jesus Christ, Gene!' her mother screamed, tugging violently at her husband as she strained to roll him onto his back. His eyes were open and glazed.

'Gene?' she sobbed, shaking him by the shoulders. 'Gene, for God's sake!'

The girl saw her mother tremble as she placed two fingers to the side of her daddy's neck.

'Oh no . . . oh no!' was all she said.

The child stepped further back as her mother straddled her husband's body and began to beat his chest, hard, hard and hard again with the heels of her hands. She continued to watch as her mother scrambled to her feet, and she heard her mother's feet pound down the hall as she ran for the front door. Her daddy still lay there with his eyes staring at the ceiling.

The sweet summer air of that New Jersey evening had drawn the neighbourhood outdoors. Kids were cycling in their front yards or playing baseball in the fields across the quiet avenue. Their fathers were mowing their lawns or clipping back the boundless green foliage of their gardens. The trim neighbourhood wives in their capris and open-necked shirts had gathered to chatter. The tranquillity of that suburban evening was shattered by the desolate shrieks of the little girl's mother.

'Help me! Please help me!' her shrill voice pleaded to the outside world. 'Call an ambulance, please! Someone help me!'

The child clung to the room's orange floral curtains as her mother stumbled back into the lounge. Once again, the woman flung herself at her husband's still form to compress his chest again and again.

More adults followed, women cupping their palms to their open mouths as they saw Gene Byrne, lying there, staring sightlessly at the ceiling. 'Let me try, Mrs Byrne,' one man said, getting to his knees as the women tried to pull Angela Byrne away. The man's mouth was a grim line as he shoved his palms forcibly into Gene Byrne's chest, and the little girl saw her mother bury her head in her hands.

'Don't worry, Angie, the ambulance is on its way,' a woman said, wrapping a tanned arm across the distraught woman's shoulders.

'It's too late, it's too late.'

'You don't know that, Angie.'

'I'm a nurse, for God's sake! Gene's gone!'

More and more neighbours pressed their way into the room, and as they did, the little girl found herself being pushed further and further out until she stood alone in the hall.

'The poor child shouldn't be in here at all,' said someone. 'Go play outside like a good little girl.'

She could still hear her mother sobbing and the urgent voices of panicked neighbours.

'Maybe we should put him on his side.'

'Keep doing the compressions.'

'Does he have a pulse?'

The child reached the open front door as the wail of a siren grew louder on the avenue. A man with rolled-up shirt sleeves flagged down the red station-wagon ambulance. The two men in white uniforms slid a stretcher from the back of the Chrysler vehicle. The child backed into the wall, flinching as the men ran by her, one by one, their boot-shod feet pounding down the hall.

She eyed the deck and stairs that led from the driveway. Clinging to each wooden baluster, she cautiously stepped her way down. People were gathering on the sidewalk, shaking their heads, speaking quietly, and glancing at every movement inside the windows of the Mountain Avenue home.

The child was shaken, confused. She twirled her fingers through her fair hair and then ran them over the chrome grill of her father's sedan. She took a few hesitant steps along the car, her fingers trailing along the curves of the shining black bodywork until she reached the driver's door. The door was still ajar.

Curling her small fingers around the door's edge, she pulled open the door and climbed onto the striped tan broadcloth of the seats. She loved being in the car. She often sat on Dadda's knee where she would grip the leather steering wheel and 'drive'. Dadda would make loud 'VROOM, VROOM' noises, and he laughed at her squeals of glee every time he blew the car horn.

The small girl pulled the driver's door shut after her with a clunk. She pushed down the black button that locked the door just like Dadda showed her. Sitting back in his seat, she was struck by the silence. Without Dadda's knee to sit on, she could no longer peer out the window or play with the steering wheel. Her dadda seemed lost now, far away.

As the ambulance men covered the man's lifeless form, his wife's ragged sobs were the only sounds in the reverential hush. Women wiped the tears from their cheeks with the backs of their hands, and the men solemnly lowered their heads. Some filed out after the stretcher and stood in silent salute as their neighbour's body was loaded into the back of the emergency vehicle.

Sometime after, Angela Byrne rose to her feet in shock.

'Where's Ann Maria?' she asked, her eyes darting around frantically.

'She's okay, Angie. We're watching her,' one woman replied.

If Angela hadn't been in such deep shock, she might have noticed that the women were unnerved; they glanced at each other before one added: 'It's just she got into Gene's car, and she's locked the door, and won't come out.'

It was weeks later before the women told Angela Byrne about the sight they witnessed. The little girl's hands were balled into fists, her head was thrown back, and the primal screams of grief that reached their ears, even from inside the locked car, shocked them to their core.

# EARLY DAYS

*What we are today comes from our thoughts of yesterday, and our present thoughts build our life of tomorrow. Our life is the creation of our mind.*

BUDDHA (563 BC–483 BC)

The note taped to the front door was an ominous sign. I knew there was little point ringing the doorbell as its powerful clang would only echo around our empty home. Peeling the scrap of lined notepaper from the door, I saw a looped scrawl that wasn't my mother's handwriting.

*Ann Maria, please call to your Aunt Betty's after school.*

Blinking back tears, I crossed the road to our neighbour's house. Mrs Walshe, who I always knew as Aunt Betty, ushered me in, her eyes full of tenderness. I hated that sympathy, that pity.

'Your mother's not well, Ann Maria,' she almost whispered, even though we were alone. 'I'm afraid she had to go away for a little while until she feels better.'

My cheeks burnt with that familiar sense of shame. Sometimes there were 'incidents' that precipitated my mother's frequent disappearances, but these were discussed among adults in low voices and never within my hearing.

But I was aware from an early age that when my mother was 'away', she was in Saint Patrick's psychiatric hospital in Dublin. The stigma surrounding mental illness in the fifties and sixties was as ancient as the institution once called Saint Patrick's Hospital for Imbeciles.

No one ever explained my mother's illness to me, but I acutely felt the humiliation of it. And I would never learn the reason she was admitted to the hospital that day. Mrs Walshe led me to the kitchen, and once she had made her hushed disclosure, she brightened.

'Now, love, you sit down here and let me get your dinner,' she said, whipping on her apron. 'I've called your Uncle Jimmy, and he says to tell you he's on his way. How did you get on in school today?' My mother had vanished again, and there was no more to be said about it.

If there was an issue with my mother's mental health during her formative years, I never heard about it. Angela Pratt was born in a house on George's Street in Templemore in County Tipperary on 3 April 1916. Her parents, Patrick and Leshia Pratt, née Mockler, were shopkeepers in the town. My mother was christened Anne Angela but she was always known by her middle name, and she was raised as one of four siblings.

More recently, I learnt that there was a fifth child, a boy, who died after fracturing his skull in an accident. The tragedy led to my grandmother being hospitalised in an asylum in Dublin for depression. It's possible my mother's struggles with her mental health were ancestral.

A series of tragedies in my mother's younger years may also have resurfaced to cause her problems in later life. Her young life mirrored mine because she was only six years old when her father died. That loss must have been magnified when she and her younger sister Nora were sent away to Ballingarry boarding school in County Tipperary.

Leshia remarried but died a few years later during childbirth. So my mother was orphaned just after her fourteenth birthday, a pivotal time in an adolescent's life.

My father Eugene Byrne's childhood was different but also filled with hardship. I have little sense of the person he was, because I never had the opportunity to know him, and my mother never spoke much of him either. All I can relate about him are the bare facts, the black-and-white biographical details of his life.

He came from a huge family in rural County Mayo. The Byrnes were farmers in a windswept place called Mountain Common in

Aghamore, between the towns of Ballyhaunis and the pilgrimage village of Knock. Eugene and his twin brother, Joseph, were born on 22 March 1902, near the tail end of fifteen children reared by Dominick and Maria Byrne.

The country was in a deep economic depression in the early decades of the twentieth century. Emigration was often the only opportunity available to rural Irish men and women. One by one, my father's older siblings emigrated to the United States and each sent funds home for the younger family members to follow. My father's twin, Joseph, emigrated to the States via Canada in 1924, and Eugene followed in the late 1920s.

By 1932 my father was working as a station agent for the Interborough Rapid Transit Company (IRT), which back then operated the New York City Subway.

Two years later he became a naturalised American citizen. The official documents, issued on 2 August 1934, describe Eugene Byrne as black-haired and blue-eyed with a 'dark' complexion. The authorities noted he was 170 lbs in weight and five foot and six inches tall. His address was listed as 64 West 83rd Street in the Upper West Side of Manhattan. A modest apartment in the same block today costs more than a million dollars.

Three years after he became an American citizen, he became a white-collar worker in the prestigious Prudential Insurance Company in New York. His new job involved selling industrial and ordinary life insurance and looking after the endowment policies of hundreds of families.

When the United States entered World War II, my father was among the sixteen million Americans who were called to serve in the armed forces. At the relatively advanced age of forty, he was assigned to a desk job when he turned up for duty in Newark, New Jersey, in 1942. As general clerk, his job was to assist his sergeant major with personnel records, mess accounts and general War Department files.

Eugene S. (Sylvester) Byrne received an honourable discharge and a Good Conduct Medal when the war ended in September 1945. As soon as he left the army, he returned to his job at Prudential.

Transatlantic passenger services resumed between late 1945 and early 1946, and during that time, my father returned to Ireland for a holiday. He travelled to County Kildare, where three of his sisters had settled, and it was here that my parents' paths first crossed.

Gene Byrne and Angela Pratt met at a dance or a 'social' at the Curragh, an area renowned as the home of the Irish Defence Forces and for horse breeding. My mother was a member of the Army Nursing Service, working at the Curragh Military Hospital.

I know little about their romance except that it was a whirlwind affair. My mother followed him to the United States, and they married in New Jersey on 26 July 1946. My father was a mature bachelor of forty-four years on his wedding day. My mother was younger but equally mature at age thirty.

They exchanged vows in Sacred Heart Church, then a small mission church near their first home in Bloomfield, New Jersey. In their wedding photos, my mother is wearing an eye-catching turquoise-coloured suit with a wide-brimmed brown hat. My father stands beside her, looking smart but solemn in a dark suit.

Photos show friends and family gathered around a rather grand white-linen and silver service wedding reception. Their mostly sepia-coloured wedding photos are mixed with snaps of the happy couple onboard a mahogany speed boat in what appears to be a sunshine-filled honeymoon. It all appears so glamorous and cosmopolitan – a world away from the grim, economically depressed times that existed in Ireland of that era. After the privations of wartime rations at home, my mother must have been dazzled by the prosperity and modernity of post-war America.

My father exudes a strong presence in all his photographs. He was a dapper man in sharp pinstripe suits with slicked-back hair and a receding hairline. He has a steely look and a challenging gaze that is reminiscent of a forties movie star. His twin brother, Joe, by comparison, exhibits a more relaxed and smiling demeanour in photos.

My mother had thick black hair and hazel-brown eyes, which were almost always concealed behind spectacles. She had a trim figure, which was enhanced by her collection of wide-flared trousers, fur-trimmed belted coats and the most up-to-date fashions of the forties. They made a stylish couple.

Fate was never kind to them, however. Most of their marriage was overshadowed by their struggle to start a family, and they must have experienced a lot of heartache as my mother had one miscarriage after another. It was eight years before their prayers for a child were answered, and I was delivered on 30 July 1954.

The very next month, my parents bought their dream family home on Mountain Avenue, West Caldwell, New Jersey. Mountain Avenue is filled with detached houses on big plots that overlook a green expanse called Mountain Avenue Fields. It's an affluent middle-class area that has some of the ambience of a country town while being conveniently close to the city streets of Newark and New York City.

Our four-storey Cape Cod-style house sat on a half-acre grassy plot surrounded by mature trees. The property was so spacious that it had been split into a two-family home. It provided an extra source of income for my parents and a home for us on the ground floor and basement. It was the perfect house to raise a family.

However, my parents' story had no happy-ever-after ending. My father had complained of a pain which radiated down his left arm. He was reassured by the doctor who dismissed it as tendonitis or nerve pain from resting his arm on the open window of his car while driving.

But on Friday, 10 August 1956, he returned from work and suffered a massive heart attack. It was the month after my second birthday when he collapsed and died in front of me. My mother only discovered him after responding to my cries.

Amid all the chaos surrounding his death, I wandered away. The neighbours found me in his car, doors locked from the inside, screaming inconsolably. From that day, I believe I've carried an imprint of grief and abandonment, which has been with me ever since. His death, which occurred at my feet, marked the first major loss in my life.

My father's funeral took place the following Tuesday in St Aloysius Church in Caldwell, and his remains lie in Holy Cross Cemetery in North Arlington, New Jersey.

I often wondered if the shock of her husband's death triggered my mother's mental health problems. In those days there was little or no support for bereavement. The curious thing, as I said, is that she never spoke much about my father. There was such a silence concerning him that I began to doubt his existence. I remember rooting through photo albums because I suspected that I was 'illegitimate', and it was only the sight of my mother's wedding photos that ultimately reassured me.

Down through the years, I developed a sense that their marriage may not have been a happy one. One relative said that they didn't always get on and that my father may have been drinking. I don't know if he was any different from others in America at the time. The decade of the fifties was a hard-living era when business lunches comprised multiple martinis, and a bottle of scotch was routinely kept in the office desk. Certainly my mother never said a negative word about my father. 'Your father was a very kind and generous man,' she used to say.

I could never draw her further. But reading between the lines, I believe their relationship may have been a rocky one. Perhaps I'm wrong, and maybe his loss was too traumatic for her to discuss. But I became adept at reading between the lines. My mother's illness taught me how to tune into people's real feelings and emotions.

My newly widowed mother returned to work as a nurse after placing me in a day nursery. Her Dublin-based sister, Nora, who stayed with her in the months following my father's funeral, insisted it would be easier to raise me back in Ireland.

'What sort of an upbringing is that for a child – in a nursery all day with strangers?' Aunt Nora argued. 'And what supports do you have here if something happens you?'

My mother loved America; the country represented progress and modernity to her, but she agreed that the best place to rear me was in Ireland, where she had the support of family. She couldn't leave America until she sold her home on Mountain Avenue, so she handed me into the care of my Aunt Nora, who took me to Dublin. That was the first of many times that I lived with Aunt Nora and Uncle Jimmy in their home in Inchicore.

Aunt Nora was then aged thirty-nine, a year younger than my mother. She and my uncle, Jimmy Lavin, who was forty-five, had no family. I became their surrogate child, and they doted on me, especially Jimmy.

For much of my early years, I lived in their home located above their drapery shop, Lavin's on Emmet Road in Inchicore. I played in their large back garden, often with Uncle Jimmy and Steve, the dog. Uncle Jimmy's cousin, Donzey lived next door, and he had two sons, Patrick and Dominic, a few years older than me. They owned Lavin's hardware shop, next door to the drapery. The adjoining shops took pride of place on Emmet Road and were a well-known landmark in the area. Patrick, Dominic and I often played together, exploring beyond the garden, running through the fields that ran down to the River Camac, a tributary of the River Liffey.

Uncle Jimmy was my reassurance whenever anything went wrong. I recall consternation on one occasion when I broke a precious Waterford Crystal glass, a wedding present to my aunt and uncle. My Aunt Nora gasped in horror as she gazed upon the smithereens of glass on the floor.

'I'm sorry,' I said quietly, my voice wavering and my eyes filling with tears.

Uncle Jimmy didn't hesitate. 'Come here, Ann Maria,' he said, pulling me towards him. 'Everything is going to be all right.' He wrapped me in a warm bearhug and squeezed all my troubles and tears into his woolly jumper.

'It's only a silly glass anyway,' he whispered, but he did it out of earshot of Aunt Nora.

Aunt Nora and Uncle Jimmy were a hard-working couple who spent six days a week in their large drapery shop. Lavin's had four staff and stocked everything from needles to brassieres and men's shirts to First Communion dresses. Soft-hearted Jimmy sold many things 'on tick', where the women of this poor, working-class area came in each week to pay off a few shillings on a Communion dress or a suit.

When my mother returned to Ireland in 1958, she bought a home for us in Mount Merrion on Dublin's southside. We moved into a comfortable, semi-detached house on Upper Trees Road, in the heart of middle-class suburbia.

She received a pension after my father's death, which allowed her to stay home in my early years. But I spent a lot of time going back and forth to Inchicore, where my aunt and uncle lived. From a young age, I knew how to catch the number 46A or the 64 double-decker bus into the city centre, and then I'd take the number 21, which would bring me out to Inchicore. From early on, I became an independent and self-reliant child.

I worked in their shop most Saturdays, but every Sunday we travelled the country together. Sunday was their only day off, so after mass every weekend we set off on an outing. It was like our weekly adventure.

'So where will we go today, Ann Maria?' Uncle Jimmy would ask.

'Maybe the beach?' I'd suggest hopefully.

On a sunny day, my Aunt Nora would pack a picnic basket and we'd go to sandy beaches like Brittas Bay in Wicklow or Courtown in County Wexford. On other days, they drove to places like Glendalough, Woodenbridge or Arklow in County Wicklow. On rainy days Uncle Jimmy would suggest lunch in a nice hotel. Sometimes my mother came with us, and other times it was just the three of us.

Every summer I'd look forward to holidays with my aunt and uncle as they travelled to France and Italy. I have photographs of us in exotic destinations like Monte Carlo, Nice and Saint Tropez.

Every time my mother wasn't well, which was often, I lived in Inchicore. For me it was like having two families. Family life with my mother in Mount Merrion was precious but also precarious. Living with Aunt Nora and Uncle Jimmy in Inchicore meant security, comfort and reassurance.

My mother had to return to the United States to renew her citizenship in 1961, but I was upset at any suggestion that I go with her. 'I want to stay with Aunt Nora and Uncle Jimmy,' I said. 'I don't want to go to America.'

Even though I was only seven years old, they listened to me. I changed school and lived in Inchicore while my mother worked in New Jersey for that year. Years later I discovered my mother had kept a small bundle of letters that I wrote to her in America. It was sad reading them. I started writing each letter with words like 'Dear Mummy, I hope you are well. I went to school today and . . .' But in each letter my handwriting ended abruptly after a few sentences.

## Carried on Spirit Wings

Clearly, I found something better to do than write to my mother.

Every note was finished off by my Aunt Nora, who made a crude attempt to forge my childish thoughts and handwriting. I still think of how those letters must have hurt my mother's feelings. No one made a telephone call to America in those days unless there was a death in the family. Those letters would have been our only contact for the year.

I loved my mother deeply, and she loved me, but even at a young age, I had a sense of insecurity when I was around her. I was always alert; watching for the first signs that my mother was becoming unwell. Intuitively I read the signals. I noticed every change in her and every shift in her mood or expression. I was able to tune in to every delicate shade of her emotional state. When she suffered, I felt it too. I lived with a certain sense of dread and fear around her.

In today's world my mother would have been diagnosed as bipolar, and in earlier decades she would have been called a manic depressive. But when I was growing up, there was a conspiracy of silence. 'Your mother suffers from her nerves,' is all that Aunt Nora would say. Uncle Jimmy would say my mother was *unwell*. I didn't understand why she suffered as she did, and no one ever explained it to me.

My mother and I had many great times together too. When she was well, she was a caring mother, a great homemaker and an excellent nurse. I remember being called to the front door on my birthday one year and seeing my mother holding the reins of a full-sized chestnut mare. She had somehow managed to hire the horse for the day. 'Happy birthday!' she said, beaming, as my jaw dropped. The animal was led through the garage into the back garden where my friends enjoyed horse rides all afternoon. She dreamt up the most original surprises. Even when she was ill, I was never neglected or abused in any physical sense. She got me up for school, made the dinner and kept the house in order.

I did, however, suffer from unintentional emotional neglect. Sometimes she functioned, but her illness made her withdraw from me and life.

'Mummy?'

Silence.

'Mummy?'
'Hmmm?'
'Guess what I did in school today?'
Silence.

Often the only symptom of her disease was that she just withdrew into herself. She disappeared into a dark world and catatonic state from which she just couldn't find her way out.

I could see the changes happening before anyone else. A kind of a tightness appeared around my mother's mouth, and a vacancy spread into her eyes. It was almost like she was worried about something and was already detaching from the real world, entering a world of inner torment and suffering. Her condition made me a hyper-vigilant child. My response was to pray for my mother, pray really hard. *Dear holy God, please make my mother better. Please, God, don't let her be taken away to Saint Patrick's.*

The concepts of God, heaven and death were a part of my life from an early age. I recall being in mass, my short legs swinging on the pew while I fidgeted with the buttons on my cardigan. My mother took hold of one of my hands and lowered her head to meet my eyes.

'Ann Maria, you have to sit quietly like a good girl,' she whispered. 'Your daddy is in heaven with God, and they are both looking down on you.'

My eyes rose to the vaulted ceiling, and I stared up in awe. I was filled with wonder at the thought that my daddy and God were watching me. It was something that stayed in my head as a small child. My love of sitting in churches and praying began. I would pour out my heart to God, especially for my mother's health, and it brought me a feeling of consolation.

My mother was religious like most people of the time, but she wasn't pious, and prayer wasn't a strong presence in our house. The first time I witnessed a family kneeling around the kitchen range to recite the Rosary was in my Aunt Alice's house in Tipperary. Uncle Jimmy often knelt at the fire to say his prayers before he went to bed, but he never expected me to join him.

My mother said prayers with me at night, and she went to mass every Sunday. She joined the occasional parish retreat and kept

Rosary beads under her pillow. But you could never describe her as fanatical about religion, and she never tried to push religion on me. Still, I found great consolation in sitting in silence, lighting a candle and praying.

I considered every move I made so that I wouldn't be a worry to her. 'You're such a good girl, Ann Maria,' people would say to me all the time. 'You must be such a comfort to your mother.' The truth was that I was afraid to do anything wrong in case I tipped her into that world of *unwellness*. I grew up with the constant fear that something terrible was going to happen to her. So I prayed. I went to churches, lit candles and said intercessory prayers pleading to God that she would stay well and that I'd be a good girl. Prayer became a solace; it helped deal with the stress of her sickness. Having God – this idealised father figure – in my life, meant I didn't have to bear the burden alone. But even my most earnest prayers didn't always work.

My mother had an old metal cash box in the house that held documents like birth certificates and my father's old war papers. The box usually lay forgotten in a desk. Within days of that tightness appearing around her mouth, I would come home from school to find the box under her arm. There would be a wariness about her, her eyes darting around, looking for unseen enemies. She was guarding the metal box and its contents from some terrible threat.

'We have to be careful, Ann Maria. They're coming for this. They're going to try and take this away from us.'

'Who's coming for it, Mummy?'

'You know very well who, Ann Maria. We must keep this box safe. Promise me you'll help me keep this safe.'

'I promise, Mummy.'

'They're coming for us. I know they are. They're going to try to take this away.'

I left her clutching her box, her eyes trained for the mysterious beings who sometimes came to haunt her, and I picked up the receiver and dialled the telephone.

'Hello, Uncle Jimmy.'

'Hello, Ann Maria. How's my girl?'

Even though I made a lot of those phone calls, the words would

always catch in my throat
   'Mummy . . . is not well.'
   Uncle Jimmy and Aunt Nora, prayer and those words – *Mummy is not well* – were the constants in my young life.

# Called to Become

EDWINA GATELEY

*A perfect creation.*

*No one is called to become*

*Who you are called to be.*

*It does not matter*

*How short or tall*

*Or thick-set or slow*

*You may be.*

*It does not matter*

*Whether you sparkle with life*

*Or are as silent as a still pool.*

*Whether you sing your song aloud*

*Or weep alone in darkness.*

*It does not matter*

*Whether you feel loved and admired*

*Or unloved and alone*

*For you are called to become*

*A perfect creation.*

*No one's shadow*

*Should cloud your becoming.*

*No one's light should dispel your spark.*

*For the Lord delights in you.*

*Jealously looks upon you*

*And encourages with gentle joy*

*Every movement of the Spirit within you.*

*Unique and loved you stand.*

*Beautiful or stunted in your growth*

*But never without hope and life.*

*For you are called to become*

*A perfect creation.*

*This becoming may be*

*Gentle or harsh.*

*Subtle or violent.*

*But it never ceases.*

*Never pauses or hesitates.*

*Only is –*

*Creative force –*

*Calling you*

*Calling you to become*

*A perfect creation.*

*Reproduced by kind permission of Edwina Gateley.*

# GROWING UP

*You can't go back and change the beginning,
but you can start where you are and change the ending.*

C. S. Lewis

The sun was blazing, and I can still see my Aunt Josie pouring warm lemonade into plastic tumblers. My mother was sitting on the green tartan blanket, her hands shielding her eyes as she gazed out across the waves.

We had been staying with my Aunt Josie and my cousin Nora in Thurles town in County Tipperary, where my aunt ran a newsagent's. 'It's such a glorious day,' Aunt Josie had said. 'Why don't we all get some fresh air and go to the beach?'

So, we packed a picnic and headed off in Aunt Josie's Morris Minor to Clonea Beach near Dungarvan, County Waterford. With its long, sandy beach and shoreline, it was always a popular spot for picnics and swimming. On fine days people from miles away converged on its shores, so the beach was a hive of activity that afternoon.

My cousin Nora and I sat on the crowded strand next to our mothers. I was twelve and Nora was a year older, and our legs were slathered in Nivea cream. We hoped to transform our milky-white legs into fashionably tanned ones. People splashed around in the rolling waves, and the sky was so clear we could see Annestown beach fifteen miles down the coast.

Nora kept an interested eye on the local boys as they emerged, torsos glistening and hair sleek from the water. I was too busy watching my mother. I had recognised the first signs of a deterioration days earlier. Aunt Josie chatted, and my mother responded with a brittle laugh, a nod or a word or two. No one else appeared to notice the quietness that descended on her when her mood turned. Aunt Josie set about unpacking the picnic, but my mother was distracted, continuing to gaze out across the water. I spotted a shadow of anxiety cross her face, and then her whole bearing changed. In an instant, she was like a coiled spring.

'That little boy . . .'

'What boy?' Aunt Josie said, looking up, with a tumbler in one hand and a lemonade bottle in the other.

'The one on his own in the water.'

The three of us looked in the direction of her gaze and squinted in the dazzling sunlight. There were many people in the water, but no small boy on his own.

'Do you mean the child in the blue swimsuit?' Aunt Josie asked. 'Isn't that his mother right beside him?'

Aunt Josie lost interest and topped up the last beaker of lemonade. But my mother remained bolt upright, her eyes scanning the water, seeing things that no one else could see.

'What's wrong with everyone?' she cried suddenly. 'Can't they see the poor child is drowning?'

In a heartbeat my mother managed to scramble to her feet and run full pelt into the sea, fully dressed in navy trousers and a white shirt. She was strong and fast, and it all happened very quickly.

The scene that unfolded runs like a horror movie in my head even today. All eyes turn towards the commotion in the water. They see a shrieking woman trying to drag a child out of the sea. The child howls with fear, and the boy's mother cries for help as she fends off this stranger 'attacking' her youngster. Bystanders are running to help, shouting at my mother. Josie and Nora are standing on the shoreline pleading with my mother to come out of the water. 'What on earth does that woman think she's doing?' says a man nearby. He is watching the chaos and using both hands to shield his eyes against the sun's glare.

I stop looking. I can't bear these chaotic scenes. My face is already burning red with mortification, and my stomach is churning in anxiety. I start haphazardly stuffing everything back into the wicker picnic basket so that we are ready for a quick getaway.

I can't bear to see the grave expressions, the solemn shakes of the head, the stares of condemnation and, worst of all, the sympathetic looks from people. *So many people!* All I want to do now is to get out of here and make that call to Uncle Jimmy. I can't stand it that my mother's illness has been exposed for all to see.

Even after all these years, that sense of shame is seared into my memory. I've also never forgotten my mother's confusion as we bundled her away from the beach. 'I don't understand, Josie. What did I do wrong?' she asked.

She only wanted to help a drowning little boy. My Uncle Jimmy and Aunt Nora came down to take my mother away, and I stayed in Aunt Josie's for a while. I saw how my mother suffered and how people sometimes disapproved of her behaviour. But none of us understood what was going on, least of all her.

My mother had very few options when she was *unwell*. Mostly she disappeared behind the high walls of the old Saint Patrick's Hospital on Bow Lane in Dublin. Psychiatric hospitals were little more than depressing places of confinement then. I visited my mother in Saint Patrick's when I was older, and my abiding memories are of the sense of gloom and the barred windows. The place had barely changed in the two hundred years since it had been built, so it was little wonder it was so grim.

My mother was a patient during the years when psychiatric hospitals used electroconvulsive therapy (ECT) without anaesthetic. It was a barbaric and cruel process where patients were forcibly restrained and electric charges were sent through their heads. Many were mercilessly dragged screaming to this 'therapy'.

My mother always emerged a crushed spirit after those treatments. Aunt Nora and Uncle Jimmy lived ten minutes' drive down the road from the hospital, so she would return there and lie in a darkened bedroom to rest afterwards. I remember looking in on her and feeling so sad to see her lying there, fragile and lost.

'Are you all right, Mummy? Can I get you something?'

Her lips were parched, and they moved but made no sound. Her eyes rolled, unfocused. I could see she was disorientated, but she made an effort to reply when she saw my anxious face.

'I'm fine, Ann Maria,' she said, her voice cracking. 'Mummy just needs a little rest.'

She went through torment when she was unwell and through more torture to get better. Outside of Saint Patrick's, she was prescribed lithium, a commonly used treatment for bipolar disorder. They gave her blood tests, and she met with a psychiatrist, but there was no counselling or therapy in those days. Simply put, her appointments consisted of: *How are your meds? Here's your prescription. See you in a month.*

When she felt well, she would sometimes go off her medication. This commonly happens because many patients feel that the drug is another form of incarceration, albeit a chemical one. Lithium has a sedative effect, which depresses every sensation. For some patients it feels like a permanent fog has descended on their mind. After she stopped taking the drug, for a while she would feel great, and I'd have my real mother back again. But inevitably the cycle would start, and one day I would arrive home from school to find that she had disappeared again.

I would pray hardest for her when she was in the hospital; I'd plead with God to make her better and let her get out of Saint Patrick's. I knew she hated to be in there. Prayer was all I could do to help her. I loved to sit and pray in the serenity of our local Church of Saint Thérèse in Mount Merrion. Later I prayed in the gallery of our school chapel in the Dominican College Sion Hill in Blackrock. When I was living in Inchicore, I slipped into the pews of Saint Michael's Church. Other times I walked that bit further to Mary Immaculate Church, where they had a full-size replica of the grotto at Lourdes. Prayer was a wonderful comfort, but I often questioned why a merciful God would allow my mother to be afflicted with such torment.

'Why does God allow innocent people to suffer, Uncle Jimmy?' I asked.

'Everyone suffers at some time, Ann Maria,' he said. 'We just have to trust in God.'

Moving between the areas of Mount Merrion and Inchicore, I started to recognise a stark contrast between the haves and have-nots. When my mother went to the United States for a year, I went to the local Goldenbridge national school, located on the site of the infamous industrial school in Inchicore.

Maybe it was my first day at Goldenbridge, but I recall wearing a pretty green dress with black bows and shiny patent-leather shoes to school one day. Aunt Nora had tied a green ribbon on my head to help tame my blonde curls. I noticed that many of the other scrub-faced little girls around me wore threadbare dresses and darned hand-me-downs. In those days, many families still occupied the nearby Keogh Square housing project, tenement slums that existed for many decades. The State provided each pupil with small glass bottles of milk and a jam, ham or corned-beef sandwich for lunch. The white bread sometimes curled at the edges, and each slice was always smeared in cheap white margarine. Yet some children wolfed down those sandwiches, and I knew it was the first meal they'd had that day. The poverty was palpable in Inchicore. I was aware of the discrepancy between my life and some of the other children in my classroom, and it troubled me.

'Some of the children in my school are hungry, Uncle Jimmy. Can I keep my ginger biscuits for them?'

'That's very kind, Ann Maria, but they mightn't want you to know that they're hungry. We give to the poor during the St Vincent de Paul collection at mass. Why don't I give you extra money to put in the box this Sunday, so that they can buy biscuits themselves?'

When I was in my Mount Merrion home, my best friend was Ann Humphrey who lived on the same road. Our childhoods were quite similar because both our mothers had dark and shameful secrets. Her very glamorous mother was an alcoholic who was occasionally hospitalised to be 'dried out', and my mother suffered from 'her nerves'. Ann's father, our family doctor, was often the one who admitted my mother to the mental hospital.

Dr Henry Humphrey was a kind man who regularly drove us around in the back of his car when he was going on his rounds. He never knew that Ann and I sneaked into his surgery to play hospital with his stethoscope, his blood pressure monitor and other equipment. He also didn't know that we were often sent on 'errands' to the local off-licence in Deer Park to buy bottles of vodka for his wife.

I think he knew, however, that his housekeeper, Mrs Kielty, could always be relied upon to mother us when our real mothers weren't able to. 'Come in here, you two,' she would say, bundling us into the warm kitchen. 'Let your poor mammies have a rest from the both of you.' She would whip off a tea cloth and reveal a tray of steaming currant scones or fairy cakes that she had baked for us.

I cried when Ann was sent to boarding school at Mount Sackville and she no longer lived a few doors down from me. We wrote long letters to each other and looked forward to the holidays.

The truth was that most of my days outside school were spent in the company of middle-aged adults. When I was at home with my mother in Mount Merrion, life was quiet, too quiet sometimes. We'd often sit in silence over dinner, and I longed to have someone small to play with.

'Mummy, why can't I have a brother or sister like the other girls at school?' I remember asking.

My mother shrugged.

'Ann Maria, you need a daddy to have a brother or sister, and you know your daddy is in heaven.'

If life was often silent with my mother, it was just as quiet in Aunt Nora and Uncle Jimmy's household. Aunt Nora, like my mother, trained as a nurse in her younger years. She met Uncle Jimmy when she was hired as a private nurse to look after his mother, the original proprietor of Lavin's drapery store.

Often the only sounds in the house were the wooden mantel clock ticking on the slate fireplace, the occasional clink of cutlery on our plates over dinner or the rustle of Uncle Jimmy's newspaper. Sometimes we listened to the radio or watched what little was available on the Telefís Éireann, the single national television channel, before going to bed early. The quietness would only be interrupted whenever my cousins from next door, Pat and Dom, called for me.

Aunt Nora never said why they didn't have children of their own, and people didn't discuss those things then. Oddly, my mother and Nora were quite different even though there was only a year between them. My mother was a very independent woman when she was well. Living in America had broadened her view of the world and made her more adventurous than Nora, who led a more sheltered life. My mother always drove a car, while Nora never got behind the wheel. Also, my mother managed her home and paid all the bills, while Nora never wrote a cheque until after Uncle Jimmy died.

Sometimes I detected a rivalry between my mother and Aunt Nora over me. Aunt Nora must have envied my mother for having the child that she clearly wanted. And I know there were occasions when I took advantage of being at the centre of a tug of love. There was a time, for example, that my mother refused to buy me a bicycle.

'Why can't I have a bicycle? All the other girls have one.'
'Because you don't need one.'
'It's for playing.'
'Bicycles are too expensive, Ann Maria.'

But shortly afterwards Uncle Jimmy went out and bought me a bicycle.

I recall another time when my mother came home with a 'surprise' for me. It was a brown skirt and jacket on a hanger.

'It's for your confirmation!'

I was dismayed. I thought the suit looked shabby and dowdy, and my eyes brimmed with tears.

'It's not new!'

'Not everything has to be new, Ann Maria. It's a perfectly good suit, and you're only going to wear it for one day.'

The first chance I had, I told Uncle Jimmy about my mother's terrible choice of confirmation outfit. I knew he would rescue me from that awful brown suit.

'Now, Angela,' he reasoned, 'the child only makes her confirmation once. We own a drapery shop, so the least we can do is to buy her something that she wants to wear.'

So Uncle Jimmy brought me to Arnotts department store in Dublin city centre where he had an account. I was thrilled when he let me browse through the rails of lovely childrenswear. My eyes finally settled on a linen suit with a delicate check print in shades of cinnamon and white. The short jacket had a Peter Pan collar, and it came with a matching pleated skirt. Uncle Jimmy beamed with pleasure at my happiness as I left the department store with my new suit.

## Carried on Spirit Wings

My mother smiled and she admired my new outfit as I spun in front of her. She bought all the accessories: a white jockey hat and gloves and new leather shoes and a bag. It is only on reflection that I realise the hurt I must have caused by rejecting her choice of outfit. I have a confirmation photograph where I'm posing in my suit outside the Church of Saint Thérèse on 24 May 1965. You can see the sparkle in my eyes, and it wasn't all about the spirituality of the occasion. The glamour of the day was clearly important to me too.

Despite occasional tensions between my mother and Nora, I only ever remember a single curt exchange of words. I don't recall what was said, or what prompted it, but it ended with my mother taking me by the hand and announcing, 'Come on, Ann Maria. We're leaving.' I remember it so clearly, probably because it was the only time that I ever witnessed a quarrel between them.

My mother's love affair with America never faded. From when I was ten years old, we started to spend our summers in New Jersey, where she would get a job in Mountainside Hospital in Montclair. My father's twin, Joseph Byrne, still lived in New Jersey with his wife, Aunt Helen. I remember being excited when they invited us to lunch at their club during our first summer in America. As Joseph was my dad's twin, I knew he was the closest I would come to seeing my father in the flesh. I recall studying him over lunch and being struck by his age. I remember thinking that he wasn't like my friends' dads. *Wow, my father is old,* I thought.

I also remember the day in August 1967 when my mother brought me to my father's grave in Holy Cross Cemetery in North Arlington. The cemetery is one of those vast park-like places with endless rows of low headstones set in neatly cropped grass. We needed a map and a plot number to find him. When we reached my father's graveside, my mother got down on her hands and knees and began pulling up weeds. I shed a few silent tears over that tender gesture of care for my father. I didn't expect it but the visit moved me deeply.

We spent the long holidays in New Jersey living with 'Aunt Tommy', a nursing friend of my mother's. Aunt Tommy, whose real name was Roberta Barnard, was also widowed. She had three children and lived in a neighbourhood called Berkeley Heights Park in Bloomfield. It was a horseshoe-shaped enclave of big, old Victorian homes that surrounded a park filled with shady oak trees. I loved those summers in America. I had a readymade playmate in Judy, my Aunt Tommy's daughter, and their house seemed like a mansion to me. We teamed up with other neighbourhood kids, Rosemary and Marty O'Boyle, Diane Polk and Beth Shapiro, and tore around under cornflower blue skies for months.

I remember sitting with Judy on the porch steps one warm night. My mother had told me she was going out with an old friend of my father's. When the friend arrived to collect her, my eyes narrowed. I noticed she was wearing her favourite pink shift dress, her pearl earrings and going-out high heels. She had even curled her hair. I was too polite to scowl at my father's friend. However, I didn't smile at him. I hoped that he'd notice.

'Please don't stay out late, Ann Maria,' said my mother as she left. 'I'll be checking with Aunt Tommy to see what time you're home at.'

Judy had a smirk on her face but she waited until my mother gave a final wave and the car pulled off.

'Oooh, your mom's on a date!'

I didn't like the idea of my mother having a boyfriend.

'It's not a date! He's just a friend of my father's!'

Judy knew by my tone that she had hit on a nerve.

'Your mommy is sitting in a tree, k.i.s.s.i.n.g.'

'Shut up, idiot.'

'Just watch, she's going to marry him, and then you'll have a new daddy.'

I punched Judy in the arm.

'First comes love, then comes marriage,' she sang. 'Then comes baby in the baby carriage.'

This time I didn't respond at all. I just glowered in silence. This wasn't something I'd contemplated before. I didn't like the idea of having to share my mother's attentions with any man. Judy lost interest in teasing me.

'I'm sick of our moms always telling us when we have to be home,' she said. 'Just think, when your mom gets married, he'll be the one telling her what time she has to be home!'

My father's friend called to Aunt Tommy's house a few times to collect my mother, and each time he came, I fumed. My mother couldn't have failed to notice my hostility to this man. In hindsight I wish I had been mature enough to encourage her to find companionship and love. But instead I resented any man who might try to steal my mother's affections from me.

All summer long, Judy and I lounged around pools, rode our bikes, went to the Jersey coast, walked the boardwalks, played tennis and lazed under the oak trees in Berkeley Heights Park. I sobbed in the car as we headed to the airport for our flight home every year.

Yet whenever my mother threatened to pack up and move to America for good, which she often did, my heart plunged. My mother went back to work as a private hire nurse when I got older, working for a long time in a large country house called Sefton in Blackrock, County Dublin. However, she was often exasperated with life in Ireland. She lauded America as a land of promise, progress and sunshine and derided Ireland as inefficient, backward and cold.

'That's it! I've had enough of this place. We're moving back to the States!' she'd say.

Even though I loved our summers in New Jersey, I'd tremble at the thought of leaving Ireland for good.

'Mummy, we can't leave. What about my school?'

'The schools are better in America.'

Everything was better in America, according to my mother. Looking back, she may have been right. The standard of living across the Atlantic was far better than it was in Ireland then. I never remember my mother being unwell during all the times she was in the United States either. Maybe it was the summer sunshine and the change of scenery, but she always seemed well in New Jersey. Yet the thought that any day she might choose to move to America made me feel insecure. I felt anxious at the prospect of leaving school and leaving behind Uncle Jimmy and Aunt Nora.

When I look in the family photograph albums, I see myself, a smiling child, in beautiful dresses, sometimes posing in far-flung destinations surrounded by adoring adults. My childhood looks idyllic, and in many ways it was. However, the loss of my father resulted in the need for a closer emotional connection to my mother, and this was absent due to her illness.

My mother was available as much as she could be, but for her, life was a constant struggle. I have immense compassion for her as an adult, but I didn't understand what she was going through when I was a child. A lot of the time, my mother was lost in her own deep emotional pain, and as a consequence I suffered emotional neglect. The combination of my father's death and my mother's withdrawal left a wound that has been difficult to heal. The reality is I was a lonely child, who was often sad and insecure.

*My father, 1950.*

*My parents' wedding day, New Jersey, USA, July 1946.*

*Our house in New Jersey.*

*Playing with Dominic and Patrick Lavin in Inchicore, Dublin.*

*Uncle Jimmy, Steve the dog and me in Inchicore, Dublin.*

*Neighbours' back garden Mount Merrion, 1959.*

*My mother and me, Holy Communion day, 1962.*

*Me, Auntie Nora and Uncle Jimmy, Isle of Man, 1964.*

*Confirmation day, St Teresa's Church, Mount Merrion, Dublin, May 1965.*

# *Thoughts of Gretchen Rodriguez*

*You have a purpose, a divine reason,*
*for being on this earth.*
*No matter how difficult the road may be,*
*never shrink away from what stirs in your heart.*

*Whatever your dream is,*
*Whatever the promise God has given you,*
*Never let it go.*
*Keep believing.*
*Keep expecting.*
*Every day, do something to move towards it,*
*Even if only in your heart,*
*For that is where all faith begins.*

# ANDREW

*Being deeply loved by someone gives you strength,*
*while loving someone deeply gives you courage.*

Lao Tzu

There was little indication when I first met Andrew that he was destined to be the love of my life. There was no lightning-bolt moment between us, no eyes meeting across a crowded office. I can't even say what one feature I found attractive about him above all else, but it was probably his eyes. It took me a while, but I saw an intensity, a sparkle and a softness that I have never seen in another man.

I met Andrew through the Free Legal Advice Centre – known as FLAC – in October 1977. Each part-time legal centre was staffed by one fully qualified solicitor aided by final-year law students. We were the same age, but he was the director of the Molesworth Street centre, which opened one night a week. I was one of the legal students working there. Every Tuesday evening we gathered in rooms in that red-brick Georgian building to meet people desperate for legal advice.

At this stage I need to rewind a few years to relate how I ended up studying law. All through my school days in Dominican College Sion Hill in Blackrock, the teachers described me as a conscientious student. Despite my efforts, however, I never did well at exams. Nerves would always get the better of me, and my performance in exams suffered.

I don't know why I got so nervous. My mother never made any demands on me when it came to exams. *Don't worry, Ann Maria. All you can do is your best.*

I studied hard for the Leaving Certificate, but I wasn't confident that I'd get results I needed to get into university. The summer of 1972 we went to America again, where for the first time I worked with my mother in Mountainside Hospital in Montclair. As a member of staff in the dietary department, I wore a white uniform and spent my days sorting and delivering trays for the patients who required specialised diets.

While I was there, the Leaving Certificate results were announced. Trembling, I rang the school to get my results and discovered I had received enough honours to go to college. The problem was that I had no idea what I wanted to study. It was a girl, whose name I no longer remember, who influenced me in my choice of a college course. She gave me Latin grinds and had such an air of confidence that I looked up to her. When I learnt that she was studying law, I decided it would be a good idea for me too. So I signed up for a bachelor of civil law in University College Dublin, in Belfield, Dublin.

By the time I met Andrew in FLAC, I was in the final year of my degree and failing most of my exams. By then I knew law wasn't the right career path for me, but I was determined to persevere and get my degree.

Andrew was a handsome man. He was tall, with a thick mane of long hair that reached the collar of the neatly pressed suit he wore for work. He got his law degree through an apprenticeship in a city-centre law firm and by studying in Blackhall Place, the headquarters of the Law Society of Ireland. He was one of the youngest solicitors to graduate from Blackhall Place in 1977, at age twenty-two.

By the time I met him, he was working for Gerard Black, on South Frederick Street in Dublin's city centre, and volunteering in the free legal aid office every week.

We talked a few times in FLAC, but there wasn't much more to it. He didn't seem my type, and I was distracted by an on-again, off-again relationship with a man called Nat McNabb. One evening, as I put on my coat to leave FLAC, Andrew appeared by my desk.

'You off, then?'
'Yes, that was my last client.'
'I'm having a party this weekend.'
'That's nice.'

'Would you like to come?'

'Oh, thank you, but I don't think so. I wouldn't know anyone.'

'You'd know me.'

Maybe it was then that I really looked at him and saw something appealing in those eyes. Much later I discovered that Andrew went home that night and hurriedly arranged a party that weekend. I was much less amused when I also discovered he'd only summoned the courage to ask me out after a colleague bet he wouldn't do it.

'You made a bet about asking me out?' I said. 'Are you telling me that you asked me out because of a bet?'

In the end it wasn't any one thing about Andrew that attracted me; it was a combination of so many things. I didn't think we shared many interests, but as we talked and danced that evening, I realised we had many shared values.

'So where did you go to in France?' Andrew said.

'You probably never heard of it, but it's the most amazing place called Taizé.'

'Of course I've heard of it, but I haven't been there.'

I was glad that he had heard about Taizé as it was such an important place to me. Prayer and church were an integral part of my life as a small child. As I grew into a young adult, spirituality became even more crucial to me. I was searching for ways to connect to the Divine. I had a yearning and a curiosity to know more about the workings of the universe.

The Jesuits ran a retreat centre for young people called Tabor House at Milltown Park in Ranelagh. I found lots of like-minded people there and spent evenings exploring ways we were going to change the world. It was there that I first heard about Taizé.

My college friend Mary Kate Egan and I spent a sun-filled summer grape-picking and doing voluntary work in Lourdes in France in 1976. Before we returned home, I persuaded her to come with me to visit Taizé. 'Everyone who has been there says that it's a magical place,' I told her.

It was meant to be just a brief stay, but straight away I was captivated. Located in beautiful Burgundy countryside, Taizé is a monastic community that welcomes mainly young people from around the world to join in prayer, reflection and meditation.

It is run by brothers from Catholic and Protestant traditions, with the help of volunteer workers called permanents and religious sisters from the order of Saint Andrew. Founded in 1940 by Brother Roger Schütz, while part of France was under Nazi occupation, the place became a shelter for Jews trying to escape into Switzerland.

After the war Brother Roger continued to live with a handful of brothers who took vows of celibacy and poverty. Their message of peace and reconciliation gradually spread far and wide, and Taizé evolved into a major site of pilgrimage for young people. I felt at home there from the very start, so when Mary Kate left, I stayed on.

The food was simple, the accommodation basic. The day was filled with prayer, meditation and communal work. I loved the music, the chants and the spirit of kindness and simplicity that flowed through this community. I was reluctant to leave, but the new college term was starting in Dublin.

On my twenty-first birthday I received funds from a small trust that my mother had the foresight to set up on my behalf. It wasn't a lot of money, but a few years later it allowed me to buy a stone cottage in rural Donard, in County Wicklow. Fauna Cottage was barely habitable, with no plumbing, no sewerage system nor heating, but it was surrounded by glorious woodland and wildlife. It sat in an acre of unspoilt land with the Lugnaquilla mountain in the background. It really was an idyllic spot, with wild deer, foxes, badgers and forest creatures of all sorts wandering into the garden. I bought it because the peace and tranquillity reminded me of Taizé and its surroundings.

At first Andrew had seemed like a man's man to me. Tall, broad-shouldered and athletic, he was into rugby and played as an out-half in Lansdowne FC. He was also a keen tennis player and was interested in lots of sports. As one of the youngest solicitors around, he was clearly intelligent. He just didn't appear to be the creative soul that I imagined as my ideal companion.

As we talked, however, I discovered a whole other side to him. He was a sensitive man, compassionate and caring. I loved that he laughed a lot. It was a gradual process, but I began to trust him and realised he was a kindred spirit.

I remember a night early in our relationship when Andrew

brought me to my front door in Mount Merrion. I had my keys in my hand, ready to turn the porch lock. There was an awkward pause at the front door, and I could see Andrew was hovering.

'Good night, so. Thanks for dropping me home.'

I gave him a shy glance, and that's when Andrew swept in for our first kiss. If I had any hopes of a Rhett Butler and Scarlett O'Hara moment in our relationship, this was not it. Andrew leaned in too fast, so instead of a meeting of lips, his nose collided with my glasses, which flew off and landed in my mother's flowerbed.

'Oh God, I'm so sorry,' he said. He immediately bent down and began to rummage in the rose bushes to retrieve my glasses. It took a second or two, but I couldn't help myself. I got a fit of giggles. Andrew looked up in surprise, and he started laughing then. When we finally stopped laughing, we locked eyes, and the awkwardness was gone.

'Let's try again,' I said, and we did.

Occasionally, I still saw my first boyfriend, Nat McNabb. We met at a Stradbrook Rugby Club dance when we were both at school. He was from Blackrock but lived as a boarder in Castleknock College. He used to sneak out, throw stones up at my bedroom window, and we would take advantage of my mother's one deaf ear to steal kisses at the front door. He was my confidant, and I was his.

We were always breaking up and getting back together again. There was an emotional link between us, a sense of comfort and safe harbour, that we were reluctant to shed. It was during one of our 'off' phases that Nat contacted me. As usual, I was glad to hear from him, and we went for a walk on Killiney Hill.

Finally, he turned to me.

'I still think about you a lot, Ann Maria. What do you think about giving us another try?'

I really liked Nat and enjoyed his company, but I was with Andrew by then. It was still early days with Andrew, but I realised there was something between us.

'Do you know what, Nat?' I said. 'I don't think we should get back together. I don't think it's going to work.'

I may have surprised myself as much as Nat, but I was falling in love with Andrew. The more I learnt about Andrew, the more

I admired him and relaxed around him. I seemed to breathe slower and deeper when he was with me. We were both young and idealistic, and he was passionate about ending injustice and poverty around the world. We began to dream about working together with the underprivileged in faraway continents.

Much of Andrew's compassion may have been born out of his own traumatic childhood. Andrew lost both of his parents within days of each other when he was twelve years old. His father was Michael 'Mick' Dunne, a man whose early life was dominated by rugby at Castleknock College and Lansdowne Rugby Club. Mick was an international rugby player and was capped sixteen times for Ireland between 1928 and 1934. He was even forced to resign from his job at the Hibernian Bank when they refused him a leave of absence to join the 1930 Lions Tour. On his return, he began to study law.

Andrew's father became a solicitor in 1934, working as a partner in the firm Thomas Crozier & Son Solicitors, on Ely Place in Dublin. Six years later he wed the love of his life, Kathleen Murphy. They seemed to have enjoyed an idyllic family life and had three daughters and three sons, the youngest of whom was Andrew.

However, the family was shattered when Andrew's father died suddenly of a heart attack on 7 February 1967, aged only sixty-one. Just ten days later, Andrew's mother, Kathleen, who was eleven years younger than her husband, was pronounced dead in Saint Vincent's Hospital. Andrew always said his mother couldn't bear to live without her soulmate and that she died of a broken heart. Kathleen was laid to rest with her husband in Mount Jerome Cemetery in Dublin.

At just twelve years of age, Andrew's life was irrevocably changed. Following in his late father's footsteps, he was sent to Castleknock Boarding School. Leaving his family home must have been a terrible wrench for a grieving boy. I think it was this childhood heartbreak that prompted his deep emotional response to suffering. He had the kindest heart. Whenever anyone needed help, he was always the first to offer it. Andrew had the most generous and giving spirit.

One of my early memories of us is walking hand in hand in Blackrock Park. We were so in love, totally absorbed in each other, and we didn't notice the dark clouds gathering. Suddenly we were in the middle of a thunderstorm and the rain was falling in torrents. Andrew was wearing a big rain cape, and he battled the wind and rain, trying to shelter both of us under it, like a makeshift tent. I remember a moment when our eyes met, and time seemed to stand still. It was so intimate, and I felt precious, loved and cared for. We laughed as the rain pelted down on us.

That was the thing I loved about Andrew – his humour, laughter and energy was so light. I was used to heavy energy about me, and his energy was so light.

The laughter dimmed for me soon after, however, as my mother made a decision that altered the course of my life.

# *The Day Sky*

## HAFIZ

*Let us be like
Two falling stars in the day sky.
Let no one know of our sublime beauty
As we hold hands with God
And burn
Into a sacred existence that defies –
That surpasses
Every description of ecstasy
And love.*

# MOTHER

―∽―

*This world is shrouded in darkness.*

*Here, only a few can see their way free.*

*These few birds escape from the net and fly away to the heavens.*

Buddha from the Dhammapada

The car was in the drive when I got home, but there was a stillness in the house as I closed the hall door. 'Mummy?' I called up the stairs. There was only silence.

I arrived home a bit later than usual because I had been to look at a car after work. It was to be my first car, something second hand, nothing fancy. By now I was working as a legal assistant in trademark law with hopes of finishing my law studies that year. I was twenty-three years old, a couple of weeks away from my twenty-fourth birthday.

I went into the kitchen, and I saw the note on the table. It was pinned under my mother's glass sugar bowl. A note was rarely good news around our house. My heart pulsed a little faster as I picked it up.

Everything becomes confused, surreal, after that. The words swam before me, not making sense. *By now . . . left this world at Dún Laoghaire pier . . . Too tired to fight anymore . . . can't go on . . . please forgive me . . . I know you will be fine now . . . the whole of your life ahead of you . . . love you so much . . . Mummy.*

I don't remember her exact words. They were full of love and heartfelt apology. Yet it was a letter that triggered so many distressing memories that I destroyed it many years ago.

## Carried on Spirit Wings

I know my first reaction was to get to Dún Laoghaire pier to stop her. I heaved a breath, my mind moving at a frantic pace. *What time did she write this? Am I too late?* But it was a warm and bright evening in July. There would be far too many people strolling in the sunshine. *If she tries to do anything before I get there, please God someone will stop her.* I rang who I always called in an emergency.

'Quick, Uncle Jimmy, come now. She says she's going to kill herself!'

My hands shook so hard I could barely turn the pages of the phone book. *Who do I call? What do I say?* The phone at Dún Laoghaire garda station rang out.

My mother had not been well and had withdrawn into herself again. She was confused and hearing things that weren't there. A few nights earlier I had helped her into the car and had driven in a downpour to Saint Patrick's Hospital to have her admitted. I pulled in at the old hospital off Thomas Street, but those wrought iron double gates that guarded the entrance were locked. Getting out of the car, I tried to see around the tall granite pillars that flanked the gates. There was a guardhouse inside, a sentry box of sorts. It was usually manned, but it was empty that night. I got back into the car.

'We'll have to wait, Mummy. There's no one to let us in.'

My mother sat, head down, huddled into the front passenger seat.

'I don't want to go in, Ann Maria,' she said. Her tone was quiet and low.

'I know, Mummy, but you need help. I should have brought you in earlier.'

We sat in silence for a while; the only sound was the steady patter of rain on the car.

I wondered if there was a phone box nearby where I could call the hospital. I checked my pockets to see if I had the coins to make a call. But I didn't want to leave my mother in the car alone. Still no one came to the gatehouse.

'Let's go home, Ann Maria. There's no one here.'

'We'll wait a while. The guard might have gone on his break.'

'I'm tired. I want to go home. I can go to Cluain Mhuire first thing in the morning.'

Cluain Mhuire was a community service in Blackrock where she sometimes received outpatient care.

'I think you need to go into hospital, Mummy.'

'Please, Ann Maria. Please. I can't bear it. I don't want to go into that place again.'

'You know they can help you, Mummy. You'll feel better once you're in there. You know you will. Just wait a while. The guard will come back.'

'Please, Ann Maria. Please, let's go home. I'll go to Cluain Mhuire, and if that doesn't help, we can come back here another day. Just please, let's go home.'

She was pleading now, tearful. I couldn't refuse her. We drove home, and she went to Cluain Mhuire the next day. She said it was helping.

The fear of my mother harming herself was an underlying tension in my life. She had suicidal thoughts, or what we refer to these days as 'suicidal ideation'. There were possible attempts over the years, a drug overdose that was put down to confusion over her dosage. We never talked about it. We never really spoke about my mother's illness at all. I remember there was one occasion when we were meant to go somewhere, but she was ill again. She could barely speak. She was too low to go anywhere.

'I'm really sorry, Ann Maria. I'm not well,' she said.

I was filled with sadness for her. I never wanted her to know that her illness affected me.

'Mummy, please don't worry,' I said, wrapping my arms around her in a hug. 'I love you. You're the best mummy in the world.' And I did love her.

Yet growing up, I always feared something terrible would happen to her. When I was older, I made an appointment to see my mother's consultant. I wanted to understand what was going on and if I needed to worry about her committing suicide. The doctor reassured me.

'Don't worry,' he said. 'Your mother may make a cry for help, but she'll never take her own life.'

I tried to calm myself by reminding myself what the doctor had said. *She'll never take her own life. This note is that cry for help.*

## Carried on Spirit Wings

*That's all it is. She even wrote where to find her. I'll get her into Saint Patrick's tonight, and she'll be fine.*

Uncle Jimmy arrived, and we reached Dún Laoghaire's East Pier in minutes. A small queue had formed outside Teddy's for ice-cream cones. Couples and parents with small children milled around. *No one could kill themselves here.* We ran down the pier, past the Victorian bandstand, desperately looking for someone with my mother's slim form, her quick stride. I looked down the length of the pier hoping to see a slight and lonely figure lingering by the water's edge. We ran and ran along the concrete surface out into the glittering bay. It was strangely silent even though lots of people were out for an evening stroll. All I could hear was the clinking of boats, the water lapping against the wall and the heavy beat of my heart. Voices seemed muted, and everyone was faceless, even though I was frantically searching for anyone remotely resembling my mother's height and build.

'Have you seen a woman, sixtyish, slim, on her own, maybe acting strangely?'

People shook their heads. I tore on down the pier, the panic in me rising with each passing second, Jimmy left in my wake. My mind was spinning. *Where is she? Oh dear God, where is she?* I reached the end of the pier, breathless and scared. She wasn't anywhere to be seen, so I turned back, running back towards Uncle Jimmy.

We saw two men in uniform ahead. *Harbour* police. We ran to them.

'Have you seen a woman? Small, slight, in her sixties. We're worried about her.'

The men understood our shorthand. The people who work around Dún Laoghaire pier have witnessed many broken souls being fished from the sea. One of the men hesitated, and then he said the words that made the blood in my veins run cold.

'There was a body taken from the water a couple of hours ago.'

The fear that rose in my throat threatened to choke me.

*Oh dear God, may it not be her. Dear God, may it not be her.*

They said the body was brought to St Michael's Hospital in Dún Laoghaire. So, Jimmy and I ran again. We ran for the car that would bring us to the hospital. I prayed loudly and with more desperation than I've ever done in my life before.

*Oh please, Jesus Christ, may it not be her. Please, Jesus Christ, let it not be my mother. I'll do anything, Jesus Christ, if you make it not her.*

It was like a mantra.

*Oh please God, may it not be her. Please God, not my mother.*

I pleaded with God, out loud and in my head, and I kept pleading right up until the instant that they peeled back the covering in the morgue.

But it was my mother. They took off the covering, and it was my mother who lay there.

The pain of seeing her on that slab was so intense, so agonising. She was so still, alabaster white and cold to the touch. I had no sense of her being at peace. All I knew was that she was gone. My mother was dead. Uncle Jimmy must have kept me upright because my whole world collapsed at that moment.

She had it all worked out. It was 19 July 1978, a warm afternoon, when she took a bus to Dún Laoghaire. We chased down the wrong pier as it turned out. She had gone down the West Pier, where it's longer, stonier and lonelier.

Maybe someone saw her go into the water. I don't know. She was found quickly, but I never talked with anyone who helped pull her body from the sea. I remember someone from the morgue gave me my mother's wedding ring in a little plastic bag. And I looked at my mother again, and thought it was odd that her earrings, delicate little gold ones with pearls that she always wore, had disappeared. I wondered if she took them off and left them on the sea wall for someone to find, but I never saw them again.

I was sick with shock in the hours and days afterwards. This was too outlandish, too horrific, too impossible to be true. My mother had committed suicide; she had drowned herself. *This couldn't be real, could it?*

But then it was like she died again to read it in black and white on the front page of the *Irish Independent* the next day. The headline read: BODY RECOVERED.

> The body of Mrs Angela Byrne, Upper Trees Road, Mount Merrion, Dublin, was taken from Dún Laoghaire Harbour

last night by Gardaí and local fishermen. The body was noticed floating in the water by a passer-by.

It felt like I was trapped in some nightmare, and if I could only wake up, it would all be over. 'Why?' I wailed. 'Why would they publish that? Dear God, why would they be so cruel?'

I felt an intense, bruising and sickening physical agony when I thought of how my mother died. I didn't want anyone to know of her suicide. I cried and cried. I was crushed by the shame of her suicide and by the guilt that I didn't save her. The stigma surrounding mental illness and suicide was terrible. No one spoke about it. No one talked about how she lost her life. Everyone was sorry for my loss, but the circumstances of that loss were carefully avoided. I carried the deep pain of my mother's loss, but there was also deep shame.

I think my overwhelming feeling, however, was one of guilt. *If only I had waited that night outside Saint Patrick's mental hospital. Why did I go home that night? Why didn't I make that phone call to Saint Patrick's? Why didn't I do something sooner? If only I came back straight from work that evening instead of looking at that stupid car.* My mind was reeling in a torturous, endless cycle of what-ifs and if-onlies. I blamed myself. I felt there were a thousand things I could have done differently.

I read her note over and over. She said I would be fine without her. It was like she believed she had finished her job, and she felt free to leave. I had recently introduced her to Andrew. Was that her cue to go? *Did she think she could just kill herself and I was going to live happily ever after?* I wandered around in disbelief.

*Why did she do this? How could she do this?*

I thought about that meeting several years ago with her consultant. 'He said she would never kill herself!' I must have said those words a thousand times. 'He told me she would never kill herself!'

The following days were a blur to me. My mother's funeral mass took place in Saint Thérèse's in Mount Merrion that Friday, two days after her death. We laid her to rest with her family in Templemore Cemetery in County Tipperary that afternoon.

The one thing I clearly remember is our neighbour, Aunt Betty, putting her hand on my shoulder and saying, 'You know, your mother was a very brave woman, Ann Maria.' I was stopped in my tracks. I thought it was a very odd thing to say. I really did. My mother's suicide note was still sitting on the kitchen table, and a neighbour was calling her brave.

It has taken many years but I know now it was true. She was a courageous woman. My mother suffered so much for a long time. She endured mental torture for years and forced herself to live until she believed I had found my way. She only stayed alive as long as she did for my sake. She waited until she thought I was old enough to survive on my own, and then she went into the sea and ended her life.

I'm the age now that she was when she took her life, and I feel sad thinking of all the years she missed. But then, if those years were unbearable for her, would I really want her to have lived like that? I know that I don't have the courage that my mother had. But it has taken a long time for me to understand that.

# *The Bright Field*

R. S. Thomas

*I have seen the sun break through*

*to illuminate a small field*

*for a while, and gone my way*

*and forgotten it. But that was the*

*pearl of great price, the one field that had*

*treasure in it. I realise now*

*that I must give all that I have*

*to possess it. Life is not hurrying*

*on to a receding future, nor hankering after*

*an imagined past. It is the turning*

*aside like Moses to the miracle*

*of the lit bush, to a brightness*

*that seemed as transitory as your youth*

*once, but is the eternity that awaits you.*

*Reproduced with the kind permission of Elodie Thomas.*
*© Published by The Orion Publishing Group Ltd.*

# MARRIAGE

---

*Love is patient and kind; love does not envy or boast; it is not arrogant or rude.*

*It does not insist on its own way; it is not irritable or resentful.*

*It does not rejoice at wrongdoing but rejoices with the truth.*

*Love bears all things, believes all things, hopes all things, endures all things.*

*Love never ends.*

1 Corinthians 13:4–8

---

Andrew and I emerged from the church as husband and wife, gazing in awe and happiness at the winter wonderland around us. Everyone's breath rose like a cloud in the frosty air. I raised my hands with joy as the snowflakes floated weightlessly down from the heavens.

Salt tears mingled with the melting flakes on my face, and I spun around, my wedding dress a matching swirl of pure white in the virgin snow.

'It's like confetti, Andrew!' I said, my face upturned in delight to the sky. 'My mother is up there, looking down, and she's showering us in confetti!'

I woke up on my wedding day to discover the world was covered in a feathery white eiderdown. It was like the universe had handed me a fresh new page for the start of my married life. It was a magical end to the worst year of my life when we got married on Saturday, 30 December 1978, five months after my mother's death.

For me nothing was ever the same after my mother died. I felt like an exposed nerve in the weeks and months after; the pain and the despair were overwhelming. Mary Kate came to stay with me in my Mount Merrion home for a few weeks; I found it hard to be on my own in a house full of memories of my mother.

'Come on, Ann Maria, you have to get up and eat,' she'd say. 'Just eat a bit of this, and then I'm bringing you out for some fresh air.'

My whole world had imploded, and I didn't know how to cope. The emotional void that was caused by my mother's loss was filled by fear and anxiety, and I experienced severe depression for the first time in my life. The fact that I wasn't enough reason for my mother to stay alive left me with no self-esteem. My mother had killed herself; she had deliberately left me. I felt a deep sense of abandonment for the second time in my life. There was no possibility of resuming normal life.

'I can't go back to work,' I sobbed. 'I know you think it will be good for me, but I can't. I can't face anything right now.'

When Mary Kate had to leave, I knew I had to go somewhere too. The only place I wanted to be in the aftermath of my mother's death was Taizé. I needed a complete retreat from the world to heal. I lost myself in the prayer, the meditation and the simple routines and repetition of everyday life in Taizé. A sense of peace settled around me like a comforting blanket.

The lifestyle of Taizé was simple and basic. At first glance, it was like any campsite, with low wooden chalets and tents surrounded by the woodlands and meadows of the Burgundy countryside. Visitors were called to prayers with the brothers in the early morning, at midday and again in the evening. The prayer services were uplifting and beautiful, and so was the singing. The songs, sometimes short Bible verses set to music, were repeated over and over as chants. Each service included ten minutes of silence for prayer and meditation.

Sometimes, we were split into small groups to sit on the grass, under the cooling shade of the trees, where we joined in Bible study sessions. The brothers or sisters introduced a Bible text, and everyone discussed and reflected on the words. Participants were also expected to do simple chores in the community. Some of us ended up in the kitchen on the washing-up team. Others held the 'silence' signs reminding people of quiet areas. More again collected rubbish or served food, and some were in the laundry. The atmosphere was one of cooperation and generosity. People did their chores with cheer and enthusiasm, and they lived in either tents or 'barracks' – rustic dorm rooms. I remember eating a lot of lentils, couscous, bread and fruit.

Andrew came to visit me while I was there. I remember feeling my heart lift when I saw his big smile, his soft eyes and that sparkle of warmth he brought with him. It was lovely to embrace him and feel those comforting arms of his again for the first time in weeks.

'It's so good to see you again, Andrew,' I said. It really was. I was happy he was with me, and that he was experiencing my safe haven in the world for the first time. Andrew immersed himself in the spiritual atmosphere of Taizé and savoured the peace and tranquillity.

'I wondered why this place has such a hold on your heart, and now I know,' he said. 'Everything is basic, but the sum of all these simple parts adds up to something so powerful and so moving.'

We sat one evening on the floor of the community's church, the Church of Reconciliation. The prayer service was over and only a handful of people lingered in the vast place. It was in darkness apart from the flickering candles. We loved sitting in that sanctuary at night, gazing upon Taizé's Orthodox-style crucifix. Andrew would soon be leaving because he had to get back to work in Dublin, but I was staying on longer.

'I just want to know that you're going to be okay,' Andrew said.

'I couldn't be in a better place for the moment, Andrew. I just need more time here.'

He held my hand and squeezed it.

'We're going to be together, forever. You know that, don't you?'

I looked at him. His soul shone through those eyes, and it was a gentle soul.

I laid my head against his shoulder.

'I know,' I said. And I did.

There was no conventional proposal on bended knee. It was a gradual process of realising that we were always going to be together. We developed an intense, emotional connection. In the months after my mother's death, it seemed unthinkable that we wouldn't always share a future together.

We attended the wedding of Andrew's brother, Peter, in November and were swept along with the romance of it.

'What are we waiting for?' Andrew said that evening. 'We know we're going to be together always, so why don't we get married now?' I was startled for an instant and then I realised that he was right. It seemed then like the most natural thing in the world to do. I was still grieving my mother's death, and I was angry with her for dying, so maybe it wasn't ideal timing. But I knew I loved Andrew and I knew, without doubt, he loved me. The word that comes to mind when I think of Andrew is 'cherished'. He made me feel so cherished.

We planned to set up home in Fauna Cottage in the Wicklow mountains. Andrew was as charmed by the cottage as I was, and it was less than thirty miles from his work in Dublin. It was still in semi-derelict condition, but we started to renovate the house. We had a shared dream of living a sustainable and self-sufficient lifestyle, of growing our own fruit and vegetables and introducing animals. We were inspired by Taizé and its ethos of simple living and homesteading.

We drove around Wicklow one weekend to find the perfect church for our wedding day. As we travelled through a remote area near Greenane, I almost missed it. Saint Columba's Church sits back off the narrow road on a slight rise.

'Back up, Andrew. I think I've seen our church!'

He reversed his rattling Renault 4, and we got out and breathed in the silence and the stillness. The old church was a simple structure, with arched doorways and windows, that was set into a copse of trees. It sat on an elevation with panoramic country views, and ancient gravestones studded its grounds.

'This is the one!' said Andrew with a smile, looking around appreciatively at the wintry landscape.

We managed to find the home of the elderly priest of the parish, a Saint Columban father who was back from the missions. We told him of our hopes to be married as soon as possible. I remember the craggy-faced old man taking out his black diary and flicking through the pages.

'So what day are you thinking of getting married?'

'As soon as possible, Father,' said Andrew. 'Is the week after next available?'

The priest peered at us over his spectacles. He may have been suspicious.

'You know, you can't get married until the banns are read.'

Andrew and I glanced at each other, neither of us sure what that entailed.

'The banns are a public announcement of your intention to marry. They must be read in your parish churches for three successive Sundays before I can marry you. I'll need letters from your parish priests to say the banns are done.'

'So after three Sundays, where does that leave us with a date, Father?' Andrew asked.

The priest pointed in his diary to the first available weekend, and it was days after Christmas. My face lit up.

'A Christmas wedding is perfect!'

We chose Saturday, 30 December, as our wedding day. We hadn't expected the delay, but we were delighted with the prospect of a Christmas wedding.

We planned a small event, with no fuss. My mother had died five months earlier, so there was to be no elaborate bridal gown or train. I bought an off-the-peg silk damask dress from a boutique in Dublin. The dress was simple, winter white in colour, with a flowing skirt that fell below my knees. It came with a matching white waistcoat. My bridesmaid, Mary Kate, laughed when I chose a pair of black, patent-leather knee-high boots for my bridal footwear.

'What about Olen?' I asked Andrew. 'I can't leave him all on his own for the whole day. There's no one left to mind him.'

Olen was my beloved red setter.

'We can bring him with us,' said Andrew. 'He can be part of the wedding, can't he?'

So I tied a big white bow to Olen's long and silky coat, and he became part of the official wedding party.

The snowfall that morning was a bonus. Some guests worried that snow drifts would block the narrow country roads, but I was thrilled. To me, it was enchanting. The countryside looked transformed with its new white overcoat, and even the bare branches of trees were laden with snow. Everything had changed, and after the trauma of my mother's death, I needed this newly washed world.

It was a bitterly cold day. As the snow fell, my cousin Pat Lavin drove me to the church in his sports car. Everyone had to huddle together in the little church for the ceremony. I remember poor Uncle Jimmy trembling with both cold and nerves before we walked down the aisle.

'It's okay, Uncle Jimmy, there's nothing to be nervous about,' I said, squeezing his arm. 'It's a small wedding. You know everyone!'

I didn't have any nerves at all. I was the happiest bride that day as I looked into Andrew's eyes and we exchanged our vows. My tears started flowing as we came out of the church and the snowflakes drifted down upon us. I missed my mother. She should have been there, but I spun around under her heavenly confetti instead.

We celebrated our small wedding in a thatched restaurant, now long closed, called Armstrong's Barn. Singer Chris de Burgh's sister-in-law, Susan Morley, and her chef husband, the late Paolo Tullio, owned the restaurant.

A roaring fire and candles lit the room. In the flickering shadows, I can still see my Aunt Nora and Uncle Jimmy, Mary Kate and our friends and family toasting our health. The converted barn was the perfect cosy setting for our relaxed day.

Andrew and I had two honeymoons. We drove to the romantic country house hotel, Marlfield House, in County Wexford. Andrew laughed as he parked his battered Renault 4 among the BMWs and Mercedes in the car park. We spent three nights living in the luxury of gilded period furniture, artwork and lavish surroundings.

Afterwards we went on holiday to Malta. Despite rain clouds hovering overhead most days, we had a blissful time walking hand in hand along lonely beaches and exploring some of the hundreds of Malta's churches.

The miracle church in Mosta stands out in my mind. We travelled to the town to see the Church of the Assumption of Our Lady. It was a chilly day in January, and the church was empty. The only information we had on the Miracle of Mosta was a paragraph in our guidebook:

> Malta was heavily bombed during World War II, and German bombs fell on Mosta's church as many hundreds worshipped inside on 9 April 1942. A huge bomb pierced the dome and landed on the floor of the church. Two more landed in the square outside, but all failed to explode.

The sacristan of the church, an old man with a nut-brown face, approached us and addressed us in Maltese.

'Sorry, we only speak English,' said Andrew, with an apologetic shrug.

'Boom!' the old man said, pointing to a dent in the church's floor tiles. 'Boom!' he said, throwing his arms up and asunder with a broad smile. We smiled back in understanding.

'This is where the bomb landed,' said Andrew, and we looked up in awe at the huge dome it had pierced. 'This beautiful place could have been reduced to rubble. Miracles really do happen.'

The honeymoon continued for a long time. Andrew had started up on his own as a solicitor, so he was able to keep his own hours. I began teaching part-time in a local Montessori school. Many of our friends had big mortgages and were starting out in demanding careers, but we had our modest little cottage in the Glen of Imaal. We had an old car, a small house and few financial pressures.

We hired a builder for the renovations to Fauna Cottage, and after a few hectic months, we started married life together in County Wicklow. It was wonderful, and Andrew was a true romantic. He often left small love notes around the house for me to find. There didn't need to be an occasion. Sometimes I'd wake up to see a note left on his pillow, or else he'd pop one in a drawer or the car. I still have some of them:

*All my love to you now and forever . . . With you, beside you and behind you. God bless you, Andrew . . . With lots and lots and lots and lots of love to you, Ann Maria, my dear wife.*

We spent a lot of time together. We pottered about, working our garden and living the rural dream. Taizé's message to simplify everything was central in our lives, and that's how we aspired to live.

We wanted to return to a more traditional way of life, and we had great ideas of being less reliant on the outside world.

We installed a replica of the Taizé cross, a glorious colourful crucifix, in our den, and we welcomed people from the community to our house. We had an open house, often welcoming people from overseas through our Taizé contacts. We had interesting guests come and stay, and we would talk into the night about ways we could improve the world. We were idealists with stars in our eyes and openness in our hearts.

Andrew always wore his hair long, even as a practising solicitor. He was never comfortable in the sharp, tailored suits demanded by his profession. He loved every opportunity to shed his shirt and tie and wear his tweed jackets and hats and big woolly jumpers. Everything for us was about getting back to nature and simplifying our lifestyle. We had all these ideas about being self-sufficient. We set out a vegetable patch with raised beds for organic produce. I can still picture Andrew, so proud of his first crop.

'Look, Ann Maria, new potatoes! Our own new potatoes!' he said, beaming triumphantly as he dangled the root crop in the air.

I wanted goats at Fauna Cottage so that we could be self-sufficient in milk and cheese. When I spotted an advert in *The Wicklow People* newspaper for British Saanen goats, I couldn't resist. After a quick viewing and an exchange of crisp pound notes, the farmer helped me pack two white nannies into the back of the car. Andrew heard the panicked bleating even as I pulled up outside Fauna Cottage.

Our two red setters circled the car, tails wagging with excitement. Andrew took one look at the anxious goats' faces pressed against the car window and burst out laughing.

'I guess we have two new Dunne family members!' he said.

We christened them Gertie and Esmeralda. Even though they were tethered on long ropes in the field adjoining Fauna Cottage, they managed to cause their own brand of havoc.

'Can you bring me in some spinach and a few carrots for dinner,' I asked one day. Andrew loved picking our produce.

Seconds later, I heard him calling out: 'Get out here quick! Gertie and Esmeralda are on the loose again!'

Running outside, I saw Gertie's head halfway through the

organic salad bed and Esmeralda breaking into the tomato tunnel. We didn't realise how agile and cunning goats can be and how easy they found it to escape from their tethers. Our vegetable plots were well screened off with wire fencing to protect our crops from the visiting deer. But fencing never seemed to be an obstacle to our two nanny goats.

Our plans for milk production worked out fine, as Gertie and Esmeralda proved to be prodigious milk producers. Our attempts at cheese-making turned out a disaster, however, and we abandoned the idea early on. We were total novices in this back-to-basics approach. We didn't understand any of the challenges involved in running a smallholding. But we had such fun trying; we were like two children living in a fairy tale.

When I think back at our happiness, we were so naive. We had no idea that our idyllic lifestyle was about to be cut short, and that all those dreams we held for the future could be so easily shattered.

# *Echo*

CAROL ANN DUFFY

I think I was searching for treasures or stones

in the clearest of pools

when your face . . .

when your face,

like the moon in a well

where I might wish . . .

might well wish

for the iced fire of your kiss;

only on water my lips, where your face …

where your face was reflected, lovely,

not really there when I turned

to look behind at the emptying air . . .

the emptying air.

'Echo' from The Bees *by Carol Ann Duffy.*
*Published by Picador, 2012.*
*Copyright © Carol Ann Duffy.*
*Reproduced by permission of the author*
*c/o Rogers, Coleridge & White Ltd,*
*20 Powis Mews, London W11 1JN.*

# THE OMEN

*Omens are a language; it's the alphabet we develop*
*to speak to the world's soul,*
*or the universe's, or God's, whatever name you*
*want to give it.*

PAULO COELHO

The darkest period of our lives started so innocently. I remember Andrew studying his face in the mirror, turning his chin, this way and that.

'I think I'm reverting to my teenage years.'

'Those spots aren't getting any better, are they?'

'No, they're getting worse if anything. I don't think I had anything like this even when I was fourteen.'

'It's strange to be getting acne at this age.'

His chin was a bright red rash of pimples for many weeks now.

'We're vegetarian, and you're eating the best of organic food. Your skin shouldn't be bad.'

We had become more conscious of health issues. There was a lot of publicity about hormones and steroids being injected into cattle. We were already trying to live a self-sufficient life growing our own vegetables, so I became a vegetarian.

'I've decided that I'm not cooking meat anymore. It's not good for us and not great for the animals either.'

'Okay, but what am I supposed to eat?'

'Whatever you like. But I'm cooking vegetarian food from now on.'

So Andrew became a vegetarian by default.

We didn't really know what we were doing in the beginning. The first vegetarian cookbook we used was called *The Bean Book* by Rose Elliot, a best-selling book in the late seventies and early eighties.

'Lentils . . . lima beans . . . chickpeas . . . soya beans. I don't even know what they are!' said Andrew, flicking through the pages in confusion.

It was unusual to be vegetarian in Ireland at that time but not unheard of. We had two good friends, Russ and Emer Bailey, who were rearing four healthy children as vegetarians in Donard.

The main obstacle to vegetarianism was eating out with friends. Vegetarianism was still regarded as faddish or eccentric in Irish restaurants. Andrew was happy to revert to meat-eating when we were out and liked to tease from across the table.

'Mm-mmm! Roast chicken, gravy and stuffing,' he'd say. 'How's that boiled turnip, Ann Maria?'

However, eating out was only an occasional treat. Andrew's diet mostly consisted of organic vegetarian food, so I couldn't understand how he could be in his mid-twenties and have acne on his face.

'It must be some sort of allergy, Andrew. It's not getting better so I think you should make an appointment with a dermatologist.'

A few weeks later, Andrew went to a skin specialist, a dermatologist in Dublin.

'What did he say?' I asked when he returned from work that evening.

'He took bloods, and he won't know for sure until he gets the results from the lab next week.'

The following week, Andrew returned home earlier than expected. He came straight from his appointment.

'So, is it an allergy?' I asked, convinced that it was.

'No, he says it's cancer.'

I stared at him in shock.

'What do you mean, cancer?'

I was incredulous. Andrew was a healthy, athletic man of twenty-seven. He had just run a marathon, for goodness' sake. He was a vegetarian. He didn't smoke, rarely drank apart from the odd pint.

He looked after himself. Andrew shrugged, and he sat at the kitchen table, looking dazed.

'The dermatologist says the blood tests indicate that it's Hodgkin's disease. He has referred me to an oncologist, but he says that it's very curable.'

And that's how we discovered there was something wrong. In hindsight, Andrew had been saying he was tired for quite a while. I put it down to driving up and down from Dublin every day. You'll always find an excuse for tiredness.

His only symptoms were feeling tired and this kind of acne on his chin. We soon learnt that one of the symptoms of the disease can be patchy or scaly red lesions that can look like a rash or pimples.

We both attended Andrew's first appointment with his oncologist, Professor Peter Daly. He was extremely positive. He told us that the cancer begins in a white blood cell known as a lymphocyte, which is an essential part of the body's immune system.

'But you've been diagnosed at an early stage, and Hodgkin's Lymphoma is one of the most treatable cancers around,' he said. 'You'll have to undergo radiotherapy and chemotherapy, but you're young and strong; you'll bounce back in no time.'

From that consultation, we believed that the cancer was not life-threatening, so we took the news in our stride.

'That was reassuring,' I said after we left the oncologist's office. 'You're going to be okay.'

'The dermatologist said the same thing, but it was good to hear it from the expert,' said Andrew.

It wasn't all good news. Professor Daly advised Andrew that he would need to take considerable time off work.

'This treatment schedule is demanding, and there will be a lot of appointments. You'll also need time to rest and recover.'

Andrew had started up his own practice, so taking time off effectively meant closing. But even that news didn't faze us because we had plans to do other things. It was like fate had shut one door, but so many more were now opening to us.

Andrew and I were also optimistic after hearing all the publicity surrounding the famous jump jockey, Bob Champion. He was recovering from non-Hodgkin's Lymphoma, when he won the 1981

Grand National. His inspirational book, *Champion's Story*, was released months before Andrew's diagnosis in 1982. It all looked so positive. We never dreamt that Andrew would be anything other than another 'Champion' and a triumphant member of the cancer survivors' club.

I have a vivid memory of going along with Andrew to his offices in Mount Merrion for the last time. He had built up a good law practice, but his cancer treatments were about to start. He said it was time to sort out his clients and to divide their cases between colleagues. We sat on the floor with a pile of files and boxes as Andrew deliberated, which of his colleagues would be best suited to each of his clients.

'This client's case is perfect for this practice, but the client is so disorganised, I don't think he'll get on with the solicitor there. I think I'd better suggest Aidan for him instead. He has more patience.'

'Okay, so I'll put this in Aidan's pile?'

As Andrew closed his law practice, it should have been emotional for us. But it wasn't as big a deal as it might be for somebody else. Andrew had no feeling of, *Oh my God, everything I've built up in business is gone.* We were philosophical about it. It felt like we had been sent a message to change direction. We saw his illness as a transitional phase.

'This is for the best,' we said. And we really believed that. Andrew would have time to get better, and meanwhile, we would spend more time together and work out what we were going to do with the rest of our lives. We felt we were destined to do something special together. We saw Andrew's illness as an opportunity to change our lives, to see more of the world. There was no sense of tragedy around closing his practice, only excitement about what we should do next.

We had many ideas about what we wanted to do. We looked at setting up a Basic Christian Community (BCC), a model that was growing in South America. We were meeting with others who were exploring that idea too. Basic Christian Communities consisted of like-minded Christians living in groupings of families, often in their own homes, but supporting each other as a community. They explored the spiritual but also discussed political and social action.

It was an exciting time, with an exchange of opinions and news from people from all around the world. We had Bible studies and celebrated liturgies in our den. Our friends Russ and Emer are Baptists, and their minister, Robert Dunlop, rotated his Bible study groups between our house and others. We hosted many inspirational people who had links with Taizé. We may have lived in the middle of nowhere, but there were always interesting people coming and going.

Andrew's brother, Maurice, who had schizophrenia, stayed with us for a short time. There were no social graces with Maurice. One day he asked straight out: 'Ann Maria, did your mother commit suicide?' For him, there was no judgement, just curiosity. He might as well have been asking me the time. For me, it was like he'd punched me in the gut, hearing the word 'suicide' said aloud. I still harboured terrible shame over my mother's death. No one ever spoke about the circumstances of her death. Andrew's sisters never mentioned that my mother committed suicide, and that was out of politeness. No one talked about it. There was social collusion around covering up suicide, and I was complicit in it.

Andrew worried about his brother's prospects for the future, and we knew there were so many other young people out there like Maurice. So we discussed setting up a centre that offered independent living and also support for those with mental health issues. We had so many ideas for the future, and all of them whirled through our minds.

As the chemotherapy went on, Andrew began to lose weight, and his mane of lovely hair fell out. He always had such a great head of hair. He bought a wig, which bore no resemblance to his natural hair with its thick and wavy curls. It was a brown wig that looked like a wig. I remember we were stopped at traffic lights while driving along the canal in Dublin. A car pulled up beside us. The kids in the back seat stared at Andrew's wig, the way that children do.

'Andrew, look at those kids!' I said. 'You'll have to get a proper wig. Even those children aren't fooled!'

Andrew looked across and, beaming broadly, he yanked that shock of synthetic hair off his head and waved it at them. The children exploded in squeals of shock and excitement, and Andrew dropped the wig back on his head and drove off. I'm sure the parents didn't know what was going on. Andrew's niece Maeve recently recounted a similar incident. When she was ten, she and her sister, Kathryn, were sitting alone with Andrew at the dining table. He suddenly whipped off his wig, and the girls squealed with fright as they didn't know he had been wearing one in the first place. Even when he was unwell, he never lost his sense of fun and humour.

Emer and Russ, who lived nearby, rang us one day. They were thrilled because, after years of waiting, they had got a telephone line. In those days, everyone had to apply to the Department of Posts and Telegraphs for a phone, and the waiting list was years long.

Later that day, Andrew dialled their number. He put a warning finger to his lips and beckoned me closer, so that I could listen in.

'Hello, is that Mr Bailey?'

'Yes, who's this?'

'My name is Shane O'Connell, and I'm an engineer with Posts and Telegraphs.'

'Hello, how can I help you?'

Andrew had lowered his voice several octaves, but I was still surprised that Russ didn't recognise it.

'I'm afraid that there has been a mistake with your line.'

'What sort of mistake?'

'I'm sorry, but I have to disconnect you. Your number was meant to be allocated to someone else.'

'What are you talking about? You're not disconnecting my line.'

I could hear the aggravation in Russ's voice.

'As I said, I'm very sorry, but there's been a mistake. Your number is allocated to somebody else.'

'There's no way you're cutting me off. I've been waiting three years for this line.'

'I'm afraid I have to. This is just a courtesy call to inform you.'

'Don't you dare disconnect me! I want to speak to your supervisor this minute.'

'There's no need to be unreasonable, Mr Bailey. It was a genuine mistake. You shouldn't have been connected at all.'

'I'm unreasonable? I'm unreasonable? I've waited three years for this telephone line, and you're cutting me off the same day! I want to speak to your supervisor now!'

'I'm sorry, Mr Bailey, but it's the supervisor who told me to cut the line.'

Andrew added, 'But don't worry, he said you should get a line in another six months or so. A year at the latest.'

That was the final insult. Russ went berserk with the Posts and Telegraphs engineer, telling him all the reasons that he better not dare disconnect his phone. Somewhere in the middle of the red mist, he must have heard our laughter.

There was silence on his end before the penny dropped.

'Who's this? Is that you, Andrew Dunne?'

Andrew couldn't even reply, he was laughing so hard.

'Andrew? I don't believe this. I'm coming over there to kill you! I swear I'll kill you with my bare hands!'

CLUNK. Russ slammed down the phone, and we cried laughing.

Russ tells the story better than anyone now, and he and Andrew bonded over that joke. Andrew had a wonderful sense of fun, which was good for me. I was too serious at times. He had a better balance.

We had a lot of fun during those days. We bottled fruit, harvested vegetables and went hand in hand on walks with the dogs. We were very content. We had hoped that Andrew's recovery would be faster, but the doctors said the tiredness and loss of weight were normal.

Something strange began happening around that time. It began early one morning when we were woken by a commotion.

'What on earth is that noise?'

Andrew sat up, at once alert.

It sounded like someone was striking the downstairs windows with drumsticks. It wasn't a bang, but it was loud, and it was constant. RAT-A-TAT-TAT! RAT-A-TAT-TAT! We pulled on dressing gowns and went downstairs. The sun was not fully up, but the noise was loud and incessant. RAT-A-TAT-TAT! RAT-A-TAT-TAT!

My heart was pounding. We looked around the kitchen door and saw a line of ravens pecking at the window glass. RAT-A-TAT-TAT! RAT-A-TAT-TAT! We shooed them away, but the noise persisted.

RAT-A-TAT-TAT! RAT-A-TAT-TAT! Every room we went into, they were there at the windows. RAT-A-TAT-TAT! RAT-A-TAT-TAT! They were lined up on all the ledges. We couldn't understand it. We chased them away, but they just came back, or they landed on another window ledge and started again.

In the following weeks, more came. They gathered at the upstairs windows too. RAT-A-TAT-TAT-RAT-A-TAT-TAT! Every morning we woke with a start to that sound. There were lines of them assembled at all the windows. There were so many of them that it was like something from the Hitchcock film, *The Birds*.

I remember lying in bed one morning, weeks later, listening to the same noise over and over again. RAT-A-TAT-TAT-RAT-A-TAT-TAT!

'I'm going out of my mind, Andrew. How long is this going to continue?'

We asked farmers and neighbours in the area, but they weren't experiencing any problem with ravens. Some said the birds were probably eating the putty around the glass. That wasn't the case at all; they pecked the glass. Some said that ravens and crows saw their own reflections in the glass as rival birds. The pecking was just their way of defending their territory and attacking these rivals.

We started sticking up newspapers and hanging teacloths on the windows every night before we went to bed. We knew they couldn't see their reflections anymore, but still they came and woke us every morning. RAT-A-TAT-TAT-RAT-A-TAT-TAT! It went on for weeks. Then, as soon as it started, it stopped, and it never happened again. It was a huge relief, but no one could explain it.

Years later, I discovered that in Celtic mythology, ravens were said to be bearers of ominous news. With their black plumage and grating call, ravens were regarded as an omen of death.

Andrew and I were still one hundred per cent convinced that he would recover. We had no inkling that he might be more seriously ill. The weight had melted away from his body; he was emaciated and needed big woolly sweaters to keep him warm. But we were told that this was all normal, *just a side effect of chemotherapy*. We had no reason to doubt the doctors.

That incident with the birds didn't last long, and it only occurred near the end of Andrew's life. It was as if the spirit world was trying to warn us. Unfortunately, we failed to recognise this omen until it was too late.

# Joy and Sorrow

## Kahlil Gibran

Your joy is your sorrow unmasked.
And the selfsame well from which your laughter rises was oftentimes filled with your tears.
And how else can it be?
The deeper that sorrow carves into your being, the more joy you can contain.
Is not the cup that holds your wine the very cup that was burned in the potter's oven?
And is not the lute that soothes your spirit, the very wood that was hollowed with knives?
When you are joyous, look deep into your heart, and you shall find it is only that which has given you sorrow that is giving you joy.
When you are sorrowful look again in your heart, and you shall see that in truth you are weeping for that which has been your delight.

Some of you say, 'Joy is greater than sorrow,' and others say, 'Nay, sorrow is the greater.'
But I say unto you, they are inseparable.
Together they come, and when one sits, alone with you at your board, remember that the other is asleep upon your bed.

Verily you are suspended like scales between your sorrow and your joy.
Only when you are empty are you at standstill and balanced.
When the treasure-keeper lifts you to weigh his gold and his silver, needs must your joy or your sorrow rise or fall.

# DEATH

*Let me not pray to be sheltered from dangers  
but to be fearless in facing them.  
Let me not beg for the stilling of my pain but  
for the heart to conquer it.*

Rabindranath Tagore

Andrew waved to me from the door of Fauna Cottage as I set off for Taizé during Easter week of 1983. He was on a break from his treatment, but he didn't come with me. It wasn't that he was unwell, but he was tired and wasn't up to all the travelling. By now Andrew had lost even more weight and was feeling the cold a lot. He had to wear lots of layers of clothes. And even though Taizé was a beautiful place, it didn't offer many of the comforts of home. Anyway, I was going on a silent retreat, which is a solitary experience, something you usually do on your own.

I didn't worry about leaving him. He was well, and we were still convinced that he would recover.

A few weeks earlier, I had discovered the Bristol Cancer Help Centre in England. They offered spiritual healing, meditation, dietary advice and other natural health-promoting activities like yoga. The Bristol Diet was vegetarian, so we were already on the same path. I was excited to learn about this additional natural type of treatment for cancer and sent for their cassette of a relaxation visualisation. I recall showing a brochure to Professor Daly and talking to him about it, but he was dismissive.

'The Bristol Diet is supported by all these vitamin companies, and it encourages you to take all of these supplements,' he said. 'It's just self-promotion for vitamin companies.'

We could have said that he and the entire medical industry support big pharmaceutical companies, but we were more naive then. We were twenty-eight years old, and we placed a lot of trust in the medical people looking after Andrew. We only heard about the Bristol Cancer Help Centre a short time before he died, so we never really had a chance to embrace everything they promoted.

I looked forward to a restful retreat in Taizé that Easter, with days filled listening to God through prayer, Scripture readings and personal reflection. Silent retreatants took part in the liturgy and prayers in the chapel three times daily. However, accommodation and meals were in a different area set aside for silence.

Because it was Easter, the emphasis was on the Paschal mystery, a central concept of the Catholic faith, based on the Passion, death and resurrection of Jesus Christ. As I made my way to the village of Taizé, located in the hills south-west of Chalon, I went with a happy heart. I expected to have a peaceful retreat and to return feeling revitalised and refreshed. Instead I had one of the most devastating experiences of my life.

While sitting in the chapel one day, I was overwhelmed by the knowledge that Andrew was going to die. It was more than a feeling or a strong sense. It was a knowing that he wasn't going to live. There was a message: *You must prepare yourself for Andrew's death.*

Some might use the words 'mystical experience' or even 'premonition'. Many religions, including the Catholic Church, refer to 'interior locutions', forms of private revelations that are distinct from apparitions or visions and more like a supernatural communication to the ear or the mind. For me, I can only explain it as a communication from the spiritual world, a message from God. It was clear. *You must prepare yourself for Andrew's death.*

It was instantaneous. I came face to face with the realisation that Andrew was going to die. It hit me as hard as a blow from a hammer. In my head, I begged for it not to be true, but in my heart, I knew it was. I had never felt so alone in my life. *No! No! I will not prepare myself. I will not prepare myself because you are not taking Andrew. Not Andrew. He's all I have in the world.* I cried as

I'd never cried before, rocking forward and back.

People crouched before me.

'What's wrong? Can we help you?'

Others stood around in confusion.

'Is anyone with her?'

'What happened to her?'

They could do nothing. I was hysterical at the thought that I was going to lose Andrew. The sister, who directed my retreat, was the only one I could talk to about the revelation, this awful message I'd received.

Like all spiritual companions, she listened in a non-directive way. She didn't offer any solutions, only spiritual guidance. 'Remain open to God's will, Ann Maria,' she said. 'God will never give us more than we can handle in life.' But I would not accept God's will. *No! No! You are not taking Andrew. Not Andrew.*

The sister read passages of Scripture in a bid to console and encourage me:

> Psalm 34:18: The Lord is close to the broken-hearted and saves those who are crushed in spirit.

> John 14:27: Peace I leave with you; my peace I give you. I do not give to you as the world gives. Do not let your hearts be troubled, and do not be afraid.

But I was hugely resistant. I didn't want God's comfort, solace or promises; I wanted Andrew alive. Every day I went back into the church, L'Église de la Réconciliation, praying to hear a different message, a message of hope, but it never came. I was exhausted by the end of the retreat and had a bone-weary sense of acceptance. There was nothing I could do. I knew in my heart Andrew was going to die. I was full of despair, but there was a small consolation that God, in some way, was preparing me for the inevitable.

Uncle Jimmy met me at the airport and drove me back to Fauna Cottage. I think Andrew must have been surprised when I hugged him harder than I'd ever hugged him before. I didn't want to let him go. I was relieved that although he was tired, he seemed well. Later, after Uncle Jimmy left, Andrew sat down and patted the chair next to him.

'Come here, chicken, and tell me all about Taizé.' I laugh now remembering how he sometimes called me chicken.

I wanted to do anything except talk about Taizé. I didn't trust myself not to get upset. The last thing I wanted was to let him know what I knew. I was devastated, but Andrew was alive. I couldn't let him know what happened in Taizé.

'You first, tell me about everything I missed in Donard,' I said. 'There's not a lot to tell about a silent retreat!'

We spent a quiet evening together, but as we were about to go to bed, I thought his colour looked rather high. I put the back of my hand to his forehead.

'Do you have a temperature?' I asked.

'Maybe I do. I'm feeling warm for a change.'

I rang the former Mercer's Hospital where he was being treated, and when they heard he had a fever, they said I needed to bring him straight in. Even though I knew that Andrew was going to die, I still thought we had more time. *Far more time.* As Andrew walked out the door of Fauna Cottage, I never dreamt that it would be for the last time.

I remember that journey to Mercer's Hospital in Dublin's city centre. We played a cassette tape of Taizé chants and sang along. The songs soothed both of us. We sang until we got to the hospital on Stephen Street Lower. They said Andrew had pneumonia. His immune system was compromised by chemotherapy treatment, so he had to be admitted. They put him in a small private room. The doctors said it was only a minor setback, and they began treating him with high doses of intravenous antibiotics.

Aunt Nora and Uncle Jimmy's home was a short drive from the hospital, so I stayed with them at night and saw Andrew every day. However, the medical team were operating on a different plane to me. As far as the doctors were concerned, Andrew was going to be fine after a course of antibiotics. I could see that he wasn't improving, and I was operating from an awareness that Andrew was going to die. I thought it was important that someone told his sister Kathryn, who was living in Brussels, so I spoke to Andrew's brother Peter.

'Kathryn needs to come home,' I said. 'Andrew is not well. I think he's going to die.'

I shocked him with that statement. Of course I did. I wasn't thinking straight. I was in shock myself. I said the same to other people, who were upset too. They consulted with the doctors who insisted Andrew would recover, so people were confused.

*What are you talking about, Ann Maria? Andrew's going to be fine. He's twenty-eight years old. He'll be fine once he's treated with antibiotics.*

My reality was different from everybody else's. So instead of being worried about Andrew, something extraordinary happened: Everyone's eyes swivelled in my direction, and they all started to be concerned about me. The doctors urged me to 'have a chat' with Mercer Hospital's psychologist.

'I hear that you are just back from France,' he said.

'Yes, I was on a retreat.'

'Was it for your nerves?'

He thought I was having some kind of mental breakdown.

'It was a spiritual retreat.'

'Was it the kind of retreat where you were fasting?'

'No.'

He must have thought I was losing the plot from not eating. The quiz continued.

'Your friends say that something happened to you when you were away and that it's worrying you.'

'I received a message that Andrew is going to die.'

'Who sent this message?'

I sighed. I knew this was not going to go well.

'It was a message from God that I had to prepare myself for Andrew's death.'

The psychologist nodded sympathetically and prescribed a week-long break with medication. He didn't actually say it, but it was clear he thought I was delusional.

'You need to know, Mrs Dunne, that your husband is not dying. I've talked with his medical team. He is not in any danger. But we're worried that his illness is all getting too much for you.'

So I was given a prescription for heavy sedation and confined to bed for a week. I was dazed by it all. No one told Andrew what I'd said, but they told him they were worried about me. He could see that I hadn't been myself since I'd returned from Taizé.

'Listen to the doctors, Ann Maria,' he said. 'Take a break from the hospital. You've been spending too much time here. I'll be grand.'

My spirit was broken. No one listened to me or believed me. I was living in a different reality from the world around me, and I was scared. Everyone, including Andrew, was worried about me. I went back to my aunt and uncle's house, and I took the medication. It did its job. The tranquillisers floored me, and I didn't get out of bed for a week.

I had a few brief moments of consciousness when my aunt came up with a tray for meals. Every time I woke, I would only ask: 'Is Andrew alive?'

Aunt Nora would assure me that Uncle Jimmy had called the hospital.

'Andrew's asking for you, and he's asking if you're taking your pills.'

These messages back and forth between my uncle and the hospital were the only contact Andrew and I had. I slept, I woke, I asked my question, I ate, and I went back to sleep.

I lived in this strange twilight zone for a week, a world where everything was distorted. I kept taking the tranquillisers. I started feeling that they were killing me, and that would be a good thing. *How can I live if Andrew dies? If I keep taking these pills, I won't wake up at all.*

And when I got messages from Andrew asking if I was still taking the pills, I thought it was a sign he was encouraging me to die with him. I was committing suicide. It was a great relief to me that this was all going to end. Tranquillisers target the chemical in the brain that controls rational thought and emotions. They certainly sent my mental processes haywire. I was convinced all that week that I was going to die, and I welcomed the prospect of death.

After a week passed and the tranquillisers wore off, I was allowed into the hospital to see Andrew again. There was little sign of Andrew improving, but his medical team were still adamant.

'Andrew's getting antibiotics, and he's going to be fine. This is all very treatable.'

I saw people eyeing me, assessing me, so I didn't mention that message from Taizé again, not until after Andrew died at least. I suppose I had calmed down. The enforced rest had been good for me. I was able to function better, but I was still living with this deep awareness that he wasn't going to live. There was never any acknowledgement from the medics that Andrew was dying until near the very end.

I went to the hospital every day, and so did a lot of Andrew's friends and family. He enjoyed the visitors, the distraction. People asked all the time when he would finish the antibiotics and when he'd be allowed to go home.

'It'll be another few days,' he would say. I'd nod, and I'd smile in agreement, even though I feared Andrew wasn't going home again.

I remember Father Joe McDermott, or Joe Mac as we knew him, calling in to see Andrew and praying with him. Joe, a man in his mid-thirties, was a director of Teach Bhríde, a house of welcome for young people located in a two-hundred-year-old convent in Tullow. We went there regularly, and Andrew was always very fond of him. Russ and Emer, our neighbours in Donard, came bearing homemade vegetarian food for Andrew. He appreciated those meals because the food was terrible in the hospital. Andrew's sister, Kathryn, also made it back from Brussels to see him. Robert Dunlop, the Baptist minister from Brannockstown in County Kildare, called in to visit. So many people wanted to spend time with him.

There was a big fuss in the hospital when the Archbishop of Dublin came to visit. Archbishop Dermot Ryan, who was Andrew's godfather, was a tall, lean, austere-looking man, but he was such a kind man and a great support to me after Andrew died. Although Andrew was getting weaker, he still welcomed friends who wanted to visit.

One night, near the end, Andrew and I were alone in his hospital room. Most nights, visitors or medical staff were coming in and out, but for a change it was just the two of us. He reached over the bed and held my hand.

'So, what happened in Taizé?' he asked. We hadn't talked about

Taizé since I got back a couple of weeks earlier. I was startled for a moment, but then I returned his gaze, and I saw something in his eyes. A sadness; resignation maybe. *He knows. Oh, my God, he knows he's going to die.* I knew this wasn't the time to offer false optimism. My eyes filled with tears, and I took a deep breath.

'You know, Andrew, I don't think our plans for the life that we thought we'd have, are going to work out. I think God is going to call you home.'

He just said: 'Yes, I think you're right.'

We both exhaled at that moment. Andrew was afraid of how I might react if he spoke about dying, and I had been the same about saying anything to him. In hindsight I think that he knew all along. Something happened to him too that Easter. While I was in Taizé struggling, I think he was also going through his own agony. Easter is about the Passion, a reflection on suffering and sacrifice, and I think he was going through his own version of the Passion that week. He never told me about his experience for the same reason that I didn't tell him about Taizé. We were trying to protect each other. He must have had pneumonia before I came home, but he waited, so we could spend some time together at home before going to the hospital for the final time.

Now that everything was out in the open, we were able to be entirely honest with each other. We cried together, prayed together, and we discussed our lives, our marriage, our happiness. There was also this sense of shock and bewilderment for both of us.

'Why is this happening, Andrew? What is going on? We always believed that God had this big plan for us to change the world together. I don't understand this.'

'I don't understand it either, Ann Maria. It seems like God has other plans.'

I always believed that Andrew and I would grow old together. And now, only four years after we married, the end was near. Emotionally, we were closer than ever. I couldn't bear the thought of losing him, of living in a world without Andrew.

Messages flowed in from all around the world. It was a consolation to us both knowing that the Taizé community were praying for him. There were so many telephone calls, letters, goodwill messages and constant prayers from a global network of people whose lives had been touched by Andrew. At night, I would drive to the Consolata Fathers' chapel on Newtown Park Avenue in Stillorgan, which was open twenty-four hours. I prayed for Andrew and asked for the strength to endure the pain of losing him.

The end came fast. The doctors stopped talking about Andrew's recovery 'taking longer than anticipated' and their expressions became grim. Andrew had more medics than ever drawing bloods and checking his vital signs. They huddled together around their files and charts and spoke quietly but with more urgency. The word 'critical' was suddenly mentioned.

The night he died, his family and I held a vigil around his bedside. We lit candles and sang Taizé chants, 'Bless the Lord, My Soul', 'Jesus, Remember Me', 'Oh Lord, Hear My Prayer', 'Stay with Me', 'Laudate Dominum'.

Andrew was aware of what was going on. It is well known that hearing and touch are important in the final stages of life. So we gathered around his bed, chanting. I was holding his hand as he took his last breath, and he passed over peacefully. He left this life on Saturday, 7 May 1983, a month after my return from Taizé, and a year after his diagnosis.

The memories of what happened after that are a blur. Andrew's removal was held in Saint Joseph's Church on Terenure Road East, which was next door to his family home, Greenogue. We brought his remains to Donard for the funeral mass.

In some parts of Ireland, there's a tradition where the funeral cortege stops outside the home of the deceased. I wasn't expecting it, but as the hearse made its way to the Church of Our Lady of Dolours and Saint Patrick in Davidstown, we stopped outside Fauna Cottage.

I was astonished when I saw the front of the cottage covered in a beautiful display of fresh flowers. An artist friend of ours, Margaret Casey, since deceased, had turned our porch into a glorious floral tribute to Andrew.

His memorial card featured Scripture from John 11:26: *I am the resurrection and the life; He who believes in me even if he dies, shall live; and whoever lives and believes in me shall never die.*

After Andrew was laid to rest in the church graveyard in Davidstown, people gathered at the cottage. Margaret, Emer and many of our neighbours had prepared trays and more trays of sandwiches and cakes. The people kept coming. The cottage was small, so they filled the kitchen, the bedrooms, our garden. It seemed that people were hanging out the windows that day.

They were chatting and laughing and doing what they usually do when people get together. I moved through them, stopping to talk, accepting people's condolences, listening to memories of Andrew. But I couldn't understand how people could laugh. I didn't think I would ever be able to laugh again. I almost resented the sound. Laughter was the sound of people getting back to normal life, and I knew life was never going to be normal for me again.

It was pneumonia that killed Andrew in the end. His system was so weakened by the chemotherapy that he couldn't fight it off. The five-year survival rates for Hodgkin's Lymphoma, which is more than ninety per cent now, was high in 1983 too. The prognosis was excellent for Andrew. I couldn't understand how my healthy young husband had died within a year of diagnosis. He ran in the Dublin City Marathon the year before he died, and he was still playing rugby.

There was never, ever any indication that Andrew wasn't going to come through his illness. Until I went to Taizé, I had no doubt that Andrew was going to recover. We always thought that we would turn things around and have a long life together. I made an appointment to see Andrew's doctor, Professor Daly, sometime after he died. I needed to try and figure out what went wrong.

'It was an extremely aggressive form of Hodgkin's disease, not the normal Hodgkin's, but we didn't know that,' he said. 'We never anticipated this outcome at all. It was very unfortunate.'

*Very unfortunate*, I remember those words so well. They felt so inadequate. It seemed there were different types of Hodgkin's, and Andrew was just unlucky.

I was in a fog of despair and confusion after Andrew died. I hardly knew what was happening except that my husband was gone and that my life as I knew it was gone forever too.

# Window

## Rumi

Your body is away from me
But there is a window open
From my heart to yours

From this window, like the moon
I keep sending news secretly.

# THE FOG

*All I know is a door into the dark.*

Seamus Heaney

For a very long time, I couldn't accept that Andrew was dead. I was cloaked in such a fog of grief; it formed a dark and dense barrier that separated me from the world. I cried so hard, it sometimes felt like the sheer force of my tears could undo his death.

Andrew died at the start of summer, and all through the following months, it seemed strange to see sunshine when my world felt so empty and cold. My life was shattered into so many pieces that I didn't think I could ever put it back together again. I had to find a way to engage with life again, but for a long time, it didn't seem possible. I was devastated.

I was also angry with God, or my understanding then of God. *How could He have taken someone so beautiful?*

After Andrew died, I stayed with my Aunt Nora and Uncle Jimmy. By now, they had sold their shop, Lavin's of Inchicore, and lived in Mount Merrion. I can't remember how long I stayed with them. I was drifting, feeling numb a lot of the time. My mind was still trying to process a future without Andrew in it.

A good friend, Noreen Cullen, who was living in Baltinglass in County Wicklow, came to visit me in Dublin one day. As she was just about to leave, she paused.

'Ann Maria, would you like me to bring you home to Donard?' she said.

It wasn't something I had thought of since Andrew's funeral. *Home.* I had to think about it because I had almost erased Fauna

Cottage and my previous life from my mind. It was almost like a revelation that I had my own home.

'Yes,' I said. 'Yes, I think I would like to go home.'

So, Noreen drove me back to Donard. I remember entering the porch of Fauna Cottage, feeling lost and dazed. But then I saw Andrew's tweed cap on the coat stand inside the door, where he had left it. The pain of his loss hit me with such a ferocity that I bent over double and howled.

As soon as they heard I was back living in Donard, the neighbours couldn't have been kinder. They brought me fruit cakes and soup and offered help with the garden or with sorting out Andrew's things. I remember finding little bunches of wildflowers on the doorstep. My neighbours' children, the Flynns, used to come up the road and leave them for me. The sight of those flowers, heartfelt offerings of love and sympathy, always prompted fresh floods of tears.

The cottage was isolated, and some of my friends thought I was mad living alone up a mountain, surrounded by forest. But one of the reasons I bought Fauna Cottage was for its remoteness. I never had any fear of living in an isolated place, and I found being in nature restorative. I went out for long forest walks, and I often walked down to the church graveyard where Andrew was buried. Sometimes I needed to see the fresh mounds of earth on his grave, to believe that Andrew wasn't coming back.

Living in a remote place didn't make me feel lonely; I was lonely because Andrew wasn't with me. His loss was a deep wound in my heart, and it prompted me to write a short and melancholy poem in my journal:

*I was the rainbow; you were the cloud.*

*We danced and played.*

*I was the sun, and you were the moon.*

*I was the body, and you were my breath.*

*And then death.*

Part of me had also died when Andrew died, and I was very raw and vulnerable. Sometimes, when the pain and the loneliness felt almost unbearable, I focused on the comforting words of Brother Roger from Taizé: *What you are incapable of doing yourself, will be done for you.*

There were times when I couldn't see any point to life; I felt so terribly alone in the world. In some ways, I felt abandoned again, and I really didn't care whether I lived or died. It was often at my lowest ebb that I had a strong sense of Andrew's presence, or a presence of love. It gave me enough hope to hang on for that moment.

It was frightening to be deprived of the person that I had relied upon for love, support and intimacy. Andrew was my support system, and everything we planned together was my future. There was a huge void in my life.

The if-onlies that I first experienced after my mother's death surfaced again. I thought about the Bristol Cancer Help Centre and its holistic programme for cancer patients. I thought, *if only I had known about this centre sooner.* Maybe, if we had followed their suggestions, it would have given him more time or even cured him. I thought, *If only we had got a second opinion and gone to another doctor.* There were all these feelings of guilt and inadequacy. *Maybe I didn't do as much as I could have to save him.*

Four months after Andrew died, a cousin invited me to her wedding in America. The thought of festivities or any merry social interaction was anathema to me. I sent back a reply to say I wouldn't attend. But my Aunt Nora and Uncle Jimmy were going, and they bought me the airline ticket to go with them.

'It will be good for you,' Uncle Jimmy insisted. 'A change of scene is the best thing for you.'

My uncle was right again. I went to the wedding in September, and while I was there, I linked up with the Taizé community in New York. Taizé had fraternities in places of poverty all over the world, and they had two brothers working among the poor in places like Harlem and Hell's Kitchen in Manhattan. Those areas are gentrified now, but they were still ghettos in those days.

I remember I took the subway to an address where the brothers were staying. Moments after leaving the station, I realised I was the only white face as far as I could see. Coming from the white monoculture of 1980s Ireland, I had only American crime shows as a reference for this alien environment. *Oh holy God, what have I done? Aunt Nora and Uncle Jimmy are going to be so upset if I end up another New York crime statistic.*

People were loitering on the street, and others were drinking beer and smoking on the steps of the brownstone tenements. All eyes were on me, this nervous-looking outsider clinging to a piece of notepaper containing a scribbled address. I trembled until one of the brothers answered my urgent rapping on the hall door.

I learnt that the brothers were embarking on a three-month Pilgrimage of Suffering and Hope to other poverty-stricken areas across America. I had been lonely and adrift in the Glen of Imaal for long enough. I seized the opportunity for a distraction.

'Can I join you?' I asked.

Uncle Jimmy and Aunt Nora went back to Ireland, and I stayed in America. For the next three months, I travelled from coast to coast, dipping over the border into Mexico, on this pilgrimage. The Taizé monks visited homeless charities, food distribution centres and educational facilities for the disadvantaged. We travelled to big cities and small towns all along the border as we made our way across to the west coast of America.

I remember visiting an orphanage called Casa de la Esperanza, Spanish for House of Hope, in Tijuana in Mexico. Little children with huge brown eyes ran around the only home some of them had ever known. It was a heart-rending sight in some ways. But this children's home was a beacon of hope in the town of Tijuana, which was then little more than a hive of drug trafficking and sleaze. We went to San Antonio in Texas, a big wealthy city, with towering glass skyscrapers. Yet it had a huge migrant population, many of whom were living in clapped-out cars or on the streets.

We travelled to ghettos in cities like Santa Fe in New Mexico, which were full of desperately poor Mexican immigrants. It was there that I first heard the derogatory term 'wetback', referring to Mexicans who risked their lives to swim across the Rio Grande to America. Those who succeeded in getting across the border were illegal aliens and were ripe for exploitation by employers.

We visited charities in communities across the United States running soup kitchens, language classes and food co-ops. In San Diego in California, I saw lines and lines of people queuing to collect brown paper bags full of tins of baked beans and basic food staples.

There was a recession in America in the early eighties, so I saw a lot of urban decay and terrible poverty. It was a side of America that I didn't know existed. I had only seen the middle-class surroundings of my friends and family in New Jersey before this. I had never associated America with poverty, so this pilgrimage was a real eye-opener for me.

My job was to coordinate group discussions for the brothers during the pilgrimage. Sometimes I'd facilitate smaller groups or lead the singing and chants. The brothers of Taizé never solicited donations nor accepted financial gifts. The idea of the pilgrimage was to raise people's awareness of poverty, to connect with the locals and to inspire them to become involved in their communities. Many social justice groups marched and demonstrated against injustice, and that was important too. But Taizé's approach was more of a contemplative way. The brothers' work resonated among people with a social conscience, encouraging them to become active in local communities.

The pilgrimage was a helpful distraction for me during the months after Andrew's death. I had a purpose and a function in helping the brothers. I was falling apart inside, but I saw that many in the world were suffering in different ways. For those three months, I prayed and I kept putting one foot in front of the other.

By the time I returned to Ireland to spend Christmas with Uncle Jimmy and Aunt Nora, my intuition was drawing me back to Taizé. It was the place where Andrew and I decided to get married. It was also there that I came face to face with the pain of knowing that Andrew was not going to live. Taizé was my refuge and a place where I hoped I could heal. I returned to live in the community in the new year of 1984, and for the next six months, I worked through the pain of Andrew's loss.

I went as a 'permanent', or volunteer, to Taizé this time. Permanents were expected to stay for six months to a year and helped the brothers with the day-to-day running of the place. In return for work, we received food, lodging and spiritual guidance. Grief seemed to make everything more complicated for me, including social interaction. I was functioning but still very wounded; my natural inclination was to socially isolate after Andrew's death. I couldn't lead groups or look after the hundreds of arriving guests each day. I still experienced those intense emotional surges that caused me to break down. The most innocuous comment could trigger tears, and I never knew where or when it would happen. Instead, I stayed in the kitchen, working in the background for the first few months. We cleared dishes after meals, swept up, did general housekeeping and gardening. Everything was done selflessly, mindfully and in the service of others.

The Sisters of Saint Andrew, a Belgian order, collaborated with the brothers in Taizé and acted as spiritual companions for female retreatants. Once again Sister Diane Reynolds accompanied me through my bereavement. A tall woman with sallow skin, she always looked even taller as she wore her dark hair in a rolled bun on her crown. Kind, wise and ten years older than me, she was a discerning woman. Many of her fellow sisters were French or Belgian, but Diane was English-born, and like me she was an only child. Now in her mid-seventies, she heads a community of twenty-three sisters in Belgium and continues her ministry of spiritual accompaniment around the world.

For the longest time, I felt empty with no hope or desire to live. I entered the darkest time that I can recall, lost in a fog of nothingness. It was a darkness that I thought I'd never escape. Living a normal life, finding happiness, seemed unimaginable. However, the daily rhythm of monastic life suited me and gave me the space and privacy to mourn. Sometimes I withdrew into a shell and was unable to connect with the outside world. Other days I exhausted myself crying.

As the months went on, Taizé's quiet and gentle lifestyle was like a balm to my soul. The combination of the daily prayer, simple lifestyle and Diane's compassionate guidance helped me to express my grief. It wasn't therapy but it was incredibly therapeutic. There were even days when I felt deep consolation and inner peace. The restorative effects of Taizé were working their magic almost without me knowing.

It must have been around this time that an idea came to me. It was a solution to my constant search for meaning in my life. It was

## Carried on Spirit Wings

probably a year since Andrew had died, and the struggle to find a way to live without him continued. I thought it had to be more than a coincidence that Sister Diane, my spiritual companion, was a member of the order of the Sisters of Saint Andrew. It had to be a sign from God. Taizé was a place that Andrew loved, and it was here that Andrew and I had agreed to marry. It was also where God revealed that Andrew was going to die. Now I was back in Taizé, working among Les Soeurs de Saint-André. The Sisters of St Andrew's mission was the education of youth and the care of the sick. This was the answer, the path I had been seeking all along.

'I think I have a calling, Sister Diane,' I said. 'I think I have a vocation to join your order.'

I was sure of it. I remember searching Sister Diane's eyes for a reaction. I think I must have hoped that she'd smile and embrace me, tell me that she was glad I had discovered a divine intention for my life. To give her credit, she didn't blink. There wasn't even a hint of amusement in her voice. She was far wiser and more sensible than I was then.

'Ann Maria,' she said, firmly grasping my hands, and looking me straight in the eye. 'You cannot consider making a decision with your life for at least two years. Haven't you ever acted rashly in an emotional moment? Done or said something you later regret?'

'Yes, I suppose.'

'Well, this is that emotional moment. It's a crucial time in your life. Don't make any major changes while you are still in mourning. You can't afford to make any major life decisions now.'

She knew me better than I knew myself, and, as it turned out, so did my Uncle Jimmy. I still hadn't abandoned the idea of a vocation by the time I returned home to Ireland. I discussed the idea with Uncle Jimmy, but his reaction was knee-jerk.

'You'll never deal with the obedience.'

'What do you mean?'

'You would never be able to keep the vow of obedience, Ann Maria. It's not in your nature.'

Of course he was right. I was a free spirit and I liked being able to pick up and go whenever I wanted. I would never have survived a religious life, pledging obedience to an order and a mother superior.

It's just that I felt so alone in the world that the idea of being part of the Sisters of Saint Andrew in Taizé seemed so appealing. I admired their spiritual work and their uncomplicated lifestyle in the gorgeous French countryside. However, I hadn't even thought about the vows of celibacy and obedience. I was twenty-eight years old and struggling to find a place in the world after my husband's death. Our future together was gone, and I was flailing around, trying to find a new life for myself.

Looking back, if I had really wanted to be a sister, I would have visited convents and gone for weekends of discernment, but I never did any of that. It was just a fanciful idea, not a practical one for me. Uncle Jimmy was right. If I wanted to be involved in the Catholic Church, I grew to realise that it would have to be as a layperson.

After months in Taizé, I came out of the kitchen and started working in the *Accueil*, the French word for welcome. This was a reception area where all different nationalities converged on arrival. I was part of the welcoming team for the English-speaking groups, orientating them, handing out timetables and the maps of the place. I was able to interact with people again without fear of bursting into tears.

The permanents of Taizé got time off on Sundays, and we tried to make the most of that afternoon of freedom. A few of us planned a cycle one Sunday afternoon to Vitry-lès-Cluny, a picturesque village nearby.

An American permanent called Thomas was among us. He was from upstate New York and probably drove a car from the time he was sixteen, but he hadn't a clue how to ride a bike. The country roads were narrow and potholed, and the bikes were old and rickety. Thomas looked like he was riding a unicycle on a tightrope, such was the concentration he needed to stay upright.

'Come on, Tom, we only have a day to get there and back!' one of the other permanents yelled.

I remember looking back as trees arched overhead, and I saw the petals of small pink blossoms falling. I was reminded for the first time in ages that I was in a beautiful place. By now, I could see that Thomas was coming down an incline behind us at speed, his expression one of rigid terror as he sped towards us. Suddenly he struck a bump in the road, and he and his bike soared into the air. For a split second it seemed that they almost defied gravity. But then he tipped over the handlebars and fell headfirst into the ditch.

I couldn't help myself. Peals of laughter surged up and escaped from deep inside me. As his hands blindly reached out from the shrubbery, I laughed even harder. I remember that day so well because it was the first time in a whole year that I laughed. *Really laughed.* It felt like a turning point.

That dense fog was lifting at last, and a sliver of light had appeared in the darkness. I was able to see a world beyond Andrew's death. That was the first time since Andrew died that I felt that maybe, someday, I could feel normal again. It gave me some hope that I might survive after Andrew.

# *How to Open your Heart*

JEFF FOSTER

Do not TRY to open your heart now.
That would be a subtle movement of aggression towards your immediate embodied experience.
Never tell a closed heart it must be more open; it will shut more tightly to protect itself, feeling your resistance.
A heart unfurls only when conditions are right; your demand for openness invites closure. This is the supreme intelligence of the heart.
Instead, bow to the heart in its current state. If it's closed, let it be closed; sanctify the closure. Make it safe; safe even to feel unsafe.
Trust that when the heart is ready, and not a moment before, it will open, like a flower in the warmth of the sun.
There is no rush for the heart.
Trust the opening and the closing too; the expansion and the contraction; this is the heart's way of breathing; safe, unsafe, safe, unsafe; the beautiful fragility of being human; and all held in the most perfect love.

# THE QUEST

*Two roads diverged in a wood, and I took the one less travelled by, and that has made all the difference.*

Robert Frost

A burst of gunshots rang out in the humid stillness of the morning. Cries filled the air, and I floundered as people scattered all around me. More gunshots. I threw myself to the ground. The explosions started then, and people scrambled over me, screams ringing out from every direction.

Heart thudding, I crawled on my belly, clawing my way through the smoke-filled air. Soldiers in camouflage rushed towards us, armed with cudgels and guns. I recall the exact place where my desire to live returned, and it was on a bridge nearly seven thousand miles away from home.

When I started to emerge from the pain of Andrew's death, I became absorbed with a search for meaning in my life. I didn't know what I wanted to do. My vision for my future had been the one I'd shared with my husband, and now that he was gone, I had to find a new path. Prayer for guidance and direction became part of my daily life. I was searching for a new identity and a way to be of service in the world.

It seemed fortuitous when I was asked to attend a month-long conference in the Philippines after returning from France. The conference was an international ecumenical event in Manila, and because of my connections with Taizé, I was invited to attend as the Irish delegate. I saw it as a possible sign that my life was about to move in a new direction.

The delegates were sent to Manila on a fact-finding mission and to attend a conference entitled The Role of the Church in the Struggle of the Filipino People. We split up into small groups and were led all over the country by Filipino activists. We travelled to outlying islands where we visited everything from cooperative projects to prisons, and we met people in shanty towns, rehabilitation facilities and women who were involved in sex work. Overnight I was propelled into levels of poverty and suffering I'd never experienced before.

The Philippines was a volatile country under the control of the dictator President Ferdinand Marcos. The culmination of our trip was to take part in a demonstration in Manila against the American-backed dictatorship.

The day before we arrived back to Manila, tens of thousands of demonstrators filled downtown, shouting slogans against the Marcos dictatorship. They marched until they reached Mendiola Bridge, which leads to Malacañang Palace, the residence of the president. The people were met by soldiers and military police and barricades of barbed wire, steel shields and water cannons. The demonstrators sat down and held an all-night vigil on the bridge.

The next morning, the international delegates arrived in support of the people. The event was to be marked with a big outdoor mass at the bridge. Being part of a demonstration was nothing new to me. I had attended lots of marches in Dublin when I was in college, usually outside the American Embassy.

So I held a banner, joined in the singing and, where language permitted, chanted slogans along with all the thousands of other people. Our fellow demonstrators included students, labourers, peasant farmers and many Catholic nuns and priests. It was a hot and humid day with showers, and my clothes were sticking to me. But there was a sense of purpose and unity on the streets, and I was blissfully unaware of what was about to happen.

No one had told the delegates that for years Mendiola Bridge had been a site of numerous bloody clashes between protesters and government troops protecting Malacañang Palace. And certainly no one had mentioned that eleven people had been shot dead at the same demonstration a year earlier.

None of us expected the subsequent turn of events. The first thing I noticed was a shift in the mood of the demonstrators, a murmur of alarm running through the crowd. I didn't understand what they were saying, and it happened so quickly that I didn't have time to react. People around me started pulling up what I thought were pretty neckerchiefs, and suddenly everyone around us was masked. My fellow delegates and I looked at each other in consternation.

That's when the gunshots started, and everyone scattered in all directions. All hell broke loose. Afterwards I learnt that more than two thousand police and soldiers charged the anti-government demonstrators outside the presidential palace. This was way ahead of where I was standing, so I couldn't see what was happening at first.

But I heard the shooting and the crack of tear-gas canisters being released. I heard the screaming as helmeted riot police, wielding clubs and rifles, began attacking the demonstrators. I felt the explosions from grenades vibrating through my body and rocking the entire city.

I remember ducking first and then flinging myself on the ground as people tumbled, scrambled all over me. It was like someone put two electric paddles to my chest and gave me a cardiac shock. I realised with a start, *Jesus, I don't want to die here, on a bridge in Manila. I don't want to die, full stop.*

That was the first surge of life I felt since Andrew died. Up until then, there were a lot of times when I hadn't cared whether I lived or died. What I felt in those moments must be what defibrillation of the heart feels like. It was the ultimate wake-up call. I was never more alert in my life, and I knew more than anything else that I wanted to live.

Lying on a wet street in Manila, I went into survival mode and vowed, *I am not going to die here.* So I crawled and clawed my way out of the chaos. I ran into the side streets of Manila, escaping the plumes of black smoke, the tear gas and the mindless mob of soldiers wildly beating everyone in their path. Even then, it wasn't over. When I finally found some of the other traumatised delegates, we were told we had to go into hiding. There were widespread arrests and we were at risk. For days we were all in hiding in a hotel, unable to go anywhere.

I can talk about it now in a very light-hearted manner, but it was a big shock to my system at the time. It took a trauma like that to make me realise just how much I wanted to live.

When I set off for the Philippines, I believed that this might be the first step in a new life for me. Maybe it was my fate to become a missionary or an overseas social activist and volunteer. That traumatic near-death episode on Mendiola Bridge in September 1984 put an end to any of those lofty aspirations. Several people were injured that day but, by some miracle, no one died. For me, it was a profound turning point in my grieving process.

I was so glad to return home to the tranquillity and safety of Fauna Cottage. Shortly after I got back, I received a phone call from Joe McDermott. He rang me out of the blue to ask a favour for one of his resident youth workers.

Joe ran a house of welcome called Teach Bhríde, and Harriet Kinahan was employed there as a youth leader under a community employment scheme. Harriet, a graduate of Trinity College, had to sit solicitors' exams for the Law Society and needed a quiet place to study. He asked if she could come and stay with me in Fauna Cottage.

'It will be so good for Harriet to be able to stay with you, Ann Maria,' he said. 'She's not getting the time to study, and I don't want to be responsible for her failing her exams. She just needs a quiet place for a few months so she can get her head into her books.'

I was used to people coming and going in Fauna Cottage, so I happily agreed. Joe arrived at the door that evening with a woman and a suitcase. Harriet had short-cropped hair and a smile that lit up her intense blue eyes. She was a young woman who radiated warmth. From the minute she arrived, I knew that I'd enjoy sharing my home with her. It was only later that she told me Joe had an ulterior motive behind bringing her to Fauna Cottage.

'I promised Andrew on his death bed that I'd look after Ann Maria,' he'd told her. 'So I'd like you to help me do that job.'

He made it sound as if I was doing him a favour, but he felt I was on my own too much and needed the company. What happened between Harriet and me was extraordinary; we formed an incredibly close bond. We also had our law studies in common, and subsequently I went back and finished the final year of my law degree.

More importantly, we were fellow seekers; both of us were on a search for truth and meaning in life. After the pain of Andrew's death began to subside, I became absorbed with that search. Prayer for guidance and direction became part of my daily life. I was seeking a new direction and a way to be of service in the world. It was providence that Harriet came to live with me as we were both looking for an authentic way of life.

My regular practice of prayer was as vital as oxygen to me and was central to my day-to-day life. I was aspiring to live a contemplative and simple life. I remember Harriet and I praying together, eating plain meals, sometimes walking together. We regularly spent twenty-four hours in silent retreat. We shared a love of Taizé as Harriet had been there too. We were ideal companions for each other, and her presence filled the loneliness in my life.

Our prayer took place in the den, an extension that Andrew and I had built on to the cottage. The room had a plain pine floor and ceiling. Our Taizé cross, a full-size replica of the one in France, sat in the centre of the floor. It was a Greek Orthodox-style cross in brilliant colours of red and gold. It looks like the San Damiano Cross, which was painted during the twelfth century and is linked with Saint Francis of Assisi in Italy.

The Taizé cross has a central image of the crucified Jesus Christ, with figures of the Virgin Mary and Saint John the Apostle on either side and the floating figure of an angel above the cross. There was a photo of Andrew in a small frame on the little altar in those days, along with the Bible, a vase of fresh flowers and other significant symbols or images that I'd brought back from other spiritual retreats.

I prayed for guidance as I continued on that inner search for meaning and a direction in my life. These days my spiritual practice is mindfulness-based meditation, but in those years, it was Scripture-based. All the retreats Harriet and I took part in were focused on readings from the gospels as we tried to discern where God was leading us.

•

It was only after Harriet moved in that she discovered that her brothers had been friends of Andrew's. It happened when she was trying to explain to her older brother John where she was living.

'I'm living in West Wicklow, in the Glen of Imaal; it's a very rural area – you wouldn't know it.'

'I know the place, all right. I went to a funeral of a schoolfriend there about eighteen months ago. A little church in Davidstown.'

'Really?' Harriet was astonished. 'That's right beside us. Who did you know in the area?'

'He wasn't from there, but he moved down there when he got married. He was in our year in boarding school. The poor fellow died of cancer. A guy called Andrew Dunne.'

Harriet's twin brothers, John and Tom Kinahan, had been at Castleknock College boarding school with Andrew. It seemed like an extraordinary synchronicity.

Harriet and I continued the tradition that I'd started with Andrew of making Fauna Cottage a house of welcome. Word got around and one day Father Eamon McCarthy, a Trinity College chaplain, called about a young woman who needed help.

'She needs somewhere quiet for a few days.'

'That's fine. She's more than welcome to stay.'

'She has something called anorexia nervosa. Did you ever hear of it?'

Public awareness of anorexia nervosa and other eating disorders had been raised by the death of singer Karen Carpenter a year earlier.

'I know about it, but I don't have any medical background.'

'I can't find medical help yet. I just need a safe place for her to stay for a while.'

The girl seemed tired and disheartened when she arrived. She joined in our prayer-based daily routine, helped in the garden and enjoyed walks on the forest trail behind Fauna Cottage. We shared meals, and she had plenty of time to rest. I didn't try to counsel her because I knew I didn't have the skills. However, she had the space to talk, and I listened. I felt a sense of achievement when she left feeling brighter and ready to face the world again.

Other wounded people arrived, people who needed a refuge or a sanctuary. I realised I needed skills to accompany these people.

Members of the clergy and sisters acted as spiritual directors or companions on most retreats. However, a new group had started training laypeople in the ministry of accompanying people on retreat. A friend and Jesuit priest called Myles O'Reilly and a sister called Rosemary Alexander were leading the next spiritual companioning course.

So Harriet and I started the Anamcharadas course in Green Acres Convent in Dublin, in the winter of 1984. It would be another decade before John O'Donohue published *Anam Cara*, which popularised Celtic spirituality and the idea of a 'soul friend'.

The training was invaluable to me. When people came to Fauna Cottage, I had some basic skills in listening and being present for someone. After the course I also started working on the retreat team at Tabor House, another house of welcome for young people. Tabor was directed by Myles and the Jesuits in Milltown Park in Dublin.

I enjoyed the work but I was still searching for a real purpose in my life. The main thrust of my life was this relentless search for meaning. I loved the final line of Mary Oliver's poem, 'The Summer Day': Tell me, what is it you plan to do / with your one wild and precious life?

What I planned to do with my 'one wild and precious life' was at the forefront of my mind. I constantly sought guidance to know what I was going to do next in my life, and I didn't have much patience waiting for the future to unfold.

I had an inheritance from my mother, which I wanted to use for good in the world. It wasn't a massive amount of money, but I felt it was enough to make a difference. I spent a lot of time contemplating an idea that Andrew and I had talked about – setting up a community-based care centre for people with schizophrenia.

Andrew was drawn to this idea because of his older brother Maurice and it appealed to me because my mother struggled with mental illness. I got in contact with the Schizophrenia Association of Ireland (SAI) and went to some of their meetings. My idea was to use my mother's legacy to start a community-based and family-style residence.

Harriet and I travelled to the Richmond Fellowship, a mental health charity in the UK that provides supported housing services. I also travelled to the headquarters of the L'Arche community in Trosly in France. This charity had also developed worldwide communities for people with intellectual disabilities. I was excited about the prospect and felt it would be great to do something in Andrew's memory.

Andrew's godfather, Archbishop Dermot Ryan, rang me from time to time. 'And how are you *really* doing, Ann Maria?' he'd ask. He had a great listening ear. There was something about him that had me pouring my heart out to him. I could never gloss over how I truly felt like I did with other people. Dermot knew that my heart was broken and that I was very lonely. He lived in Stillorgan, where I used to meet up with him sometimes. I enjoyed his company and I valued his counsel. His sudden death in Rome from a heart attack only twenty months after Andrew's death was a shock and a loss.

One day I met up with Dermot with the express purpose of discussing my plans for a community-based care home for the Schizophrenia Association. I told him about all the research that I'd conducted and explained the concept of the house.

'It's something Andrew and I talked about before he died,' I said. 'Andrew's brother Maurice is kind of the inspiration behind the project.'

I felt sure that Dermot would whole-heartedly support the project, especially because Andrew had been involved in its origins. Instead he shook his head and sighed.

'Look, Ann Maria, let the Dunnes look after Maurice.'

I remember the words so clearly because it really deflated me. Until that moment I thought I was on the right track and believed it was a good plan. But he was unequivocal. *Let the Dunnes look after Maurice.*

'Why do you not like the idea? I've put a lot of research into it. I think it's something that's badly needed and could work very well in Ireland.'

'Just don't get too attached to any plans like this, so soon,' he said. 'You shouldn't rush. You need to take time and see which direction your life will go.'

He discouraged me very emphatically, and I sort of lost confidence in the project after that. I think he was saying, *Maurice is not your responsibility*, which I knew, of course. Maybe he thought I was trying too hard to weave something of my life and Andrew's into my future. Perhaps Dermot thought I was too young to be committing my resources to something like this. Maybe he thought the whole idea was far-fetched.

I don't know what he thought. The idea of that community-based care centre still ran around in my head a lot after that, but so did Dermot's counsel. It was Archbishop Dermot Ryan's advice that really closed the door on that idea and really put a stop to my life going in that direction.

# The Summer Day

## By Mary Oliver

Who made the world?

Who made the swan, and the black bear?

Who made the grasshopper?

This grasshopper, I mean –

the one who has flung herself out of the grass,

the one who is eating sugar out of my hand,

who is moving her jaws back and forth instead of up and
　down –

who is gazing around with her enormous and complicated
　eyes.

Now she lifts her pale forearms and thoroughly washes her
　face.

Now she snaps her wings open and floats away.

I don't know exactly what a prayer is.

I do know how to pay attention, how to fall down

*into the grass, how to kneel down in the grass,*

*how to be idle and blessed, how to stroll through the fields,*

*which is what I have been doing all day.*

*Tell me, what else should I have done?*

*Doesn't everything die at last, and too soon?*

*Tell me, what is it you plan to do*

*with your one wild and precious life?*

'The Summer Day' from House of Light *by Mary Oliver,
published by Beacon Press, Boston.
Copyright © 1990 by Mary Oliver,
used herewith by permission of the
Charlotte Sheedy Literary Agency, Inc.*

# POUSTINIA

―― ∾ ――

*We all have an inner dream if we have
the courage to let it unfold.*

Julia Cameron

The monk held up a lantern in the half-opened door. I could see he was wearing the iconic brown robes with a cincture, the simple corded rope around his waist.

'Buona notte, Padre.'

That was the extent of my Italian. The light illuminated a beaming smile as the monk pulled open the creaking wooden door.

'Benvenuto! Benvenuto! Vieni, signore.' *Welcome! Welcome! Come in, ladies.*

He ushered us into the old stone building set into the town walls. His sandals slapped on the ancient stone, and our breath formed white plumes in the freezing night air as we followed him through dimly lit corridors. He threw open the door into a small room. His lantern illuminated a narrow bed, a crucifix above it and a small shuttered window. He lit a candle and the shadows danced on the wall. It was as austere and cold as any monk's cell, yet my smile was as wide as the friar's.

Harriet and I hoped for a sense of travelling back in time, of taking a pilgrimage to thirteenth-century Italy, when Saint Francis walked the streets of Assisi, and our dream was coming to life. We were experiencing a tradition of hospitality that had been extended to pilgrims for the past fifteen hundred years.

We flew to Milan on 29 December 1985, arriving in the railway station at Piazza Dante Alighieri, two miles south of Assisi, in darkness. Assisi is a hill town in central Italy's Umbria area, and a blanket of snow covered the region.

'Why don't we do as the pilgrims did and walk to Assisi?' I suggested. We followed the direction of the lights on the hill, but it took longer than we expected to reach the town in the snow. We made our way down the silent Via San Francesco to the monastery. Our first impressions were of frosty cobblestone streets, tiny alleyways and snaking stone staircases amid a huddle of medieval homes. It was bitterly cold in Assisi, but we were enchanted and excited to be there.

The more I read about Saint Francis in the days that followed, the more I was inspired by his life. The brown robes he wore, now the most recognisable religious habit in the world, reflected the clothing worn by the peasants of his time. Brown dyes and sackcloth formed the wardrobe of the poor. I learnt how the rope that the Franciscans wore at their waist had three knots that represented poverty, chastity and obedience, the three cornerstones of the order.

Moved by the Franciscan spirit, we dined on simple meals of bread and cheese. We revelled in our spartan accommodation in the monastery and the silence of Assisi in mid-winter. I prayed to Saint Francis for guidance in doing God's will and recited his prayer again and again: *All highest, glorious God, cast Your light into the darkness of our hearts. Give us true faith, firm hope, perfect charity and profound humility, so that with wisdom, courage and perception, oh Lord, we may do what is truly Your holy will. Amen.*

My seventh wedding anniversary took place in Assisi. To do something special to mark the day, I went to nine o'clock morning mass in the Basilica of Saint Clare. Regarded as the spiritual twin of Francis of Assisi, Clare was inspired by Francis to leave her wealthy family and to found the Order of Poor Clares. She and her sisters vowed to live in poverty, austerity and seclusion from the world.

The Basilica contains the San Damiano crucifix that Saint Francis knelt before as he heard the words: *Go now and repair my church, which, as you have seen, is falling down.* Afterwards, Harriet and I trekked to San Damiano Church, the first monastery of the Order of Saint Clare.

My journal from that time reads: *Thoughts of Francis's life dwell within me, and Francis prays that God would give all men and women courage to be themselves, instead of what others expected them to be.*

Saint Francis didn't encourage everyone to enter the brotherhood or to join Lady Clare and her sisters. He urged people to be free to be what they wanted because he believed God spoke differently to everyone. I was still weighed down with the decisions about the future and how I was going to live my life.

We spent long days in prayer and meditation, in between meandering around the town of Assisi and the Umbrian hills. We walked to the nearby Basilica di San Francesco, where we admired Giotto's frescos of Saint Francis's life and descended to the crypt to spend some time at his tomb. We wandered through the streets of Assisi to see the sites that played a role in Francis's life. We saw his parents' house in the Plateola di San Francesco and the little church of Porziuncola, around which Francis established his brotherhood.

Our pilgrimage to Assisi was memorable, full of light and peace and such a magical escape from ordinary life. It was only ten days, but the serenity and the sacredness of the trip have stayed with us in the decades since.

Soon after we returned to Donard, I was astonished when a Franciscan nun asked if I would host a retreat for three novices in Fauna Cottage. I was still working on the retreat team for Tabor House. However, it was quite unusual at the time for a layperson to lead a retreat for a religious order. I was so startled by the request that I hesitated. After talking it through with Harriet, I decided it was a God-given opportunity. I thought it also might be a signpost to my future.

After Andrew died, I had considered two ideas for the future: developing a community care home and building a 'poustinia' – a hermitage – next to Fauna Cottage. For a while I was at a crossroads, awaiting a signpost to know which way to go. When Archbishop Dermot Ryan discouraged the care centre, I began to put more energy into the idea of the poustinia.

The Anamcharadas course equipped me to go in either direction, but the arrival of the novice nuns seemed to be a sign in the direction of the poustinia. I was inspired to build a hermitage by reading a beautiful book called *Poustinia: Christian Spirituality of the East for Western Man* published by Russian-born Catherine Doherty.

The word 'poustinia' means desert in Russian. It's a type of hermitage from the Eastern Christian tradition, a place to meet God in silence, solitude and prayer. A poustinia can be any type of domestic dwelling in which a hermit lives. The idea was to build a house where people could spend a few days in isolation and contemplation. It would have been a place where anyone, from any walk of life, could go for a day or several days of silence, solitude and prayer.

The Franciscan novices' arrival seemed like a sign pointing towards the poustinia, but I had more immediate concerns. We only had two small bedrooms in Fauna Cottage. *Where am I going to accommodate these women?* I wondered.

Gene O'Grady's holiday home came to mind. I met Gene one night after reading at mass in the nearby Church of Our Lady of Dolours. It turned out to be his wife's anniversary mass. She loved the Glen of Imaal so much that she was buried in the local church graveyard. Harriet and I grew very fond of Gene, and he used to refer to us as the Little Sisters of Fauna. He was amused when I asked if we could use his unoccupied house to accommodate three real novice nuns, Eleanor, Dymphna and Sandra. The arrival of the women seemed to be a very clear sign that a hermitage or poustinia was a good idea. Yet something caused me to hesitate. Even after the Franciscan retreat, I waited for some clear guidance on which path to follow in life. There were a few pieces of Scripture that were important to me during this time; one was from the Old Testament:

> Jeremiah 29:11–14: I know the plans I have in mind for you, plans for peace not disaster, reserving a future full of hope for you. Then when you will call me, and come to plead with me, I will listen to you. When you seek me with all your heart, you will find me.

I read that again and again, knowing there was some plan, but still searching for a road map. Since the mystical revelation in Taizé that Andrew was going to die, I felt there was something I was meant to do. I felt I didn't have the full picture. So I ploughed on with the idea of the poustinia, hoping to build it in a field to the side of Fauna Cottage, surrounded by forest. An architect drew up beautiful plans. It was an octagonal building with a bedroom, a bathroom, a kitchen, a living area, a prayer area and an open fire. There was also a lovely deck with views of the surrounding area.

I envisioned it as a place where people could stay for a day, a weekend, or even a week. If they didn't want to fast, they could self-cater in the kitchen. I wanted it to be open and available to anyone who needed a restorative break from the world. Excited about the drawings, I applied for planning permission.

In April 1986 I went to Manresa Jesuit Centre of Spirituality in Clontarf for a thirty-day silent retreat known as an Ignatian retreat. Before a Jesuit makes his final formation, he must complete this retreat which involves prayer, reflection, silence and daily meetings with a director.

In the Anamcharadas training, we used the term 'spiritual companion'. But in Manresa, they used 'spiritual director', and I had Jesuit priest Brian Grogan as my spiritual director. Each day I would meditate on a piece of Scripture and talk about my prayer experience. I was open to where the spirit of God was leading me and hoping to find the guidance that I was seeking.

In my journal from that time, I wrote: *During my time of prayer, I desire to know God personally and desire to know His plans for my life . . . I prayed for an openness: Lord, for You to probe me, to know me. You know my words before I say them; You know me through and through. I pray to be open to You, to Your word . . . My heart carries hurt within it. I'm weighed down at times. And I pray for healing* [over Andrew's death].

I used the daily meetings with my spiritual director as an opportunity to discuss my idea of a poustinia. I told Brian about the architect's drawings and the planning application and about how I envisaged it would work. I was a bit shocked by his response. He was as dismissive about the poustinia as Dermot had been about the care centre. Spiritual directors are not supposed to be 'directive' when they're listening, but Brian's reaction was surprisingly off-hand.

'Do you really want to tie yourself into something like that?' he asked. 'It could be very restrictive.'

# Carried on Spirit Wings

It wasn't the response I was expecting, and it disappointed me. Brian's attitude took some of the gloss off my dream of a beautiful poustinia in the Wicklow hills. His comments weren't enough to turn me off the idea altogether, but it certainly made me rethink my plans.

Days later I was attending mass in Manresa, when a priest appeared and beckoned me to follow him. I knew this wasn't good news. No one ever disturbed us at mass.

'There has been a call from your aunt. She's very upset and looking for you, urgently,' he said.

Uncle Jimmy was now in his mid-seventies and had suffered a stroke earlier that year. It was a severe stroke, which rendered him paralysed down his left side and without any power of speech. He was in Carysfort Nursing Home in Glenageary, where we hoped, with therapy, he might start to recover. I rang the nursing home. Aunt Nora was distraught.

'Oh thank God, Ann Maria! Please come quick. Jimmy's very bad, very bad. He's had a fit, some kind of seizure. The doctors are with him now, but I don't think he's going to make it.'

I got into my car and drove to Carysfort, praying that if God had to take Uncle Jimmy, that He wouldn't let him suffer. I met Aunt Nora in the hall, and we both spoke with the doctor. He didn't hold out much hope for him. When I saw Jimmy, my heart sank. He was a big man, but he seemed so frail now, tucked under the nursing home sheets. I sat by his bed and took his hand and started to pray. When I looked up, his eyes were wide open and focused on me. I gasped. He was fully alert. I wasn't expecting that, and my heart pounded with fright. 'How are you feeling, Uncle Jimmy?' I asked before I remembered he couldn't speak.

It was soon apparent that Jimmy wasn't in any immediate danger, but the thirty-day retreat was at an end for me. I needed to be around for my aunt and uncle. I continued instead with a process called the nineteenth annotation, sometimes called an Ignatian retreat, in daily life. It's a version of the spiritual exercises designed for people who can't commit to spending thirty days in a closed environment. The exercises, weekly prayer practices, readings, and meditations are spread over several months rather than thirty days.

As soon as twinkling fairy lights started to light up the streets of Dublin, and the supermarkets started to fill with festive tins of sweets, Aunt Nora had an idea.

'What do you think of taking Jimmy home for Christmas?'

I was astonished but I loved the idea of bringing him home.

'Really? Can we? I can't bear the thought of him being in a nursing home for Christmas.'

Aunt Nora rang her GP to see if he could help organise Jimmy's return, but Dr McCafferty opposed any plans to remove him from the nursing home.

'Nora, it's not a good idea. If Jimmy comes home, you'll end up dead before him,' he said. 'All the stress and the responsibility of looking after Jimmy is going to fall on you.'

Nora was disheartened. She hadn't worked as a nurse since she married Uncle Jimmy, but I knew she understood the level of care he needed.

'Don't mind what the doctor says, Aunt Nora,' I said. 'We'll manage. Tell me what we're going to need, and we'll get it.'

So we organised a hospital bed and a hoist from the Eastern Health Board and made the sitting room into a bedroom for my uncle. We managed to find a neighbour, Mrs O'Dowd, who came in and washed and shaved Uncle Jimmy every morning. We also had a local nurse helping with his care. I stayed in Mount Merrion a few nights a week, and between everyone, we found a system that worked. Uncle Jimmy came home for Christmas and never went back to the nursing home.

Jimmy was relieved to be home, but I could see that he suffered a lot. His mobility was very restricted, and he was bed-bound or chair-bound most of the time. He could feed himself because he had the use of his right hand. But losing his speech was difficult for him. At times it seemed words were clear in his head but they eluded his grasp. When visitors arrived, he would extend his good arm and shake their hand. But once he tried to speak, he couldn't get those words out. He used to sigh with frustration. It must have been even worse for him when some people talked about him as if he wasn't present or as if his mental faculties had been impaired.

We did all the exercises that the occupational therapist

recommended. They gave us squares, shapes and what seemed like childish games to work and stimulate his brain. I sensed his despondency and his frustration. It was painful seeing him struggle.

It was my big red setter, Olen, who prompted Jimmy to speak again. Olen must have stuck his snout around the door of the sitting room and spotted Uncle Jimmy in bed. Olen loved lots of things but he especially loved people and beds, and he saw an irresistible combination in the sitting room that day. Without warning, he burst through the door and leapt upon Uncle Jimmy in the bed. Uncle Jimmy let out a terrible roar.

'Oh, Jaysus!' he cried.

The two words rang out so loud that Aunt Nora and I came running. We found Olen lying on Uncle Jimmy, tail wagging furiously, and poor Jimmy's eyes out on stalks with the fright. Aunt Nora and I bent over with the laughter; we thought it was hilarious. Jimmy's outburst also gave us great hope that he would recover his speech. It was the first time that he had spoken since he had the stroke six months earlier. As it turned out, Uncle Jimmy lived for a long time after, but those words, *Oh Jaysus!*, were his last ever.

# Accepting This

## MARK NEPO

We cannot eliminate hunger,
but we can feed each other.
We cannot eliminate loneliness,
but we can hold each other.
We cannot eliminate pain,
but we can live a life
of compassion.

Ultimately,
we are small living things
awakened in the stream,
not gods who carve out rivers.

Like human fish,
we are asked to experience
meaning in the life that moves
through the gill of our heart.

There is nothing to do
and nowhere to go.
Accepting this,
we can do everything
and go anywhere.

*Our wedding day. With Andrew, Greenane, Wicklow, 30 December 1978.*

*Andrew with Esmeralda and Gertie the goats, Fauna Cottage, circa 1980.*

*Andrew and me, Sitges, circa 1980.*

*Andrew with our dogs at Fauna Cottage, circa 1980.*

*Taizé Cross icon at Fauna Cottage.*

*BCL graduation with Aunt Nora and Uncle Jimmy.*

*Taizé visit to village in Tamil Nadu, 1985.*

*The official opening of Chrysalis, June 1989.*

*Early days of Chryslis.*

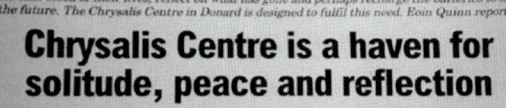

**NEWS SPECIAL** *nearly everybody needs a quiet place at some time, where they can withdraw and take stock of their lives, reflect on what has gone and perhaps recharge the batteries to face the future. The Chrysalis Centre in Donard is designed to fulfil this need. Eoin Quinn reports.*

## Chrysalis Centre is a haven for solitude, peace and reflection

*Dick McHugh SJ, Sadhana Lonavala, India.*

*Mataji Vandana, Himalayas, India.*

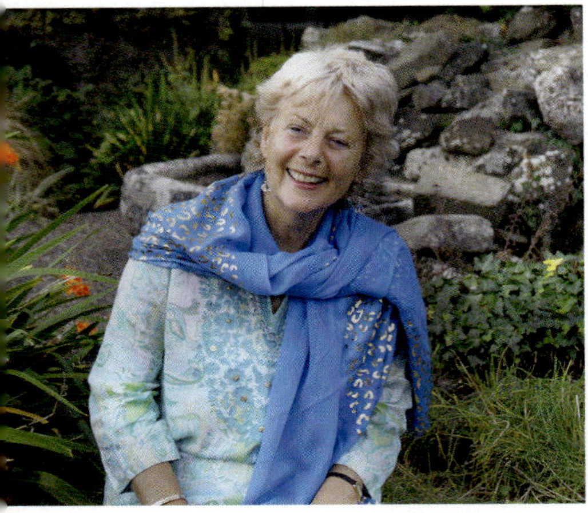
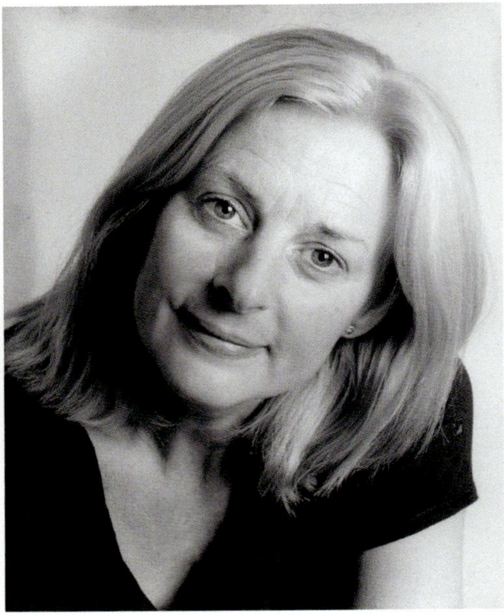
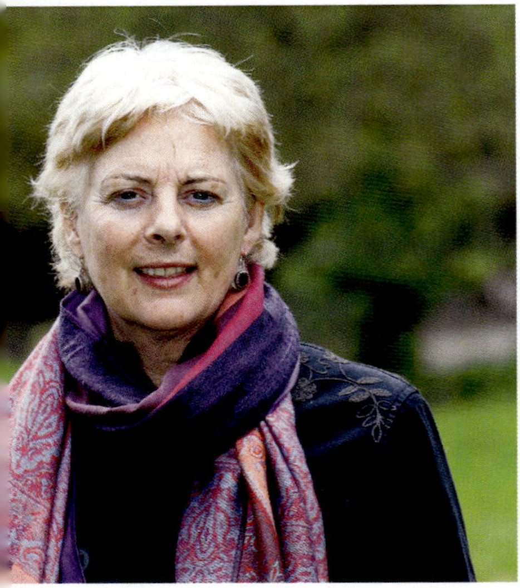
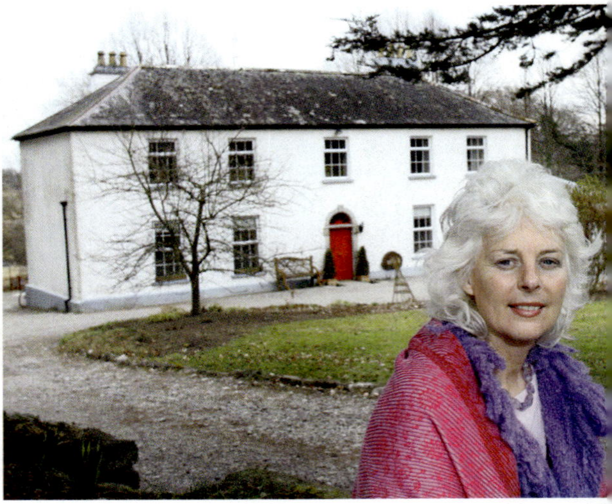
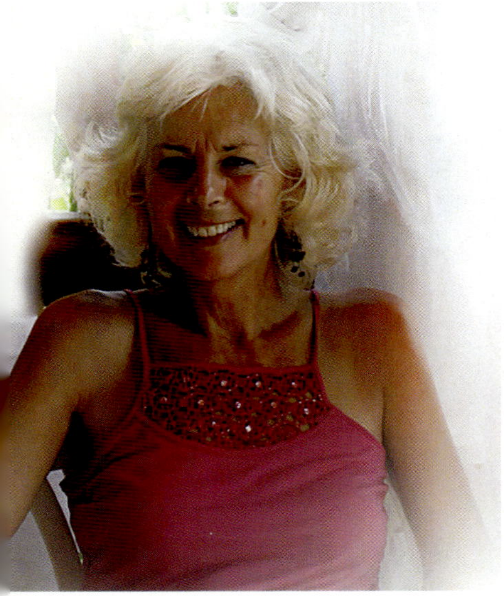
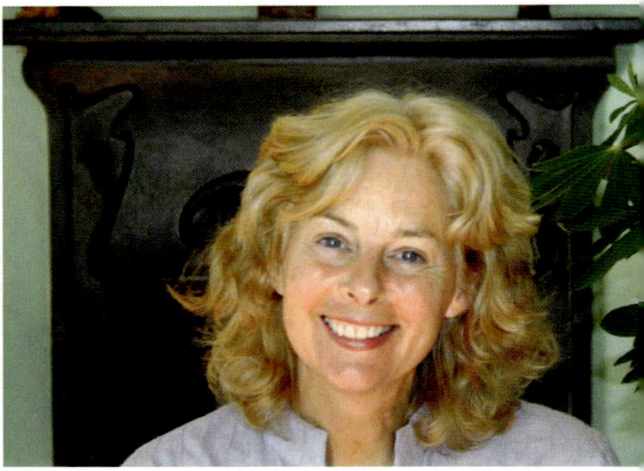

# TO LOVE AGAIN

―――― ↭ ――――

*Never stop dreaming.*
*If you can dream it, you can do it.*

JULIA CAMERON

For a long time, following Andrew's death, I had no thought or desire for any other man in my life. I had male friends and good relationships with men but I had no interest in an intimate relationship.

But gradually I began to feel the gentle tug of my heartstrings when I saw couples walking hand in hand. I felt a deep yearning when I caught expressions of affection between lovers. A squeeze of a hand or a hug could prompt a sigh or bring a sentimental tear to my eye. I began to feel a need to connect with someone on a deeper level.

I wanted to fall in love again, to have a loving relationship with another man and to fill the emptiness and loneliness. Yet, even though I tried to be open to love again, I had a lot of conflicting feelings about having another relationship. There was the fear of another loss and separation. Having loved and lost with Andrew, I had a lot of anxiety at the thought of investing my fragile heart in another relationship. There was also a feeling of guilt. When Andrew and I married, I believed we'd be together for life and that I'd never love another man. Our marriage lasted less than five years, but there was a sense that by seeing someone else, I was being unfaithful to Andrew. I still missed my husband. I wondered, *Can I ever commit myself wholeheartedly to another person? Will I ever be free to love again?*

And then it happened when I least suspected it. This man was a friend and then he became more than that. I let him into my life and opened myself physically and emotionally to a new relationship. It was difficult. I felt terrible pangs of disloyalty to Andrew, and it felt worse somehow that Andrew knew him. But I threw caution to the wind. I needed arms to embrace me, and I needed to be understood, accepted and loved.

This relationship was only significant because it was the first time that I opened myself up to another man after Andrew, and because it was a tremendous emotional upheaval for me. In my journal, I wrote: *Does he really know or understand or is this too much to expect? My being has been soothed, touched, healed, tormented, all at once.*

I know now that I wasn't emotionally ready to move on; like many new relationships after a great bereavement, I still harboured feelings of guilt and fear of loss. I was vulnerable at that time, and the relationship only lasted a few months. Maybe he thought I was too needy, or he knew that I was still too emotionally involved with Andrew. Or perhaps we weren't even suited, and I would have figured that out if I had been able to see clearly at the time.

Whatever the reason, he finished the relationship, and it hit me extremely hard. I was absolutely shattered. For a while, it was like going through another bereavement. Grief for someone is usually felt in direct proportion to how much you love them and how connected your lives had become. This grief was not proportional to how I felt about him or to the length of our brief relationship. At most I should have been experiencing a hollow sense of regret or a vague sadness that he was gone.

But after he left me, all sorts of emotional pain came to the surface. Everything I felt when Andrew died hit me again: anger, loss, loneliness, emptiness, a sense of abandonment. I attributed all this angst to the break-up, but of course it had nothing to do with the situation. The relationship never warranted this kind of reaction; it just triggered unresolved deep feelings within me.

A lot of other things were also going on at that time. I was feeling lost. My plans for a care centre were over, and my enthusiasm for the poustinia had waned. Harriet was gone now too. She had been a caring presence in Fauna Cottage for the past two years. She wasn't there all the time but she always ended up back in the cottage, and it was a wrench when she left for France in 1986. She moved to Lourdes to study a programme about faith formation and lay vocations in the Catholic Church.

I was working in Tabor House in Milltown Park, for the Jesuits and Myles, but I fell into a prolonged depression. I have a note in my journal that reads: *Crying with Myles because of my loneliness. I'm feeling so empty. Nothing seems good. I just feel very desolate. I'm feeling so lonely.* There were more expressions of depression in December that year: *These past months have been dreadful. At mass had to leave Tabor because of the tears welling up. Tears seem to be on the verge all the time. Imagine, I forgot Andrew's birthday.*

The first time I experienced depression was after my mother died, and I was crushed by darkness after Andrew's death. However, there seemed to be an underlying current of depression in my life all the time now, and it had washed me back into its black depths again. Triggered by the break-up of a relationship, I was once again in the throes of an emotional upheaval. I think I was depressed too because I was struggling to find a direction in my life. It was three years since Andrew died, and I still felt rudderless. My journal notes: *I'm feeling desolate and depressed most of the time. I can't pray these days.*

But one thing was becoming clear: my work on the retreat team in Tabor House taught me that training in spiritual companioning was not enough. I was coming across people with complex problems, and I needed more skills to be able to help them. I started to investigate further training opportunities. In September 1986 I started a course in Humanistic Psychotherapy at the Institute of Creative Counselling and Psychotherapy, Dún Laoghaire. One of the course requirements was for students to enter one-to-one psychotherapy. I began seeing a therapist called Patrick Nolan. It was my first time in therapy and the first time that I worked on emotional issues like unresolved grief and feelings of abandonment.

I was able to discuss for the first time the dilemma of wanting closeness while fearing rejection and more pain. Somewhere within me was the desire for a loving relationship, but the idea of more loss and separation was too much to bear.

There are lots of ways to handle grief, and life brought me plenty of grief to deal with. Some take prescription medication to numb their feelings, while others turn to alcohol or substance abuse. I never travelled down those paths. I first went the spiritual route, seeking healing through prayer and contemplation. However, there was an element of what's called 'spiritual bypass' with that route. Spiritual practices rarely target unresolved emotional issues and psychological wounds. I recognised I needed help with deeper issues. My journey of healing went in a new direction once I started training to be a psychotherapist. From this time on, I explored the psychological roots of my emotional issues to improve my well-being.

These new explorations started with my training in psychotherapy and my therapy with Patrick Nolan. Eager to learn more, I attended a five-day residential workshop on bereavement led by Dr Elisabeth Kübler-Ross, a fascinating Swiss-American psychiatrist. She wrote the seminal book *On Death and Dying*. A pioneer in treatment for grief, she was way ahead of anybody here in Ireland. Her theory was that if we block our feelings, we become frozen and trapped with those feelings. She supported a model of identifying buried emotions, working through these negative feelings and finally releasing them.

Her workshop was experiential. Each person in the room was encouraged to let go of resistance and to release repressed feelings, memories or long-held traumas. However, participants weren't left to cry into their handkerchiefs. Instead, they were handed a bat and invited to take out their grief and anger on a cushion. There was a strong emphasis on discharging anger.

I was in a room with maybe thirty other people, all releasing pent-up emotional wounds in a therapeutic setting. If someone wandered in the door, they might have thought they had walked in on the scene of a tragedy. They may have been shocked by the sight of people crying, screaming or shouting. All kind of shrieking obscenities filled the room as people released festering wounds and liberated themselves from the pent-up emotional pain they had held for years.

Initially I was overwhelmed and remember, at one stage, feeling ill. I found it all too much. I couldn't take any more of anyone else's grief. It's ironic that within a couple of years I began facilitating and leading workshops like this myself. However, at that time I had never witnessed that volume of rage and pain in one room before. I walked out, my heart beating fast with anxiety. I was followed by one of the therapists.

'Let's try working on our own for a while,' she suggested.

She began by exploring my background, inviting me to talk about my grief and regrets.

'So you're blaming yourself for Andrew's death, Ann Maria, is that it? Are you blaming yourself for your mother's death too?'

'No, but I feel I could have done more to save them.'

'Are you a doctor?'

'No.'

'Did Andrew and your mother have professional medical people looking after them?'

'Yes.'

'Did Andrew and your mother follow their medical advice?'

'Yes.'

'Who did they expect to make them better?'

'The doctors.'

'But they didn't make them better, did they?'

'No.'

'So who is really responsible for their deaths?'

'I suppose, in a way, the doctors.'

'You must be feeling angry at them. They failed Andrew. They failed your mother. You are living in this pain, and Andrew and your mother are dead. The doctors have moved on with their lives.'

'Yes, I suppose. Andrew should be alive now.'

'Who had the power to keep him alive?'

'The doctors.'

'So who should you blame?'

'The doctors.'

'This is a doctor,' said the therapist, brandishing a cushion. 'This is the doctor who looked after Andrew. He told you and Andrew that the chemotherapy would cure him. He told you he knew best. He told you what to do, and he filled Andrew's veins with chemotherapy. How do you feel about this doctor now?'

'I'm angry, really angry. He was wrong. He destroyed Andrew's immune system.'

The therapist continued with these images, about the doctors, about Andrew, about my mother. I was shocked by the anger that I began to feel rise from deep within me. I didn't think I had it in me. The therapist encouraged me to breathe deeply into my abdomen, to really experience the energy of this pent-up rage.

'Okay, take this bat and raise it right up, high to the ceiling, then bring it down on this cushion.'

I did it, and I felt a rush.

'Do it again.'

I did, but then I didn't need any more encouraging.

My anger was explosive, and it was directed at the medical profession. It was probably misdirected, but it was an anger that I held deep within me. I was furious at the doctors who prescribed the chemotherapy and drug treatments that weakened Andrew's body and destroyed his immune system. I lashed out at the psychiatrists who had treated my mother, fried her mind with ECT and who told me that she would never kill herself. I lashed out at God.

I had never before understood the level of fury inside me. The amount of physical and emotional energy I used to beat that cushion left me feeling exhausted and drained. Then the tears erupted, and I cried intensely, howling at times, releasing years of unexpressed grief. After I had time to rest and recover, I felt a new flow of energy; a sense of liberation I hadn't experienced before.

At the end of the Elisabeth Kübler-Ross workshop, we had a ceremony with a big outdoor bonfire. Everyone threw a pinecone on the fire as a symbolic gesture of starting anew. We were asked to complete these sentences 'I leave behind . . .' and 'I leave with . . .' as the pinecones went in the flames. My words were: *I leave behind my sorrow and fear, and I leave with the hope of freedom to love again.*

It felt as if I could finally let go of Andrew and have the freedom to love again. The workshop made me aware for the first time of a distinct pattern in my life. Everyone I loved, my father, my mother and Andrew, left me or died. The first man I'd loved since Andrew left me too.

I wrote around that time: *I am working on my fears of getting close and forming another love relationship. One of my fears is that I will be abandoned, left alone, vulnerable and broken. It seems there is a pattern in my life. If I get close to someone and need them, the person will leave me or die. This fear and pattern have blocked my freedom to enter into a committed love relationship since Andrew's death, which was four years ago.*

And then love happened again, in a most unlikely place. Over the summer break from training in humanist psychotherapy, I found my thoughts drifting towards one of my fellow students. When the course resumed, I was glad to see Peter O'Sullivan again. I knew from the light in his eye and the warmth of his smile that my feelings were reciprocated.

During our second year of the course, students explored personal issues in group therapy sessions. A greater sense of empathy grew between us. We had both been wounded by life, and the attraction between us grew. A relationship developed, but the pace of it was slow. I still grappled with the fear of intimacy and loss. Yet when our eyes met, I enjoyed the feeling of my heart quickening again.

My life was turning a corner as a new vision for my future career was also taking shape. As a result of my psychotherapy training and the Kübler-Ross workshop, I was exposed to a whole new world of healing. I became interested in the Human Potential Movement, which was just starting in Ireland. Advocates of the movement believed there was huge untapped potential in everyone. They thought that if people were helped to reach their potential, they could experience increased happiness, creativity, and fulfilment. Falling under the New Age umbrella, the movement combined Western therapies with Eastern ones like yoga. It was an early form of the self-help and personal growth movement, and I felt very at home in it.

My vision of what I wanted to do was expanding. Previously my focus was prayer-based, but now I had discovered a wider dimension to healing. My training as a psychotherapist broadened my understanding. I was learning to use bodywork and other therapies to deal with my emotional wounds. I became aware that a balanced, healthy existence requires the healing of body, mind and spirit.

There were holistic treatment centres across America, but nothing like that existed in Ireland in the eighties. I started to envisage a centre that could provide spiritual and therapeutic support. It would be an Irish retreat centre for spiritual renewal and personal growth, the first of its kind in the country.

I had stumbled across the perfect location for this vision too. Canon Stiles, the former Church of Ireland minister, had lived in the church rectory, a rambling old country house, not far from Fauna Cottage. After Canon Stiles' death in the eighties, the house lay vacant for quite a long time.

I often wandered into the gardens, exploring the grounds and peering in the small windowpanes that dated back to 1711. I felt drawn to this house, known locally as the Old Rectory. It continued to lie idle, and I didn't know what was happening with the property. I spent hours wandering and sitting in the gardens. Peter thought it was a pipe dream when I first showed it to him.

'Let's get out of this place before we're done for trespassing!' he said, laughing.

But I couldn't let go of the dream. I approached a solicitor friend and asked him to write to the Church representative body to say he had a client who was interested in buying the property. The reply said they were waiting to select a new minister.

'Please assure your client that if the property ever goes on the market, it will be sold by public auction,' the letter read.

When the new rector, Pat Semple, was finally appointed, he and his wife Hilary looked over the house. Canon Stiles and his wife had only lived in a small portion of the house, and the rest of it had fallen into disrepair. You could see blue sky through one of the rooms upstairs. The Semples shook their heads and said they didn't want to live in the Old Rectory. I breathed a sigh of relief when I heard. Somebody in the parish donated a site, and the Church of Ireland began building a new presbytery nearby.

By now I was in love with the house and could envisage its potential. I gazed upon that place and wandered the land there for over a year. I used to sit under a tree in the garden visualising a retreat centre. Shakti Gawain wrote a book called *Creative Visualization* about using the power of your imagination to create what you want in life. She believed thoughts have a magnetic pull that attract similar energies from the universe around us. Years later, when I attended one of her workshops, I realised I had been doing that without knowing it. I was visualising the house's potential as a healing centre and manifesting my dreams into being.

# The Truelove

## David Whyte

There is a faith in loving fiercely
the one who is rightfully yours,
especially if you have
waited years and especially
if part of you never believed
you could deserve this
loved and beckoning hand
held out to you this way.

I am thinking of faith now
and the testaments of loneliness
and what we feel we are
worthy of in this world.

Years ago in the Hebrides
I remember an old man
who walked every morning
on the grey stones
to the shore of baying seals,

who would press his hat
to his chest in the blustering
salt wind and say his prayer
to the turbulent Jesus
hidden in the water,

*and I think of the story
of the storm and everyone
waking and seeing
the distant
yet familiar figure
far across the water
calling to them,*

*and how we are all
preparing for that
abrupt waking,
and that calling,
and that moment
we have to say yes,
except it will
not come so grandly,
so Biblically,
but more subtly
and intimately in the face
of the one you know
you have to love,*

*so that when we finally
step out of the boat
toward them, we find
everything holds us
and everything confirms
our courage, and if you wanted
to drown you could,*

*but you don't
because finally
after all this struggle
and all these years,
you simply don't want to any more,
you've simply had enough
of drowning
and you want to live and you
want to love and you will
walk across any territory
and any darkness,
however fluid and however
dangerous, to take the
one hand you know
belongs in yours.*

*Reproduced with the kind permission of David Whyte.*

# MYSTICAL INDIA

―――~―――

*The most terrible poverty is loneliness and the feeling of being unloved.*

MOTHER TERESA

The relationship with Peter was difficult from the start, and it certainly kept me in touch with my fears. That old dilemma of wanting closeness while fearing abandonment was there all the time. We grew closer during the second year of the course, as we began to learn a lot more about each other's backgrounds.

As part of our psychotherapy training, we participated in group therapy sessions which were facilitated by staff. Class members took turns to share personal issues they were working on. We focused on unresolved issues in our lives: childhood abuse, grief, anger, loss, whatever problems came up. As time went on, a trust built up in the group, and the level of sharing went deeper. Peter and I developed greater empathy for each other.

Peter is candid about his life. He was the second oldest of a family of fourteen children and grew up in enormous poverty and deprivation. Against the odds, he succeeded in his professional life, to become an electrical engineer, building and developing ESB power plants. However, the trauma and neglect he experienced in his childhood had a huge impact on him. When he was sixteen, anxiety issues came to the fore, and he was treated with benzodiazepines. He subsequently developed an addiction to prescription medicine. He also became addicted to alcohol, which, combined with the medication, was a dangerous cocktail.

He unsuccessfully tried battling his demons in Saint John of God's hospital and through Alcoholics Anonymous. By his early thirties, he was in bad shape and was admitted to Saint Ita's Mental Hospital in Portrane in Dublin. By then Peter was convinced he was mentally ill, a psychiatric case. After six weeks of terrible withdrawals in Portrane, a doctor helped him move to a newly opened addiction clinic called the Rutland Centre, in Knocklyon in Dublin. Peter had a very intense and profound experience during the ten weeks he spent in the Rutland Centre. The centre turned his life around. His recovery felt so miraculous that it prompted him to join our course in humanistic psychotherapy. He had a desire to work with addicts.

At some level, as I listened to his unfolding story, I was attracted to Peter's honesty and vulnerability. He admits he felt an affinity for me for similar reasons. He felt a certain sympathy with me because of the losses and tragedies in my life. So, my wounded self met his wounded self, and therein lay much of the difficulty in the years ahead. He brought a lot of baggage from his past, and I had a lot of issues from mine. It was always going to be a bumpy ride, but I was blind to that in the beginning.

For me the biggest dilemma facing my relationship with Peter was the fact that he was married. Although he was separated from his wife, he was still married because there was no divorce in Ireland in those years. Even if he did manage to get a divorce, the Church wouldn't recognise a civil dissolution of marriage. Nothing except an annulment could dissolve the Sacrament of marriage in the eyes of the Catholic Church. The relationship brought a sense of turmoil to my life as it conflicted with my strong Roman Catholic values at the time.

At one stage I went to Glenstal Abbey, in Murroe, County Limerick, for some reflection on the relationship. I talked to one of the Benedictines there about my predicament. He was not sympathetic.

'The Ten Commandments warn us twice about interfering with the Sacrament of marriage,' he said. 'The sixth commandment is "Thou shalt not commit adultery" and the ninth says, "You shall not covet your neighbour's wife or husband."'

I didn't understand why everything had to be so black and white.

'I know all the Commandments, Father, but Peter and his wife are separated a long time, and his wife has moved on too. Doesn't God want his children to be happy?'

The Benedictine could not be swayed.

'We can only fulfil our needs to be happy through the love of God. No one person like this man can meet the greatest desires of our heart. That's something only God can do.'

I had spent a long time loving God, but it didn't stop me yearning for a loving relationship with a man. But the priest was categorical.

'You are committing adultery by entering into this relationship, and if you are in a relationship with a married man, you can't be part of the Catholic Church,' he said.

Deciding to be with Peter was a huge internal struggle for me because of my strong faith. For such a long time I yearned for the intimacy of a loving relationship, and it was Peter who answered that longing. In retrospect, I think I was seeking a rescuer, a white knight who would sweep away my loneliness. But his marital situation was a complication that left me agonising about what to do. It was a rocky road, trying to navigate my feelings for Peter and the religious restrictions of the Church. There was a rebellious streak in me that wanted to cast off the Church's rules and live my life as I saw fit. But I was imbued with deep faith, and it was difficult for me to turn my back on the Church. My entire way of living was connected to the Church. I was falling in love with Peter, despite knowing the road ahead was going to be hard. I didn't fully anticipate just how challenging it would turn out to be.

In the early days of our relationship, I was distracted by my dream of a retreat centre in the Old Rectory in Donard. The Church of Ireland finally put the property and lands up for auction after it lay unoccupied for over a year. I started getting organised in advance of the auction. I received loan approval from the bank, which I combined with the funds that I inherited from my mother. I was apprehensive because I still didn't know if I could secure the property within my budget. I had never been at a public auction before, so I engaged Andrew's solicitor friend, Pearse Mehigan, to represent me.

The auction was held in the Downshire Hotel in Blessington, County Wicklow, on a Wednesday afternoon, 25 May 1988. The

Downshire was a charming two-hundred-year-old hotel on the main street, which closed many years ago. The auctioneer invited bids on a parcel of thirty or forty acres of land that was to be sold separately to the house. The hammer came down quickly, with a local farmer securing the acreage.

I visibly shook as the auction for the Old Rectory began. The lot contained the old house with three reception rooms, five bedrooms, a kitchen and surrounding gardens of two and a half acres of land. The auctioneer's gavel struck the desk and the auction was over in no time. Pearse turned and pumped my hand in congratulations. I was stunned to find myself the new owner of the Old Rectory, the house I'd dreamt of for the past year.

Only days later, Pearse rang.

'I've great news for you, Ann Maria. A solicitor rang me on behalf of a client who missed the auction. He's willing to offer you several thousand pounds more for the Old Rectory than you paid for it.'

'Who's his client?'

'He won't say, but you could make a tidy little profit in a matter of days.'

I was stunned, but I didn't even hesitate.

'Pearse, it's not for sale. I've only just bought the Old Rectory. I'm not selling.'

Pearse rang me back within days.

'Okay, the solicitor says his client is willing to raise his bid by another five thousand pounds if you sell to him. It's a great offer. You'd be crazy to turn it down, Ann Maria.'

'Call me crazy then, Pearse, because I've no intention of selling!'

To me this was a sign from the heavens. That other solicitor's client had much deeper pockets than I had. If he had made it to the auction in the Downshire Hotel, I couldn't have outbid him. It seemed like the universe had conspired to keep him out of the auction room that day. I was convinced the Old Rectory was meant for me. I felt it was an act of providence.

However, the house was nearly three hundred years old. It had rising damp and wet rot, and the roof needed repairs. Peter started getting people in to look at the cost of making the house habitable. Meanwhile, I applied for full planning permission for change of use and alterations. Peter recalls seeing me arrive with a step ladder and a tin of paint at the Old Rectory soon after I bought the place.

'Where are you off to?'

'I've bought a lovely bright shade of pink, and I'm going to make a start on one of the bedrooms.'

He stopped himself laughing out loud.

'Ann Maria, there's an awfully long list of things to do before we get to the painting. I'm pretty sure it'll be another year before we get to that stage.'

I wondered what he was on about. *What's wrong with making a start and painting a bedroom?* I had no idea of the complexities of renovating an old house. I was very naive. In the weeks that followed, I started looking at the costings of redoing the windows, the electrics, adding plumbing and a heating system.

I started to get cold feet and was plagued by worries. *Oh my God, what have I done? How am I going to manage? This place is huge. How am I going to afford it? Can I really turn this into a retreat centre?* Fear took over, and rather than feeling excited, I was filled with anxiety.

I had reason to be worried. It was a massive job, and when I look back on photographs, they show that the house had to be taken back to a shell. The floors had to come up for a damp-proof course, and all the internal walls needed treatment for rising damp. The plastering had to be redone. The chimneys needed repairs and ceilings had to be replaced in parts. The windows needed replacing or repairs. It required full plumbing, electrics and a heating system. As Peter predicted, it would be a whole year later before the house was ready for my tin of bright-pink paint.

Sadly Uncle Jimmy died in Saint Michael's Hospital, Dún Laoghaire, on 5 September 1988, just three days before his seventy-seventh birthday. The removal and funeral mass were held in Saint Michael's Church in Inchicore, and he was laid to rest in Glasnevin Cemetery. Afterwards I was drawn back to Taizé, the place where I always grieved. I could feel my soul being soothed by just being in the community again.

Towards the end of the retreat, Sister Diane asked if I'd consider going to Madras, now Chennai, in India. She needed help preparing for a Taizé meeting called the Pilgrimage of Trust on Earth. Brother Roger held a European meeting every year, but this was a big intercontinental meeting, which was only held every five years or so. At any other time I would have leapt at the opportunity to travel, but the renovations were starting on the Old Rectory. Regretfully I told Sister Diane that I couldn't go, and I returned home to deal with the builders. Planning permission was granted, and work began in earnest a few months later. That's when Sister Diane called me about India again.

'I need you to reconsider, Ann Maria,' she said. 'One of the women who committed to go to Madras has pulled out at the last moment. We could really do with your help.'

I hesitated only for seconds. *The builders don't really need me here now, do they?*

'Yes, I'll go, Diane. Tell me what you want me to do.'

I met with the architect, Dave Lennon, to tell him I was leaving for India.

'India? Are you serious? We're starting this build.'

'I know, but I have to go.'

'For how long?'

'Three months.'

Dave's face fell.

'How are we supposed to do this when you're not here to make decisions?'

'Peter has offered to help you.'

Peter and I were still in the early stages of our relationship, but we had grown closer, and he was more involved in my life. He offered to help with the building project in my absence. In retrospect, he says I was very trusting because I handed him my chequebook. He agreed to pay the builder his stage payments and to buy anything else that was needed. Peter took on an enormous amount of work in the house.

'Look, I'll be here,' he said. 'I'll help out any way that I can.'

Selflessly, he drove down to a shell of a place every weekend that winter and undertook all sorts of work. I couldn't have done it without him. He still had a full-time job, but all his spare time was spent in that house in the dark and the cold. He rewired the entire building, which was a huge undertaking. He had a lot of building skills, so he was digging trenches and laying pipes, doing all sorts of work. There were lots of volunteers helping too, and he worked in the middle of them. He was a great support to me.

Meanwhile from November 1988 until February the following year, I was travelling around India. Communication with Ireland was difficult in an era before email or mobile phones. I remember returning to our base in Madras one night to find a telegram waiting for me: *Discovered wet rot in front room. Please advise.*

Donard was a million miles away from the world I had entered in India. I remember receiving my first briefing from Brother Ghislain in Madras and feeling a sense of panic and fear set in. I was heading into the unknown. I hadn't realised the vastness of India and gasped when I discovered my first destination required a twenty-eight-hour train journey. They despatched me to Calcutta, now known as Kolkata, more than a thousand miles away. The teeming city of Madras had already assaulted all my senses. City life in India was overwhelming with its the narrow alleyways and bazaars, its putrid smells and the wretched poverty.

On the train I glimpsed the breathtaking beauty of the Indian countryside for the first time. I was enchanted by the women at work, their saris like exotic flowers in the paddy fields, the men on buffalo-drawn carts and the lush tropical foliage. I was suddenly excited to be heading to Calcutta even though I was uncertain where I'd be staying. I wrote in my journal: *Placing trust in God and ask for the grace to be more and more open to Divine will.*

I remember the train screeching to a sudden stop in a rural backwater in Orissa State. We had reached Kaitanga Road Station, a tiny stop, and the thermometer outside soared over thirty degrees Celsius. The minutes ticked on, and the sun beat down on the carriages and still, there was no movement. People started climbing down from the carriages to see why we were being held up. We discovered that locals were protesting on the railway tracks because of the long train delays. My fellow passengers shrugged and snoozed while I grew more and more impatient in the heat and humidity. The locals remained impassive. I didn't know it then, but their reaction was mindfulness in action. They lay back, relaxed, resigned to the situation, while I silently fumed.

My mission in India was to provide information and to encourage people to attend the intercontinental meeting in Madras. Thousands were expected to participate in the Pilgrimage of Trust on Earth, but many of the people we hoped would attend hadn't left their rural villages before this. It was a big ask for them to travel all the way to Madras. I was among many Taizé volunteers who were sent out in pairs all over India. My partner was a girl called Helen McGowan, a newly qualified nurse from Liverpool. She was always smiling and was full of enthusiasm for our mission.

The sisters of Taizé had arrived in Madras months earlier and had meticulously planned our routes. It was much later before I learnt that purchasing train tickets in India was such an ordeal that many Westerners paid locals to do the queuing for them. Our train tickets were handed to us. We only had to bring our bags and our itinerary. When we arrived at our destination, we were met at the station and brought to a local house. In the evening we hosted the information meeting in the village. Everyone interested in hearing more about the intercontinental meeting in Madras gathered. Our job was to help and encourage people to come to Madras and join us.

Every few days Helen and I set off on another train to a new destination, receiving incredible kindness and hospitality along the way. The people, some very poor, were so gracious, generous and remarkably curious about meeting us. I remember arriving in the small town of Basanti and being surrounded by children, who were giggling with excitement about meeting two Western women. Basanti had a population of just a few thousand people, but the streets were the same in every town and village we went through. The crush of people and the smells of poverty were staggering at times. The hot and dusty roads were full of beggars, hovels, public urinating and abandoned heaps of stinking garbage. Stallholders called out their wares of spices, teas and leather goods amid the chaos of rickshaws, taxis, motorbikes, hawkers and hucksters. The noise and the throngs seemed as unending as the exhausting heat.

A cyclone hit the Bay of Bengal the night we arrived in Basanti, and as I returned from the information meeting, the rain came down in torrents. I'd never before experienced rain like it. I was drenched to the skin. The water washed through the streets, and it was the first time I saw roads in India that were deserted and peaceful.

I was deeply affected by the poverty around me, but I knew I couldn't dwell upon it. I had to get on with the task I'd been charged with. But there were many times when the crowds, the colours, the smells, the cacophony of noise felt overwhelming. At one stage I settled into Monica House, a guest house for volunteers, managed by the Saint James Church in Calcutta. This was to be my home for a week. I remember I was hot and ill, suffering from a vomiting bug, and feeling imprisoned under my mosquito net. Outside my window was the non-stop sound of horns blowing and endless traffic passing. I felt miserable and yearned for the peace and the coolness of Fauna Cottage.

The next day I was sent to meet women at a handloom exhibition. I was still light-headed and feeling sick. After the information meeting, I took a rickshaw back to Monica House because there was no way I could find my own way back through the maze of city streets. It was never pleasurable to ride in these two-stroke, three-wheeled auto-rickshaws in the clamour of fumes and traffic. It was particularly unpleasant when feeling unwell. As the journey dragged on and on, it began to dawn on me that the rickshaw driver didn't know the way either. I felt so frustrated and homesick during some of those days in India. I thought about Donard, and the silence of winter seemed so inviting. I wrote in my journal: *I'm getting tired of constant noise, dirt, beggars on the street; and taking care not to fall into open drains on footpaths, or worse.*

The house where Mother Teresa lived, the Missionaries of Charity, was located just across the road from Monica House. Many of the volunteers, who travelled thousands of miles to work for Mother Teresa's cause, resided in Monica House alongside me. Seeing their commitment, I knew I didn't have what it took to look after the poorest of people and the terminally ill. The volunteers rose early and returned late, exhausted and drained from the emotional intensity of their days.

Having made it all the way to Calcutta, I hoped to catch a

glimpse of this global symbol of compassion known as Mother. The opportunity arose just before I was due to leave for Madras when I was sent to an event called the Profession of Sisters in Saint Mary's Church. It was a ceremony where dozens of young women from around the world made their first vows to Mother's order. The candidates' family members jostled for space with the many priests and sisters who also gathered at the event.

Afterwards I joined an enormous queue to meet Mother Teresa. Graciously and patiently, she met everyone who wanted to see her. She was a tiny figure, smaller and more stooped than I ever imagined. Her nut-brown skin was a startling contrast to her crisp white sari with the blue-striped borders. And then I was before her, that iconic lined face I'd seen on the news bulletins and on the cover of *Time* magazine. I had seconds to gaze into her remarkable golden-brown eyes and witness all the warmth that inspired her to care for those shunned by the rest of society. She said she formed her congregation to care for: *the hungry, the naked, the homeless, the crippled, the blind, the lepers, all those people who feel unwanted, unloved, uncared for throughout society.* Mother Teresa smiled, blessed me and handed me a prayer leaflet, and her sense of humility and her grace remain with me today.

# *Peace*

#### Author Unknown

*Today may there be peace within.*

*May you trust that you are exactly where you*

*are meant to be.*

*May you not forget the infinite possibilities*

*that are born of faith in yourself and others.*

*May you use the gifts that you have received*

*and pass on the love that has been given to you.*

*May you be content with yourself just the way you are.*

*Let this knowledge settle into your bones,*

*And allow your soul the freedom to sing, dance,*

*praise and love.*

*It is there for each and every one of us.*

# AWAKENING

―――∽―――

*Meditation is the art or technique of quieting the mind,*
*so the endless chatter that normally fills our consciousness is stilled.*

BRIAN L. WEISS, MD

The morning mists were receding into the slowly rising sun as I lay in Savasana on the sandy beach at Ennore, the very south-east of India. Savasana, also known as the corpse pose, is a yoga position where you lie on your back, arms inches from your body, palms upwards and feet dropped open. This beach on the Bay of Bengal at dawn was the perfect place for yoga. The only sound was the lapping of the gentle waves, allowing me to relax completely. Savasana is a way to calm the mind, improve sleep and reduce stress and fatigue.

The prodding of something hard into my arm jolted me back to the real world. As I opened my eyes in alarm, several figures around me hurriedly stepped back. As my eyes became accustomed to the light, I realised five men were watching me, including one who was holding the stick that he had used to jab me.

'What do you think you're doing?' I said, rubbing my arm, furious at the intrusion.

They started chattering all at once in a local language, probably Tamil, and wildly gesticulating as they pointed from me to their fishing village. 'We think you are dead,' one explained in English.

I gradually learnt that one of the men had spotted me in the distance and thought I was a body washed up on the shore. He went back to the village to get others to help take in the 'body'. I saw the funny side then and laughed, and they laughed too. But they were still bewildered why I was lying on a beach at dawn. Yoga may have originated in India five thousand years previously, but these fishermen didn't seem to have heard of it.

Lying on the beach in Ennore helped me recover from the long and winding journey from Trichy, my previous destination. After many meetings in Trichy, I went to see the Rockfort Temples. The temples are the most prominent landmark in the city, built on top of ancient rock, nearly three hundred feet tall. Near the entrance, I stroked the painted temple elephant, his swaying head and trunk decorated in paisley swirls of pink and gold. From there, it was a steep, barefoot climb on scorching steps carved into rock that is said to be four billion years old. The ascent to the final temple, Ucchi Pillayar, dedicated to Lord Ganesha, rewarded me with a panoramic view of the river and city.

I was determined to explore every town and village that we visited. However, the constant travelling meant it was hard to avoid the infamous stomach condition known as Delhi belly. Helen and I couldn't always prepare our own food, and there was no bottled water for sale in those days. A sick stomach was a constant threat to every Taizé volunteer.

The day we were due to travel to Madras for the big intercontinental meeting, I stayed in bed with a high fever and a churning stomach. I still felt delirious when I arrived a day late in Madras, and I didn't know how I was going to survive the three-day event. My job was in the registration tent, tackling the endless queues of arrivals. In the end, more than ten thousand people gathered on the campus of Loyola College in the city for the meeting. Everyone assembled under a massive open-sided pandal with a straw roof. The first day was a blur, but later I felt gratified that all our pre-conference meetings had paid off. I was reunited with so many people from Calcutta, Basanti, Trichy and everywhere Helen and I had travelled.

This monster rally of people, the Pilgrimage of Trust on Earth, had no caste system, and despite all the nationalities, no language barriers. It was an extraordinary time, and the spirit of pilgrimage was in the air. So many people assembled, all to hear the inspirational daily words from Brother Roger. There was chanting, group discussions, prayer meetings, a lot of laughter and a lot of hope for the future. There really was a sense of absolute peace and bliss under that makeshift pandal. This unique spiritual gathering touched everyone.

I remember all the hugs, the embraces and the tears when the conference ended on 31 December. After the many months of organising, the three-day event was already behind us. Yet there was no sense of deflation because we were walking on air. Everyone returned to our base at the Good Shepherd Convent in Madras for a farewell meal. Some volunteers prepared to leave India, while others, like me, planned to continue travelling. I felt privileged to have shared in the experience and felt a renewed sense of self and purpose. Fellow volunteers, Helen, Anne and Georgina, saw me off at the train station, and even though I was travelling alone, I felt a surge of excitement as the train pulled out. I was ready to explore more of India

It was New Year's Eve, 31 December 1988, a vastly different one to previous ones. My journal notes: *A baby sleeps peacefully opposite me, a beautiful sight. I will spend New Year's Eve travelling, thinking about past New Year's Eves, and many people come to mind.*

My destination was Shantivanham Ashram, a Benedictine monastery outside Trichy founded by Father Bede Griffith. Based on the traditions of Christian monasticism and Hindu Sannyasa, it was a meeting place for people of all religions or none at all. I caught a bus from the station at Trichy, which brought me twenty-five miles into the countryside. As I alighted the bus in a small village called Tannirpalli, I thought I saw a familiar figure. *It couldn't be*, I thought, but I looked again. It was like an apparition. I was six thousand miles from home and across the road was a close friend of mine from Ireland.

'Patricia!' I hollered. 'Patricia!'

She looked over and appeared equally confused.

'Ann Maria?'

I met Patricia Leahy in Tabor House, where I was her spiritual companion during a retreat. We became good friends afterwards. She went to India many months before me, but I had no idea where she was in this vast country. And then alighting from a bus, I find her in the middle of nowhere waiting at the bus stop on the opposite side of the road. It was a beautiful encounter. We hugged each other and I burst into tears. I was overcome to see a friendly face when I least expected it. I hadn't known she was based in Shantivanham with Father Bede's Ashram. The synchronicity was extraordinary.

Father Bede, an English Benedictine monk, said he went to India 'in search for the other half of his soul'. A famous spiritual teacher and noted yogi, he honoured the wisdom of both Eastern and Western traditions and became known as Swami Dayananda in his later years. I never expected him to be accessible, but I requested an audience with him and it was granted. He lived on the grounds of the ashram, so I met with him in his rustic thatched cottage. Father Bede was a great thinker, theologian and mystic. Yet sitting there in his saffron robes, with his rosy cheeks, long white hair and beard, he had the manner of an indulgent grandfather. I talked about my spiritual life and my plans to open a retreat centre, and he was interested and encouraging. It was a privilege to bask in such a beautiful, warm presence for a while. I knew I was in the company of someone extraordinarily special.

'Just follow your inner calling, Ann Maria,' he said, 'and you are on the right path to discovering what is truly valuable.'

The silence of the ashram was restorative after the hurly-burly of Madras. Entering into the rhythm of each day, I immersed myself in the early morning meditations, yoga, Nama Japa chants, silent periods and working in the ashram. I remember the beautiful open-sided pagoda in the gardens where afternoon tea was served and where people from all over the world gathered.

One of those people was Sister Vandana Mataji, leader of Christian ashrams located at the foothills of the Himalayas. She hosted a discussion on the integration of Christian and Hindu spirituality. I remember her playing the most enchanting music on the sitar. 'Silence is above all the language through which India reveals herself . . . and imparts her essential message, the message of interiority, of that which is within,' she said.

I felt I could have listened to her for hours, so even though my retreat centre in Ireland didn't yet exist, I invited her to it. The invitation lit a spark in her eyes, and she responded enthusiastically. After a week in Father Bede's ashram, another destination in India beckoned. I headed a thousand miles away to the city of Bombay, now known as Mumbai, on the other side of the country.

The journey by train involved a gruelling twenty-eight hours in the 'ladies' carriage'. There was a dorm-like camaraderie to the carriage, with lots of chatting and sharing of food packed in tali metal dishes. The women were friendly and curious about an unaccompanied young Western woman travelling across their country.

At every station, chai wallahs or tea vendors would cling to the outside of the carriage shouting in the window: 'Chaa-ye, Chaa-ye!' They wound their way nimbly down the carriages, their trays bearing shot glasses or red clay cups filled with tea. They also offered dishes of sticky sweetmeats and jalebi (Indian sweets) for a few rupees.

Others offered fills of tea from their aluminium kettles into ceramic cups that the women held out the windows. 'Kitane paise hue, bhaiya?' (How much money, brother?) the woman would ask, before passing a few rupees out the window in exchange for a chai. The chai was invariably made by brewing tea leaves, shovels of sugar and pints of milk together in a large cauldron or a big aluminium kettle over an open fire somewhere around the station.

Our beds, hard wooden platforms that folded down from the wall, were a test of endurance. As sleeper passengers, we battled hot and sticky conditions, fatigue and rank odours from the toilets. Fleeting glimpses into the alien world outside broke the monotonous chugging of the train. This world was filled with shanty-town homes, cross-legged Brahmins, washerwomen at their work at the rivers, markets and bazaars, workers bent in paddy fields and abundant green foliage.

Every few hours, bullocks, cows or goats wandered onto the tracks, and the train would grind to a halt, brakes squealing. The air that wafted through the windows, providing the only form of air-conditioning, would also stop. Everyone would wilt into silence in the oppressive heat. Still, there was no sense of frustration, only a calm acceptance of the delays. As soon as the track was cleared, the train would continue its journey, and the good-humoured chatter would resume. There was never a rush; no one ever seemed to have deadlines. I still found it challenging to adapt to the pace of life in India.

I left my fellow travellers at Pune, a few stops before Bombay city, submerged in hugs, kisses and blessings from my travelling companions. My purpose in Pune was to visit a controversial ashram led by the Indian mystic Bhagwan Shree Rajneesh, also known as Osho. He was also known as the 'free-love guru' and the 'Rolls Royce guru' because he owned a fleet of around ninety of the luxury cars. The ashram was advertised as 'a place where the mind, body and soul can play harmoniously together', and those staying in the ashram had to have a HIV test before they were admitted.

The only requirement as a day visitor was to wear a wristband and to be accompanied by someone from the ashram throughout my time there. The woman didn't let me out of her sight as I wandered around in awe. It was like a garden paradise filled with ornate marquees fit for the Maharajas. These giant tents were lavishly decorated with richly coloured fabrics and were filled with people doing workshops. Day visitors were not allowed to join the workshops, but I glanced into one as we passed and saw hundreds of people performing an amazing synchronised dance to loud music. I didn't see any of the nudity that was supposed to be part of the ashram. Neither did I see any sign of the spiritual rock star, Osho, himself. My curiosity about the ashram was quenched. It seemed like a lavish Indian-themed Club Med in a glorious setting. However, I was still intrigued by the experiences that lay beyond the walls of other ashrams.

Before leaving for India, back in Tabor, Myles O'Reilly had given me some advice: 'If you're going to India, make sure to try a ten-day Buddhist Vipassana retreat,' he said. 'It's tough, but it's worth it.'

My journey's end was Igatpuri, a scenic hill station and village in the Western Ghats about seventy-five miles after Bombay. The area was known as a haven for trekkers and as the location for many of Bollywood's big outdoor musical scenes. It was also known as the world capital of the ancient Vipassana meditation. The International Centre for Vipassana, also known as the Dhamma Giri, was in a broad valley in the Sahyadri mountain range. The golden spire of the Dhamma Giri's pagoda soared above everything else in the area and was surrounded by eighty acres of colourful flower gardens and fruit trees.

Influential meditation teacher, Satya Narayan Goenka, often referred to as S. N. Goenka or Guru-ji (revered teacher), led the centre. A world-renowned Burmese-Indian meditation guru, he addressed the United Nations, the World Economic Forum at Davos and other prestigious conferences during his lifetime.

When Vipassana retreats are held in Europe, people bring their cushions, mattresses and blankets for this ten-day test of stamina. The format for Vipassana is the same whether it's held in Goa or Galway, but in Dhamma Giri, there were no comforts. The participants sat on a hard floor, with thin rattan matting in the meditation complex, known as the Shanti Pathar or Plateau of Peace. Located on the highest part of the eighty-acre community, the Shanti Pathar was divided in two, with hundreds of men on one side and hundreds of women on the other.

Vipassana is a Buddhist term which translates as 'special-seeing' or 'insight'. There is no mantra or prayer in Vipassana; it's all about silence, clearing the mind and 'anapanasati' or 'mindfulness of breathing.' We were instructed to observe our natural breathing during long meditation periods.

The day began with the wake-up gong at four o'clock followed by two hours of silent meditation in the Shanti Pathar. Participants spent a total of eleven hours each day in silent meditation, with breaks for silent, simple meals of plain rice and dhal. We had an hour to listen to S. N. Goenka's teachings every evening before a final meditation, which ended at nine o'clock. It was lights out at half-past nine.

I anticipated the discomfort of sitting on a floor for long periods. What I didn't expect were the other physical reactions I experienced. Vipassana was mind-opening for me. We were told to shut our eyes and to remain still while concentrating on our breathing. For a while, this was quite pleasurable, but by the second day, I felt searing pain moving up and down my body. It was extreme at times. My body shook violently with spasms and tremors, and my limbs involuntarily jerked. I felt excruciating stabs of pain. I had never experienced anything like this before and found it very unsettling.

I was on the verge of fleeing the 'Plateau of Peace' on many occasions. But then someone would whisper, 'Annica, annica,' in my ear; it was an instruction to let the sensations arise and pass away. 'Annica' translates as 'impermanence' and was a reminder that both the physical feelings and the surges of emotion would pass. 'Anapana, anapana,' was sometimes also whispered to me as a reminder to concentrate on my breathing rather than the pain.

I still found it difficult at times. On one occasion, my right foot felt as if it were burning, and I experienced uncontrollable spasms in my body. They were like jolts of energy. I tried to breathe through the sensations as instructed, but my limbs continued to jerk wildly. On this occasion, one of the facilitators whispered that I should lie down. But I pulled myself upright, concentrated on breathing and managed to find some composure again by the end of the meditation. I have since learnt that such experiences are not uncommon in Vipassana retreats. The surges and spasms are understood to be emotional releases, a sign of the nervous system trying to release trauma, blocked energy flow and tightness in the body.

On the tenth and final day of the retreat, we were invited to engage with our fellow participants for the first time. By then, I didn't feel like talking, but two Indian women approached me. We exchanged the greeting, 'Namaste', with a slight bow and hands in prayer position. It's a lovely greeting, meaning 'I bow to the Divine in you' in Hindu.

'I hope you don't mind us asking,' one of the women said, leaning in to me, 'but I'm a doctor, and I couldn't help noticing you in meditation. Do you suffer from epilepsy?'

The woman saw my startled expression.

'I'm only mentioning it because I was concerned for you,' she said. 'There were times when you shook so much, I thought you would fall over and hurt yourself!'

I was utterly taken aback and felt part-mortified and part-offended. We were instructed to close our eyes during meditations, so I felt very invaded. I had followed all the rules for the ten days, but these women had been watching me twitch and jerk in all manner of involuntary gyrations. The women's remarks were only a minor irritation, however. I found the whole experience a beautiful introduction to Buddhist teachings and to meditation. Doing the Vipassana opened doors to a new way of spirituality and reflection for me.

When the ten days were completed, my mind felt clear and present to the world around me. There was a sense of release. I was astonished at the difference. All the spasms and the discomfort were forgotten, and it felt like I had transcended the blocks that caused me so much pain. I feasted on the sight of the mountains, the clear air and light around me. It was like I had been through a type of purification process and had a lightness and liberation that I had never experienced before, some inimitable sense of clarity. I felt recalibrated. I left with a smile on my face, a light in my eye and the sense of new spiritual wings. My trip to India had broadened my mind and my vision and brought me one little stepping stone further on the path to enlightenment.

# Hindu Prayer for Peace (Shanti)

*Brihat Aranyka Upanishad Hindu Sacred Scripture*

*Oh God lead us from the unreal to the real*

*Oh God lead us from darkness to light*

*Oh God lead us from death to immortality*

*Shanti, Shanti, Shanti unto all*

*Oh Lord God almighty,*

*May there be peace in celestial regions.*

*May there be peace on earth.*

*May the waters be appeasing.*

*May herbs be wholesome,*

*And may trees and plants bring peace to all.*

*May all beneficent beings bring peace to us.*

*May thy peace itself bestow peace on all,*

*And may that peace come to me also.*

# CHRYSALIS

*When a person really desires something,
all the universe conspires to help that person to realise his dream.*

Paulo Coelho

The calendar lay on the desk and I flicked idly through its pages, hoping to spot a date that resonated with me – an auspicious date. I paused on 24 June, Midsummer's Day. The day coincides roughly with the summer solstice, a time that has been celebrated since the Stone Age. In ancient times it was associated with the sacred, with ceremony and the sun god. Midsummer's Day has also traditionally been a day of celebration with festivals, bonfires, feasting, singing and dancing. It seemed like the auspicious day I was looking for; an opportune time to celebrate the beginnings of a sanctuary and a place of sacred healing, personal growth and renewal.

So the official opening date for the new retreat centre was set for Sunday, 25 June 1989. It was probably a rash decision. The date was chosen four months in advance because it fell on the midsummer's weekend, not because the builders were likely to finish by then. The date didn't reflect in any way the amount of time needed to complete the house.

By the time I returned to Ireland in early February, building work on the Old Rectory had more or less come to a standstill. Overnight my life went from the mystical and fantastical experiences of India to the mundane and the practical issues of a building site in Donard. A myriad of decisions had to be made, and it seemed everyone was waiting for me to make them.

My builder and architect told me 25 June was an impossible

deadline, but I persisted. Announcing the launch day seemed to motivate the builders, and a network of friends and groups of volunteers rallied around too. Progress began to hasten on the site.

I never worked so hard in my life, running at breakneck speed from early morning to late night. I knew I was a total amateur when it came to project managing, but I put my trust in the universe and threw all my energy into it. Taking a deep breath, I oversaw the conversion of a rundown country house into a retreat centre. With Peter's help, I managed to juggle builders, subcontractors, builders' providers, volunteers and all the hundreds of problems and unexpected issues that arose over the next four months.

From early on I chose the name Chrysalis for the centre as a symbol of renewal and rebirth. A chrysalis is the final stage before the butterfly emerges from its cocoon. The winged form of the butterfly was also a symbol for the human soul in Irish mythology and for the ancient Greek and Aztec civilisations.

The analogy between a natural chrysalis and a healing retreat was perfect. The butterfly begins as a soft and vulnerable caterpillar, which cocoons and transforms within the protective shell of the chrysalis. When conditions are right, and the air is warm and welcoming, the butterfly emerges, and its bright wings unfold. My vision of Chrysalis was a safe place where people could cocoon and begin transformative journeys with newly learnt skills or by letting go of old patterns and behaviours. I hoped to see people emerge from Chrysalis reborn like butterflies, flying light and high, with an ability to see a familiar landscape from a whole new perspective.

The name Chrysalis was also perfectly in tune with our surroundings. Flamboyant butterflies – red admirals, tortoiseshells and peacocks – fluttered all around the gardens of the Old Rectory every spring and summer. They alighted on flowers and bushes, wings beating in the summer air, as fragile as a spider's web but as beautiful as painted silk. Chrysalis seemed like the perfect name for this retreat in the wilderness of County Wicklow.

As the opening date for the centre hurtled towards me, it felt like a higher power was taking over. Something outside myself was looking after my needs and the new centre's needs. Everyone around me seemed to be inspired by a sacred energy too. Whenever

I despaired about the progress, friends appeared with great hearts and willing arms or tradesmen would turn up unexpectedly. We needed a lot of furniture, and I remember people arriving with chairs, tables, beds and assorted furniture tied to their car roofs. A friend who was emigrating to England brought a car-and-trailer-load of household goods to equip the centre's kitchen.

Through dogged persistence and with the help of many generous souls, the Old Rectory was transformed. What had been the Church of Ireland rectory was now the spiritual home and grounds of Chrysalis. When Midsummer's Day arrived, I looked around, and by some miracle, we were ready to greet the two hundred and fifty guests attending the official opening. Like so much in my life, it felt like I had got there carried on spirit wings.

The day is etched on my mind as a riot of colours, music, dancing and laughter. My memories are of the ecumenical opening ceremony, the blessings, the colourful balloon release, the delicious food, the children, the face-painting, the circle dance on the lawn and the melodic simplicity of a harpist's strings filling the air. My dream of a retreat centre had become a reality, and my desire to be of service in the world was being fulfilled.

I couldn't quite believe that I'd succeeded in opening Ireland's first lay retreat centre, a haven of therapeutic healing and personal and spiritual development.

But there was no time to sit back or to revel in the success of reaching this milestone. Once the centre opened, all my time and energies were consumed with the organisation and running of the place. When I look back, I don't know where I got the stamina that I needed in those early years. But Chrysalis was my passion, and I poured everything I had, physically, mentally and financially, into it.

That summer unfolded with a skeleton programme of workshops and retreats, and Peter and I were spending more time together. I had come to rely on him, not only for emotional support but also for the practicalities of everyday life. When the sink was blocked, the lights went out or the heating didn't work, the first person I called was Peter.

By now I had qualified as a psychotherapist and worked as a part-time student counsellor in Saint Patrick's College, Maynooth.

As soon as I completed my hours in Saint Patrick's, I got into my car and rushed back to Donard.

In the early days, I did all the cooking, washing, cleaning and administrative work at Chrysalis. It was a one-woman show for a long time. There were residential weekend courses and week-long courses or longer. At weekends, it was all-hands-on-deck as friends would come down and help me out.

Ireland was a very different place in the late eighties. When Chrysalis first opened, some locals didn't understand what we were aspiring to do. There was a certain level of suspicion about the work there, and some people even believed the centre was some kind of cult. We had sweat lodges, so there was even talk that people were 'going around naked down at that place'. Once the local priest, Father Lyons, began announcing some of our events from the altar on Sundays, we got the veneer of respectability we needed. As soon as the locals started attending our events, all the suspicion dissipated, and Chrysalis became part of the community.

In many ways Chrysalis was ahead of its time. When it opened, we were still living in the eighties when the grand house, the fast car, the high-powered job and status were priorities for many. That was the era of right-wing Thatcherism, Yuppies (young, upwardly mobile professionals) and Donald 'The Deal' Trump. Church attendance was on the decline, and the world seemed to worship at the altar of Wall Street. 'Greed is good' was the celebrated catch-cry of the trader Gordon Gekko. The world of the 1980s seemed like a harder, more mercenary place. I remember attending a directed retreat that year, and the director was bewildered about my plans for Chrysalis.

'Retreat centres are closing all around the country; why would you want to open one?' he asked.

But I knew this was part of my destiny, this was what I had to do. I felt a strong sense of support and guidance, and I never lost heart. I knew not everyone was driven by an insatiable desire for wealth. There were people out there who were spiritually hungry too. Many people had grown disillusioned with the traditional Church structures and were looking for an alternative way to live. I had an intuition that there was a new spirituality emerging in Ireland.

Chrysalis was definitely a trailblazer in the field of holistic treatment, spirituality and personal growth. Today, with health food stores and alternative therapies available at every corner, it's hard to imagine how innovative the concept of Chrysalis was back then. There was an element of 'build it, and they will come', and thankfully, people did.

When we first opened, we hadn't enough people to keep a yoga class going a few times a week. Within a year we hadn't a room big enough to fit everyone who wanted to be in every class. Chrysalis took on a life of its own from early on, and it became a destination within spiritual and therapeutic circles extremely fast. Some people came to Chrysalis for healing and others were seekers, searching for something new and meaningful in their lives. It was never about people coming for a weekend and then leaving on a Sunday saying: 'Oh, so that's what my life is all about!' But every course Chrysalis offered had some element of spiritual healing to it. Some chose to go to our Eastern workshops like Indian yogic spirituality, and others attended traditionally directed retreats with a Catholic priest. But even a birdwatching weekend with the Irish Wildlife Conservancy added to the richness of people's everyday lives.

From the beginning, Chrysalis had a very holistic approach to helping people to heal. I started with the concept that there are three elements within every person to be nourished: the mind, body and spirit. The aspiration was to create an environment that integrated and cared for all three. Every course was designed to some extent to help personal development, psychological healing and the journey to the spirit. Above all, the workshops were designed to nurture the senses, nurture the body, and nurture the soul. The word 'nurturing' permeated everything we did in Chrysalis.

In the early days many of the courses reflected my own journey. I knew the facilitators personally because I trained with them, worked with them or met them on retreats. In Tabor House, for instance, there was an outstanding bereavement programme, so I brought those bereavement weekends to Chrysalis.

From the start Chrysalis was nondenominational, and we invited teachers from many different spiritual traditions. There was a sort of a universal spirituality at the centre. We invited teachers from

Christian, Buddhist, Hindu and Islamic traditions, which made the place quite special.

One of the first programmes in the centre was a workshop called Adult Children of Alcoholics, which was facilitated by Dr Ellen Sher from the United States. This type of experiential workshop was new to Ireland, and one of the first news stories about Chrysalis appeared in the media as a result. I also found well-known therapists in America doing workshops on inner-child work, who agreed to come to Ireland. I was at a Chieftain's concert when I met a woman who had recently returned home after spending twenty-five years working with families and children in the United States and Canada. Lucille McDonald, now one of my closest friends, was one of the first qualified therapists working on co-dependency issues in Ireland, when she began facilitating workshops in Chrysalis.

In the early days I never had to pay airfares for the international facilitators, only for their time on the workshops – so many people from around the world were looking for any excuse to come to Ireland. As the centre developed, we had more and more facilitators from abroad come to share their skills with us. We had a facilitator who trained with the Cherokee-Irish shaman, Harley Swiftdeer-Reagan, who hosted a workshop called Sacred Laws and Psychic Gifts. Dutch therapist, Zelda Hall, who trained in rebirthing and body-oriented psychotherapy, facilitated a workshop called Inner and Outer Worlds. From London, we had Nigel Hamilton, leader of the Sufi Centre, who held a retreat called Journey to the Home of Your Soul. Pat O'Leary, a well-known teacher from the USA, facilitated popular Enneagram weekends.

Of course there were also more conventional courses on the programme. Michael Casey from the Irish Ramblers Club held hill-walking weekends. There were painting weekends held by Bob Lynn who studied art at the Edinburgh College of Art.

Then as more staff and volunteers began to work in Chrysalis, the programme expanded to reflect their interests too. One of them, Claire Harrison, suggested a vegetarian cookery course. I never thought that there would be enough interest in vegetarian cookery in those days, but that turned out to be a huge success.

I started attending many more workshops and retreats to soak up all the new concepts and teachings out there. At one stage I didn't know if I was becoming enlightened or bewildered by all the varied beliefs, theories and practices I was learning. It was an exciting time because the Human Development Movement was blossoming. Any workshops or facilitators that I found helpful on my own personal journey, I sought to bring to Chrysalis.

One of those people was Jesuit priest, Richard (Dick) McHugh, an American who spent decades in India. He worked in Lonavala, a hill station on the west coast of India, with renowned Jesuit spiritual guide, Anthony de Mello. Dick, who had a doctorate in psychology, was a very gifted therapist. He came to Chrysalis to teach a nine-day residential programme called Freedom from Conditioning through Neuro-Linguistic Programming (NLP). Dick had an extraordinary ability to capture the imagination of a group, challenge participants and help them discover their inner resources.

'There's something inside us stronger than us; there's a life we are not even aware of,' he used to say. 'The resources necessary to find an answer are within each person.'

Dick held his first NLP programme in Chrysalis during a heatwave in August 1990. Suddenly we had a full house of people and no water. The water pressure was so low that only a trickle was coming from the taps downstairs and even less upstairs.

'Oh my God, Peter, what am I going to do?' I said. 'This is a disaster. No one can even flush a toilet, and they are supposed to be living here for the next nine days!'

Peter checked the well, which serviced our water supply. It was located on adjoining land, and he found the levels were low.

'There's nothing that can be done if the water isn't there,' said Peter. 'Improvise. Get buckets and get them filled somewhere else. What's the water pressure like at Russ and Emer's place?'

Panicked, I dashed to the local hardware shop in Baltinglass to buy a load of plastic buckets for flushing the toilets. Clearly flustered, I apologised to Dick for the water situation. He was a tall, lean man, with silver hair and bright blue eyes which twinkled with humour and intelligence.

'You forget that I lived in India for a long time. I'm perfectly at home without running water.'

I was grateful that he was making light of the situation, but I knew the participants would not be so sanguine.

'The problem is the rest of the group have never lived in India,' I said. 'And we don't have enough staff for bucket-filling duty.'

'I'm sure if we ask nicely, everyone will help out,' he said.

So Dick explained my predicament and asked for volunteers from the group to collect the water. No one could refuse him. They trekked down the long avenue, crossed the road to Russ and Emer's house and heaved back all the buckets and basins of water that were needed. That was the only way we could get an essential water supply to the bathrooms for the nine days. Some of them even had their showers in our neighbours' house. I learnt a valuable lesson. By that autumn I had another well drilled in the garden, so we always had plentiful water after that.

Dick continued coming to Ireland in the following years to facilitate groups in NLP in Chrysalis and other venues. He passed away aged eighty-seven in 2018, and I remember him fondly as one of the most inspirational and popular facilitators on our programmes.

After my experience in India I was drawn to the wisdom of both Eastern and Western spiritual traditions. I first met Sister Vandana Mataji, one of the great spiritual mothers of modern India, during my time in Shantivanham ashram.

She led the Christian ashrams, Jiva-Dhara, in Rishikesh and Jeevan-Dhara in Jaiharikhal, both in the foothills of the Himalayas. Born into the Parsi faith, she was ostracised by her family when she converted to Christianity and joined the Sisters of the Sacred Heart. I was thrilled when she agreed to visit Ireland in 1992 to host a workshop on Indian yogic spirituality in Chrysalis.

Sister Vandana was one of those rare people with the ability to listen with a compassionate heart and without judgement. White-haired, bird-like and gentle, she was a warm, comforting presence in any room. Simply being in her presence, you felt a sense of being loved and accepted.

Decades before it became fashionable, she was advocating mindfulness and was the first teacher to introduce me to the practice of living in the moment. Everyone loved Sister Vandana and her gentle Hindu-Christian spirituality. She wasn't interested in proselytising. Her teachings were eclectic as she embraced the Hindu way of life and the teachings of 'Christ the Guru', as she called him. She brought Eastern and Western spirituality together in her Indian yogic spirituality retreats. She quoted from the Bible and from Hindi sacred scripture such as the Bhagavad Gita, the Vedas and the Upanishads.

By the time she came to Chrysalis, she was in her seventies, but she was a yogi, with a body as supple as an elastic band. She introduced us to yoga asana poses, to Nama Japa (chanting the name of God in meditation), and Yoga Nidra or deep body relaxation. She worked to open the heart and awaken the Divine in everyone in an atmosphere of stillness and silence. She liked to quote Johann Angelus Silesius, the German Catholic priest, mystic and religious poet: *The longest way to God lies through the intellect. The shortest way lies through the heart.* She was trained in Indian classical music and often played her sitar while singing mesmeric Indian bhajans or devotional songs.

I remember her bringing us on silent walks around the area. Sometimes the neighbours watched and wondered what we were at. She'd stop and focus our attention on a wildflower and bring us back to the moment. She was inspirational, a free spirit. She was kind of zany too, feather-headed in a lot of ways. You could never let her get a bus or make her way from the airport – she could end up anywhere.

Just watching her helped me realise that I had a long way to go on my spiritual path. When I said this to her, she reminded me, 'The journey to reach your goals far exceeds the goal itself.'

After her first visit, Sister Vandana became a frequent facilitator at Chrysalis. Her workshops were called Be Still, Stop, Breathe and Smile. I have a photograph of her in Donard with a cake iced with the title of her workshop, and she is beaming out of the image. Everyone smiled in Sister Vandana's company. She left this world in 2013, aged ninety-two, and her teachings remain with me to this day.

Jesuit priest Tony Baggot was also a great mentor to me, as well as an inspirational facilitator and healer. He trained with Dr Frank Lake in England, an innovator in the field of pastoral counselling who went beyond the constraints of talk therapy.

Tony came back to Ireland to run retreats that explored traumatic life issues. They weren't your run-of-the-mill retreats. I think he found Chrysalis a safe place to practise because it wasn't under the auspices of any church or organisation. County of the Spirit was the name of his workshop, which doesn't tell you much. But people who worked with him once always wanted to continue. His workshops were very popular.

The participants, usually around fifteen or sixteen people, lay on mattresses, and Tony would play music and lead them in a visualisation to their 'original wound'. People came for many reasons, but no one had to explain why; everyone was on their own inner journey. During the visualisation, people would often start crying, and he or an assistant might put his hand on their belly or chest and say, *breathe into it*. His mantra was: *Breathe into it and trust your body. It will take you where you need to go.*

And I used this with my own clients. If we really breathe, it brings us in deeper to our feelings and pain. Whether it was grief, anger or sadness, he led you back to it.

There's a value to talk therapy because everyone needs to tell their story. However, in my opinion this form of therapy has its limitations. Sometimes in relating painful life events, feelings are not expressed. For instance, a child who was abused never had the chance to fight back or to be angry. Tony led people back, exploring unexpressed painful feelings back to the original wound. He created a very safe environment to go beneath the surface and release and heal traumatic repressed experiences.

Anyone new to therapy would never start with a Tony Baggot workshop. It wasn't a workshop for the faint-hearted. People would often flail about, thump cushions, wring towels or scream obscenities. Not everybody wants to go to a deeper place, and that's their choice, but it provided a catharsis and a healing space for many people.

I have an abiding memory of Tony standing on a chair in the office in Chrysalis with a plastic bag trying to trap a poor bat, which was flying laps around a light shade on the ceiling. I really valued Tony's work and his counsel in my life. He died in March 2001 at the age of seventy-seven. For many years he was a supportive and healing presence in my life.

Chrysalis had a strict vegetarian ethos, which seemed to pose a problem for a lot of our residents in the early days. I lost count of the times that I had to say, 'No, you can't bring your ham sandwiches with you.' We could accommodate up to sixteen people, but when we had an overflow of guests, we sent them to two local guest houses nearby. However, that resulted in a chink in our vegetarian-only policy. 'I'd a mighty feed of rashers, sausages and pudding this morning,' someone would invariably announce.

There was a great sense of camaraderie throughout the whole place, a feeling that we were pioneers in healing and therapy. The kitchen was run in the days before food safety management procedures and HACCP (hazard analysis and critical control point) regulations. I made up giant trays of vegetable lasagnes for the freezer without a hair net on my head. I baked steaming apple tarts and stirred up pots of porridge in the mornings. Everyone just rolled up their sleeves and got in there, but everything was clean and safe. When all the health and safety rules arrived, things became more formalised. It took away from some of the fun and the spontaneity of the early years.

We had wonderful staff who worked tirelessly to make Chrysalis the success it was. Claire Harrison was an answer to my prayers. She was working as a volunteer at a summer festival in the north of Ireland, when she met my friend Emer Bailey. Emer told her that I was looking for volunteers, so Claire arrived in September 1991 in her little brown Mini Metro, packed to the roof with all her earthly belongings. She had intended to continue to Cork if things didn't look promising. We chatted in the garden for a while and I invited her to stay the night. Claire ended up staying for more than twenty years. I remember she was like a human dynamo around Chrysalis in her first week. She proceeded to feng shui the place, throwing out all sorts of things, most of which I retrieved from the bins! Claire proved to be an excellent organiser and, in time, took over the management of Chrysalis. We worked well together as a team, and we complemented each other in our different styles of working.

There were a lot of people like that who appeared unexpectedly and never left. We had people in the office, housekeepers, a gardener, chefs. As we progressed, my earlier dreams of a poustinia were fulfilled by building two hermitages on the grounds. These octagonal stone houses with self-catering facilities were totally separate from the main house, allowing people to get away from the restless momentum of modern life.

Our creative gardener, John Pilling, developed a Zen, or meditation, garden, a contemplative place where people were asked to remain silent. Stepping stones were placed in ways that helped people slow down so that even walking was a meditation for mind and body. When guests closed their eyes, they could hear the birdsong, the bleating of sheep, the wind rustling the leaves in the trees, and they could smell the scent of the grass and the flowers. The garden cultivated stillness. When people become still in the body, usually the mind follows, and stress and tension evaporate. One of our Chrysalis postcards featured a lovely verse about gardens by Dorothy Frances Gurney:

*The kiss of the sun for pardon,*

*The song of the birds for mirth,*

*One is nearer God's Heart in a garden*

*Than anywhere else on earth.*

The old house had an extraordinary atmosphere too. The scent of incense and fresh flowers filled the air as participants came through the door. It was a welcoming and cosseting environment. The words of an eleven-year-old visitor called Nicola Walsh were framed and hung in the library. The picture read: *Chrysalis is a house of peace, where people grow friendlier towards each other and get closer to God.* For me, it was the perfect assessment of the place.

People who attended our programmes entered a world of possibilities for healing and personal development. During an era when dissatisfaction was almost a way of life, Chrysalis offered a place of sanctuary and refuge. It was a reflective healing space, a place where people could calm their anxious minds, find support and learn new life skills.

Our ethos was one of mutual respect and confidentiality so that people only shared when they were comfortable doing so. We were never trying to push an agenda or convert anyone to anything. We simply offered people space to explore their inner selves. I've always believed that therapy and healing should be made available to everyone, not just those who could afford it. Initially, Chrysalis wasn't set up as a business, so after a few years I applied for charitable status. We offered reduced fees for some people and courses could also be paid by instalment over six months.

People came back again and again to our house of healing to become the people they wanted to be. They retreated from the frenetic pace of modern life and took stock of their lives and where they were going. People came to Chrysalis for many different and personal reasons. It wasn't realistic to expect that the centre was a panacea for all ills or could help people find a direction in their life in a weekend. But at least, they left with new insights into their inner selves and the realisation that they weren't alone in their pain.

Chrysalis was a dream for me, and the universe supported it. It became a little haven of peace and spirituality that touched many lives and scattered seeds of healing light all over Ireland and out into the world.

*Wedding day with Peter, New Rochelle, New York, July 1991.*

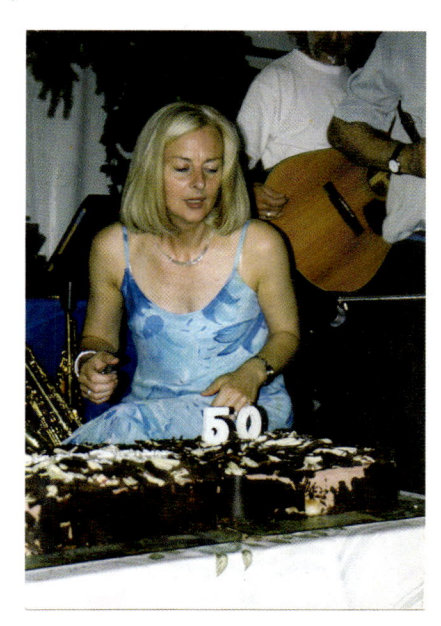

*Fiftieth birthday party, July 2004.*

*American Conservatory Theater, San Franscisco, 2001.*

*Daughter of the Caza Ceremony, Abadiânia, Brazil, 2008.*

*Elephant sanctuary, Sri Lanka.*

*Govardhan Ayurveda Hospital, Mumbai, October 2019.*

*Heather, David, me, Angela and Norah at Casa Nirvana Abadiânia, Brazil.*

*School visit, Govardhan, India, November 2019.*

*Swami Sharananda Korko Moses SJ, Dhyanavanam Ashram, India, November 2019.*

*Mozambique dolphin retreat, 2016.*
(Credit: clarelouisethomas.com)

*One of my pilgrimage groups in Asia, 2007.*

*Playback performance, the Mill Theatre, Dublin, 2007.*
(Credit: dakphotography.ie)

*Hang-gliding, Rio de Janeiro, 2007.*

*Buddhist temple, Chiang Mai, Thailand 2011.*

*Buddhist temple in Thailand.*

*School for Life Orphanage, Chiang Mai.*

# *If I Can Stop One Heart from Breaking*

EMILY DICKINSON

*If I can stop one heart from breaking,*

*I shall not live in vain;*

*If I can ease one life the aching,*

*Or cool one pain,*

*Or help one fainting robin*

*Unto his nest again,*

*I shall not live in vain.*

# HEALING STORIES FROM CHRYSALIS

―⁂―

*The past has no power over us.*
*It doesn't matter how long we have had a negative pattern.*
*The point of power is in the present moment.*
*What a wonderful thing to realise!*
*We can begin to be free in this moment!*

Louise L. Hay

## *Derek's Story*

The first time they put me away, I was sixteen years old. It was the first time I ever experienced wearing underwear. It was also the first time I had a quilt and a pillow to myself and a single bed. I had my own little cell that I could keep clean. I had cornflakes for the first time, and I got three square meals a day. I was in heaven.

Saint Patrick's Institution for young offenders on the North Circular Road became my home for the next five years. I was in and out of Saint Patrick's – but mostly in during those years. I was in for joyriding and driving cars without tax and insurance. I got twelve months for fighting too. But they were just the things I was caught doing.

There was a prison officer in Saint Patrick's who I got on with; he took a liking to me. I used to get into trouble just to go back in and see him. I remember when they said I was being released early for good behaviour, I cried my eyes out. I said to this fella, the prison officer, and the governor of the jail that I didn't want to go. I didn't want to leave prison. 'Can I stay? Why can't I stay?' I asked. I knew what kind of a life was waiting for me back outside.

Life outside was just rotten. I was the youngest of nineteen children. The house we lived in, there was nothing but physical, emotional and mental abuse. The Christian Brothers' school that I went to, there was loads of sexual abuse going on. I went through that when I was younger. The part of Crumlin I grew up in was just like a war zone. It was all about survival. The main emotion I lived with as a child was anxiety; I never knew what was going to happen next.

I used to sleep under a bed because there wasn't enough room in the bed. Drink dominated my house; all the money used to be spent on alcohol. I'd hear my mother crying when we had no food. So I'd go to Walkinstown where there was a lot of shops, and I'd hide and wait for delivery trucks to come. I would run up as soon as the delivery guy was in the shop and rob whatever was on the van. It could be a box of eggs or a sack of potatoes or frozen food. And then I used to travel to where there were loads of greenhouses and farms. I was so skinny then that I could fit between the bars around the farms and take heads of cabbage, carrots and whatever I could carry. I could come home with anything really.

I was so skinny that my brothers used to pull me out of bed in the middle of the night, and they would throw me in the windows of houses. They'd push me through tiny little openings, and I would open the back doors, so they could go in and rob. Whatever the need was in the house, I would try and deal with it. When I brought the food home, my mother used to say: 'You shouldn't be doing that!' But she cooked it anyway.

When I was twenty-one, the prison guard in Saint Patrick's said, 'Derek, you can't come back in here anymore. You're an adult now. You're going to Mountjoy the next time.' He said: 'Get a job because you're a great worker.' So that's what I did. I got a job, and I started working for a builder, a man who built extensions. I was the foreman *in no time. After I turned twenty-one, I never went to prison again. But I lived hard and fast; I had a lot of demons, and drink became my number one drug.*

I first learnt about Chrysalis in 1999 when I'd been in recovery for seven years. I gave up the drink when I was twenty-eight, around the time I started to struggle with my mental health. It was a woman from the AA meetings who told me about Chrysalis. I went down to Wicklow and I walked around the gardens, and the first thing I noticed was that I was able to breathe, really breathe properly for the first time. I did two courses and I made a lot of progress, but I still found it hard to talk.

Then I did my third workshop, a Co-Dependent No More course. That was a seven-day residential course. I was left until last in that group. The facilitator, Peter O'Sullivan, was watching me, monitoring me for the whole week, and on the second-last day, it was my turn. And he knew that I had so much frustration and so much rage built up inside me. He told me, 'That stuff that you're carrying is lethal. It really is lethal if that comes out in the wrong way.' He did some bodywork with me, and I started crying and screaming. I screamed for a good hour and a half straight until I collapsed with exhaustion. I collapsed from just screaming, and Peter said to me: 'That's only the beginning.'

And that's when I started to reflect on what kind of a life I lived. I was clean and sober at this stage, no substance abuse, nothing. I went to a therapist in Dublin, and they got me to write letters to say what my life was like growing up as a child. And when I read it all back, it was really hard to recognise the story as me. It read like it was the story of Oliver Twist. Really, that's the way I look at my life now. My life growing up as a child was like Oliver Twist. Only far worse.

Ann Maria was like the first lady I ever met, the first well-spoken lady I ever met. And I knew she was genuine. I just knew that I was in the presence of someone really special. And it's what I'd been craving all my life. I basically fell in love with everything that was at Chrysalis, and I used to look for any excuse to come back down. I promised Ann Maria that I wouldn't get into any trouble. That I'd stay away from any kind of crime or drugs or drink because I wanted to be accountable to her.

Ann Maria was always an 'out' for me. If I ever wanted to get away, I could ring her and go down to Chrysalis. I became a gardener because of Ann Maria. For years, I was a skilled labourer, because all I knew was how to work hard. I started to volunteer in the garden. When she saw I liked gardening, she got Peter O'Sullivan to give me a mower from his garden. It was my first ever petrol lawnmower, and I used it to set up my own business.

I used to go and tell her what I was doing, and she'd say, 'That's amazing, Derek. Well done.' That was the best drug I ever took, to get that recognition from her. I owe that woman my life, really, for what she's done for me the last twenty years. Ann Maria has been there at the worst of times like when my son died. And when I reacted badly to prescription drugs, she was there for me. I knew she trusted me, and she liked me.

There was a time when I really got bad, mentally and emotionally, from all the medication that I was on. Ann Maria got me into a treatment centre in Kerry, and she arranged for someone to pay for it. Later Ann Maria drove me from Dublin to Cavan to another treatment place where I could stay. But then I left and I rang her and said: 'I didn't like it.' She never gave out to me. She only said, 'That's okay. What do you want to do?'

I said, 'Can I come down and stay? I'll cut the grass, rake out the beds and plant the flower beds. Just let me do that. That'll get me better.' She was like a maternal figure that I never had. As part of getting better, I needed to apologise to a lot of people that I hurt in my youth, but some of them were dead. She told me to write a letter and read it at their graves. She gave me solutions to problems.

When I was in the garden, she used to say to me: 'Breathe Derek, breathe, just breathe.' I'd say, 'I can cut all this hedging back and still breathe while I'm doing it.' I loved to work there and build walls and paths and try to pay back something to the place that had given me so much. But she used to want me to stand still. Anytime I rang her, she'd be there to listen. Because I really thought that I was a headcase, a psychopath at times. I was going around like a wounded animal and carrying so much hurt in me. But Ann Maria saw right through that.

I used to love when I was leaving, the hugs she used to give me. She'd just wrap her arms right around me and hold me. It wasn't a quick hug-and-let-go. She'd just wrap her arms around me, and that would keep me going for about a week until I started getting withdrawals because I need to go back down again.

I achieved what I've always wanted to achieve. My main goal in life was to be able to say, 'I don't drink, I don't smoke, I don't take any kind of medication, tablets of any shape or form. And I'm okay. I'm sane.' And that's what I can tell you today. I help a lot of people around me, and I'm still gardening. My mind is at peace. So that was the goal, and twenty years later, Ann Maria is still in my life.

Chrysalis meant a lot to me because of two things: because of Ann Maria's physical presence, and that garden she has around her. That garden kept me alive. And just her presence alone made me feel safe. I knew I was in the presence of greatness when I was around Ann Maria, and where she lived, helped me to breathe properly. It really was a blessing from God for me to land there.

# *Patricia's Story*

My eyes dart left and right, but there's no sign of life as I make my way to the end of our council terrace. There are ten more minutes before I make it to the safety of the school entrance. My fists are clenched, and my nails dig into my palms as I reach the bend in the laneway. Then I see them.

My heart lurches, and a wave of nausea rises in my throat. They're all gathered at the corner, waiting for me. I can hear their sniggers. There's nowhere for me to go except past them. I blank them out, pretend they're not there. There's four, maybe five, of them, and I feel their cold stares boring into me even though my eyes are fixed on the road. The first stone lands just in front of me and splatters mud on my shoe.

'Dirty Brit!' they jeer. 'Golliwog! Look at the state of her. Bony Brit! Skinny Brit!'

'Thin Lizzy!' one of them cries, and they all laugh at the wit of it.

Sticks and stones may break my bones but names will never hurt me. I tell myself that over and over in my head, but the names hurt more than the stones. I don't even flinch as more stones follow. They're armed with fistfuls. They hurl one stone after another in my direction. I walk straight, shoulders back, chin up, trying to feel and look taller.

'Brits out! Brits out!' they chant.

I refuse to run even as the stones sting my legs and arms. One of the bigger, faster boys runs after me. He shoves me roughly. The others egg him on, and he shoves me again. I try to shrug him off as they surround me, pushing me so hard that I stumble to the ground. The ringleader grabs me. I won't give them the satisfaction of tears. I fight as he drags me along the road to a pothole filled with black rainwater. Wrestling my head down, he shoves my face into the watery filth. They're laughing like it's the funniest thing they've ever seen. I'm spluttering, trying to pull the wet hair from my face.

'Jaysus, lads, the dirty Brit is really dirty now!'

I'm surrounded by laughter while I fight back the tears. I don't *say a word because my accent is just something else for them to mock. They saunter off, laughing, satisfied for now. But I know they'll be back.*

I thought my family's move from England to a small Irish town in the seventies would be a great adventure. I was only nine years old, too young to know anything about the Troubles. So were the children who tormented me, but that didn't stop them. They bullied me because I was different. I was from England, so I didn't belong.

Some think that the torment endured by bullied children is gone as soon as they leave that environment, but the damage can leave an imprint on their life. The feeling of not belonging followed me everywhere.

It didn't help that in many ways, I felt distant from my family. I seemed so different from my younger sisters that it felt like I came from another planet. I was the oldest, and my parents, who were at work, expected me 'to set a good example' and 'to be in charge'. As a result, my sisters called me 'bossy boots' and 'party-pooper'.

I couldn't wait to leave and fulfil my childhood dream of being a nurse. However, I wasn't a party animal, and I didn't drink, so I didn't fit in with the student nursing fraternity either.

Twenty years later, as a qualified psychiatric nurse, I suffered postnatal depression after my second baby. Because of the stigma attached to mental health issues in those days, I felt I couldn't admit to it. So I felt more like an outsider than ever.

It was at that stage that I investigated complementary medicine rather than take prescribed medication. My counsellor recommended two things: 'Take up yoga and go to Chrysalis.'

I took up yoga, but it was ten years before I found myself at Chrysalis. I had all the excuses about childcare issues and the long drive (one hour!). Meanwhile, Chrysalis sent out brochures twice a year, describing all their events. I spent a decade reading that brochure from cover to cover, getting to know all the courses, and by the time I eventually arrived, I felt I already knew everything about the place.

By then I was no longer working, and my marriage had broken down. All those issues of self-esteem and self-confidence arose again. *Where do I belong?* The first course I attended in Chrysalis was based on the Louise Hay book *You Can Heal Your Life,* in 2004. My best friend had bought me the book, and it's still my Bible. Hay's approach is to identify the mental root causes of disease or 'dis-ease', including stress and unhealthy thought patterns and beliefs.

I went to Chrysalis thinking that a one-day workshop would sort out my life, having read the book for years. But that day I realised: 'Oh my God, this is only the tip of the iceberg.' So, I did a longer eight-week version of the course. Then I did another eight weeks. And another.

It's like a Russian doll, hiding itself within itself. When you've spent decades beating yourself up, not feeling good enough, you don't wake up one day and think, *I'm grand now.* And that's what Chrysalis did for me. It gave me the courage to keep looking deeper into myself, closer to that sense of belonging.

I also attended money and spirit courses, meditation and conflict management, among others. I always looked forward to it. I'd drive through Donard village, and as I approached, I'd see the house's gable-end first. That's when my heart would lift. Then I'd go through the red gates, pass the prayer flags hanging on the trees, and once I heard the crunch of the gravel under the tyres, I felt as if I'd come home. No matter what issue I had in my head leaving Dublin, I knew as soon as I saw that gable-end, everything was going to be okay.

The welcome was always especially warm: a cup of tea, a smile, and most of all, a soft purple blanket to snuggle into, making me feel safe and secure. It didn't matter how challenging the issue was, I always knew I'd go home feeling better.

It was Chrysalis that prompted me to open my own retreat space, which I later started in my home. I went on to train in energy and angel healing as well as yoga teaching. I'm now a yoga therapist, group facilitator and holistic event manager, teaching a lot of self-care and mental health awareness programmes.

When Chrysalis left Donard, I was gifted with their purple blankets. Now the healing energy of Chrysalis lives on with my clients and me, and for this, I feel very blessed and am ever grateful to Ann Maria.

I did fun courses in Chrysalis too, like drumming and singing.

But every activity, including a belly-dancing workshop, had some sort of healing energy.

When my sister was getting married in Malta, someone dared me to belly-dance at the wedding. Something prompted me to throw caution to the wind and agree to be the surprise entertainment at my sister's wedding. My marriage had broken down only months before the wedding, and I arrived by myself with the kids, my self-esteem on the floor. I didn't know how I was going to get through the week.

On the evening of the wedding, the guests fell quiet as the lights dimmed. They wondered what was happening as sensual Arabic music filled the air. I appeared through an archway, my face covered in a blue chiffon veil, my hands above my head in the prayer position. Very few in the room knew it was me. I shimmered in pink and blue chiffon skirts, a blue gemstone glittered in my navel, and gold bells and a sequinned top highlighted my belly. Exotic earrings dangled and jangled with every movement.

Hands crisscrossing over my head, I began the sinuous dance movements of the Middle East. The guests clapped and cheered as I whirled and swayed seductively around the room, wiggling my hips. For the grand finale, I circled the groom and draped my veil around him. And that was when everyone saw my face for the first time. The funniest thing of all was my mother's face. Her jaw had dropped. I could see the scandal of it all in her eyes. *Is it any wonder your husband left you, carrying on like that?*

But my sister loved it, and so did my new brother-in-law. And for me, it felt fantastic!

That was sixteen years ago, when I was forty, with three children and newly separated. After a lifetime of not feeling good enough or belonging, I had summoned up the confidence to belly-dance in public. It was so liberating, and like so many of the best things in my life, it started in Chrysalis. It's a place that needs to be honoured, like Ann Maria, this special lady who founded it and who, over time, has become a precious friend.

Chrysalis was my sanctuary. A place I called home. The place that helped me feel that I do belong. And with gratitude, I know Chrysalis is a treasure that will always remain in my heart.

# Brendan's Story

*My parents said that we were going for a drive to see the countryside. We set off, they in the front seat, we two small boys in the back. I was aged four, my feet dangling over the edge of the back seat. Patrick was a little older, maybe six. I had pale white skin and white hair; he had dark skin and tight black curls. We were complete opposites and we were inseparable. We were mad about football and climbing; Patrick could scale any tree or building. I looked up to him like he was my older brother, my only brother. A fostered brother who came into my life to make me happy, my hero.*

*Light turned to darkness on our trip 'to see the countryside'. My mother asked Daddy to pull over to the side of the road. She got out, opened the car boot, and took out Patrick's best Sunday clothes. She ordered him to get dressed by the ditch. Patrick began crying as he changed, and I joined him with frightened tears inside the car. Back in the car, he asked again where we were going, but she told us to stay quiet.*

*They drove on again. The old period building we approached was huge, with metal bars on the windows. My parents brought us into a white marble hall, a space that was as big as it was cold. An old nun came over to talk to my mother, then two more nuns came down the stairs and took Patrick upstairs 'to try on new pyjamas'.*

*I began to panic when Mammy and Daddy led me out of the big house without Patrick. We walked out into the lashing rain and down the steps toward the car. I started pulling away from my parents' grip, and my father had to lever me into the back seat. 'What about Patrick, Daddy? What about Patrick?' I screamed. I stood on the back seat, looking out the rear window, as the car began to pull away down the long, dark driveway. Patrick seemed to have come out of nowhere, barefoot, running after us; he was running in pyjamas, chasing after the car, trying to catch up with us. I screamed: 'Stop, Daddy! Stop! Look, Patrick's coming! Patrick's coming! Stop!' I screamed it over and over, as many tears rolling down my face as the raindrops outside. As I wiped the condensation from the rear window with my hands, I begged them to stop for Patrick. 'Look, Daddy! Look, he's catching up! Stop! Stop!' But they kept on driving into the darkness until he was out of sight.*

That traumatic night was one of many childhood events that only resurfaced in my adult years. As a child I was beaten and terrorised by a violent and abusive mother, a psychotic woman, while my father somehow lived in denial.

My childhood was chaotic, and I went to five schools. By the time I was a teenager, I was 'too much of a handful' and was thrown out of home. Even though I failed my Leaving Cert, I managed to wangle my way into Trinity College in Dublin and worked hard to get a degree in marketing.

By the time I was in my thirties, I was a capitalist success story. I held an elevated position in a blue-chip financial organisation, and I drove a sports car and a vintage car. I owned two houses and was engaged to a beautiful young woman. I had already had a child from another amicable relationship, and it was obvious to all that I was very happy with being her father. I adored her. To the outside world, I was living the dream. In reality, I was suffering heavily from depression. I was coping with the help of drink, dope, and being a workaholic. Athletics offered some relief too.

From outward appearances, I was doing incredibly well, but internally, I was falling apart. I knew it was not going to last; I felt I could crack at any stage. I have a very good friend, Paul, a doctor, who felt concerned about me. He wanted me to take antidepressants, but I didn't want to go down that road. I saw my mother turn into a zombie on antidepressants. Antidepressants offer relief for depression, but they're not a cure. I wasn't looking for relief. I wanted a cure. I was always rather ambitious.

I started going to a meditation class held by a Jesuit priest called Tony Baggot at Gonzaga College in Rathmines in Dublin. He told me of a place called Chrysalis, which offered different kinds of retreats to heal those damaged parts of your psyche. He was holding a deep conscious breathing workshop in Chrysalis over a bank holiday weekend.

I went along to his breathwork workshop. It was challenging to dive into one's inner consciousness and uncover old wounds. We lay on the ground and breathed deeply till old 'stuff' arose. Deep breaths on the other side of the room sometimes became howls or groans, and then this noise became contagious. The process was an intense catharsis for releasing repressed memories. Afterwards, participants had a greater sense of calm and connectivity. It was quite challenging but transformative. By the end of the first workshop, I was a bit shocked to discover the level of pain inside myself. I was quite naive in my expectations at the time – I expected to go there and have my depression sorted by the end of the weekend. But I did feel I'd released something. I'd got in touch with something that told me my depressive behaviour wasn't all my fault. So there was an element of forgiveness to it. I'm now convinced that that is the first and essential step.

After about two of these breathwork weekends in Chrysalis, I started having flashbacks of Patrick for the first time, of him running after a car. Because of the trauma of the event, I must have blocked everything related to him out of my psyche. Many more incidents would resurface, and they can still surprise me to this day.

It turns out that Patrick was fostered by my parents. He was a child whom I became emotionally attached to. But they brought him back to an institution because, like me, he was 'too much of a handful'. I actually did track him down forty years later, but he had had a life that was hard and filled with abuse. He has no memory of being my hero, or even visiting our family, and sadly shows no interest in me getting to know him.

Over the next four years, I went to about twenty different courses in Chrysalis. A few of these were Buddhist meditation weekends. In time these weekends triggered something in me, and I cast off my old lifestyle and changed direction entirely. I called off the wedding to my fiancée and went on a year's retreat, mostly in silence, in a place called Dzogchen Beara in West Cork. That led me to do a three-year retreat in France and a masters in English, to try to catch up on some of the education I regrettably missed.

In the years since, I've worked in top marketing jobs in the Middle East and taken many holidays to visit the Dalai Lama and other masters in India.

# Carried on Spirit Wings

Something had to change when my good friend, out of genuine compassion, tried to persuade me to take antidepressants. I no longer suffer from depression. Chrysalis didn't clear my depression, but it was the catalyst that started the journey. This journey led me to Buddhism and has since brought me much inner peace.

# Iris's Story

When my mother told me that I wouldn't be going to school that day, I felt anxious. I was eleven years old and in my final year at primary, and I was never allowed to miss school. But I learnt from an early age that it was best not to question my mother and just do as she said. I had a vague idea that I was going for a hospital visit, but I didn't know exactly where we were going or why.

We got the bus into the city centre and walked a short distance to a wide street with Georgian houses on either side. We went down steps into the basement of one of these houses. I knew this wasn't a hospital, and I still had no idea what we were doing there.

Inside, it was dark and gloomy with a gas cooker ring lighting in one corner. The blue flame seemed to be the only light in the room. A tall middle-aged woman was waiting for us, and she told me to lie on a small bed on one side of the room. I was unsure, nervous, but I did as I was told.

This woman stood at the foot of the bed, and my mother sat on a stool beside me. This woman was wearing rubber gloves, and she put her hands up my skirt. I didn't know what she was doing, but I knew that I had to be a good girl and stay quiet.

I felt an uncomfortable sensation, like something cold had been inserted into me. Now I was frightened. I had no idea what was happening. I started getting pains in my stomach. They became more and more severe. It felt like my stomach was being torn apart. As the pains got worse, I started screaming and trying to get off the bed. I remember my mother was holding me down by my shoulders. I didn't understand what was happening to my body, and I wanted to get out of this place. I was distressed and in horrendous pain. I had a feeling of something grabbing my insides, twisting them tightly and then yanking them out of my body. I thought I was going to die from the pain. Then there was a release, and the pain eased, and I fell back gasping for breath.

The woman, who was still at the foot of the bed, had something in her grip. My mother leaned forward to look. I automatically looked too. To my shock, I saw she was holding a baby. It wasn't fully formed; it was clearly a baby, my baby.

She was holding him by the back of his neck; his little body dangling a few feet from me. In my memories of him, his arms and legs seem short and thin compared to the size of his body, and his head a little large and misshapen. But I knew that this was my baby, and he was dying. I knew what I was seeing and experiencing, yet it was almost too much for me to take in.

As I stared at my baby, I felt what I can only describe as a shaft of energy, that travelled from his heart to mine. It pierced my heart, and the feeling took my breath away. I looked away as it was too much for me to see my baby suffering like this.

That shaft of energy is difficult to describe with words. It was a moment of connection, of unconditional love between a new mother and a new baby. It was also an acknowledgement between us that we were both in pain and helpless. That momentary energy was the only connection I ever had with him. I never saw him again.

I remember my mother helping me put on my coat and leaving that place. When we reached street level, I was struck by the brightness, and I felt my knees give way. My mother held me up as she flagged down a taxi. We got out of the car a short distance from home. In those days, a taxi was a luxury. Pulling up outside our house would have roused the curiosity of neighbours. When we got home, we had tea and custard slices. My mother told me that we would never mention this again. She said this like she was doing me a great favour, and then she told me to go to bed.

I can recall lying on my bed, staring at the ceiling and crying and shaking. I was overwhelmed. So much had happened in one morning, I couldn't take it all in. I didn't understand how this had happened. How I could have had a baby? It was all beyond my understanding at that time. I was still in shock from seeing a baby that I hadn't known existed; a baby that I couldn't save. I prayed for someone to help me. It was all too much for one little girl to cope with.

I had been in therapy for a few years when memories of my first baby resurfaced around 1999. The sense of shock and loss was overwhelming. I know now that my first baby, Ian, came into this world briefly in October 1973.

He had never been acknowledged, had never been remembered by anyone. That instant in time when I first saw him and that shaft of energy between us was all that I thought about at first. How could I have forgotten that?

Then I became haunted by thoughts of what happened to him afterwards. I felt a deep sense of shame because I never did anything to help him. I began obsessing about what happened to him. Where was he when I left that room? Was he still alive, lying discarded and alone when he breathed his last breath? What happened to his remains? These questions are all very distressing for me, and I know I will never know the answers. It breaks my heart to think of him abandoned and alone, dying slowly without a mother's care.

Every October, after I remembered Ian, I found myself going through a period of intense grief. I felt an enormous sense of loss and helplessness. When I saw Chrysalis was hosting a six-day residential workshop for survivors of sexual abuse in 2004, I decided to attend. I planned to talk openly about Ian for the first time.

I was a nervous wreck for a week before I attended the workshop. My husband was the only person I told. There were six of us that first morning, and the tension was incredible. Slowly Ann Maria helped us realise we were in a safe space where no one would judge us and that everyone had a story. We were all in the same boat. Everyone listened with respect as we all told our stories for the first time in our lives.

On the second-last day of the workshop, I told the group my story. I explained how I had been raped by a man who worked in the local library, but I had no understanding of what he was doing to me. I told how my mother was angry and abusive when she realised that I was pregnant. And then, I told the story of the day that Ian was born. I ended up lying on the floor, hugging a soft toy, sobbing over and over, 'I don't know where my baby is. I don't know where my baby is.'

Ann Maria suggested that it might be helpful for me to have some sort of ceremony for Ian. I knew instantly that I wanted a burial for Ian. She suggested that I work with one of the facilitators as the group went to organise the ceremony. When all preparations were made, the group came back and gave me a soft bundle for my arms. Together we walked to a secluded part of the garden.

When we reached the spot that they had chosen, I saw they had opened a new 'grave' in the ground. There were fresh flowers, candles and a cross woven from twigs and entwined with blossoms. I was so moved to see the work the group had put into this ceremony for Ian and me. Before I placed my 'baby' in the ground, I told him that I loved him, I would never forget him, and I was so sorry that his life was so short and so cruel. The grave was filled in and covered by candles and flowers while Ann Maria sang a beautiful song.

It was such a moving and spiritual experience for me that I contacted Ian. I felt his presence for the first time since that day in 1973, and I knew he was safe. At the end of the retreat, I sat alone under the trees in the spot where we had buried Ian. I felt Ian's presence again, and he told me that he was now happy and free. He said not to look at the ground or at his grave because he was above me. I looked up to the treetops and the blue sky above, and I felt at peace.

I will always be sad about what happened to Ian, and there is a part of me that longs for him. Yet, since that service, my intense grief and isolation have eased.

I am eternally grateful to the members of that group and Ann Maria and Barbara for providing the space, arranging the service and for taking part in it. After the ceremony, and as everyone left this workshop, they pledged to carry the memory of Ian with them. That meant so much to me. My baby, Ian, has been acknowledged, and he will be remembered.

# *Geraldine's Story*

On a cold, wet Friday in January 1996, I arrived at Chrysalis for a weekend workshop called I Never Told Anyone. I was full of apprehension about the workshop, but I was also very frightened because I had no real understanding of what was happening to me. Memories of childhood sexual abuse by my grandfather were emerging, and the nightmares and flashbacks were growing more vivid and terrifying.

Ann Maria and Mags ran the workshop. They were supportive and calming as they helped us make that fearful, first deep dive into our memories and emotions. I cried as others in the group told their stories, and they cried when I admitted aloud for the first time that something happened to me as a child. The rain beating down outside reflected the tears shed by our group that weekend.

It was the start of my journey and the beginning of a long relationship with Chrysalis. Unearthing the truth and dealing with the consequences of that has taken many years. After that first weekend, Ann Maria became my therapist. It was like putting the pieces of a jigsaw together. More of those memories came back to me in fragments.

Fears and emotions that I'd never experienced before overwhelmed me. Ann Maria made an analogy between the way I'd been living and a jack-in-the-box. For years I had shoved everything in, all the trauma, all those memories. I was also experiencing the anguish of my mother's terminal illness and the pressures of a new business. I kept shoving everything in, until eventually there was no more room, and everything popped out at once. But the trauma of those memories of my grandfather was so painful that my mind didn't want to accept the truth.

Every week, I left my busy life in the rear-view mirror on that hour-long drive from Dublin to Donard. I always arrived early, parked under the trees and spent a few minutes trying to centre myself, asking the strong and shady trees for help and support.

As soon as I entered the hall door of the Old Rectory, the home of Chrysalis, the waft of incense filled my senses. Inside, it was homely, with whitewashed walls that reflected the sunlight and made everything brighter. I would wait in the library for Ann Maria, fighting the urge to run away. Every time I went for counselling, I had butterflies in my stomach. I felt fear and dread, but I persevered. I knew I needed to do this to heal myself.

The sessions were always hard, often overwhelming, sometimes frightening. I never knew what to expect, but Ann Maria's loving presence was there throughout the healing process. There were so many emotions and memories that it was like being a big ball of tangled wool. We would pull a thread and see where it brought us.

My grandfather died about ten years before these flashbacks began. Before that jack-in-the-box popped open, my predominant feeling for him was love. That was the biggest struggle because there were parts of me that really loved him and parts of me that really hated him. How do you allow for two opposing memories of a person to be present at the same time, knowing that each of them is true?

I felt that I shouldn't love him, but I did love him dearly. And I know at some level he loved me. And that what he did was some way outside of his control or beyond him. When I was in a much calmer place, and I thought back, I think he was remorseful.

Before I went to Chrysalis, I was very high-functioning but numb most of the time. The strongest feelings I had were fear. And when I started going to Chrysalis, I began to allow myself to really feel. Not alone could I feel the bad feelings, but I also started to experience joy, and really experience love, probably for the first time in a long time.

As a journey, it's like I started in a frozen state, and then I entered a stage where everything is wet, watery and teary as all these emotions rise to the surface. Today I feel like I'm floating as light and free as vapour or steam in the air. Chrysalis was the beginning of my journey home to myself. It's been a long journey to go from frozen to floating like vapour in the air!

I still have a few lifelong friends who I made there, including one special person I met on the very first workshop. My life is so much richer from having these wonderful friends in my life.

In truth Chrysalis was never any one person or thing. It was the people, the interaction with nature and the old house. It was the wonderful welcome, the great food, the kind-hearted people who worked there, the warm beds, the chatter with old friends, the making of new friends and the work and those beautiful gardens.

It was the sum of many people, kindness, land, trees, Zen gardens, hermitages and an old rectory. They were all part of the whole magic of the place.

The gratitude I feel towards Chrysalis and everyone associated with it is beyond words, and in a lot of ways, the work I did there is beyond words. It helped me regain the freedom in my mind, body and being that I buried as a small child. Today I can experience a full range of emotions without feeling overwhelmed by any of them. I'm free to experience joy like I never did before. 'I never told anyone' before I went to Chrysalis, but I'm so glad that I did tell and that they were there to listen to me.

# Reflections of Claire Harrison

## Staff member and manager for twenty years

Do you remember Fusco rolls, the piggy bin, hanging out laundry, programme-packing parties, Milltown Park conferences, feedback forms, Musgrave shopping, Fancy, special diets, affirmation cards, bus pick-ups, Gift to Yourself, the magic trolley, HACCP, cushion-beating, face-painting, school retreats, Hermitage planning, Lotus room treatments, new septic tank, tree planting . . . and the deep quiet when all guests left?

Do you remember the first time you arrived at Chrysalis? I do. It was 4 September 1991, and I had left job, relationship, mortgaged flat and London a few months previously. Dissatisfied with corporate PR, restless with inner questioning, thirsty for a fresh start, I arrived in Ireland with no plans. Brown Mini Metro car packed with all my belongings, I pulled up at the Old Rectory, intending to drive on to Cork if 'this didn't work out'. I was guided there by a series of chance encounters and Emer Bailey handing me a brochure at the Corrymeela Summerfest, where I was volunteering.

Ann Maria and I sat in the garden, chatting. Might I be able to contribute? I noticed the tape cassettes in the kitchen needed sorting; soup needed making for the weekend group. It was getting late, and I stayed the night in the tiny Peacock room. Reader, I stayed for twenty years. Looking back, it was like a giant personal development workshop. Complete with excitement, breakdown, change, fun, grief, breakthroughs, soul connections, anger, inspiration and reflection.

The world seemed to come to us – fellow seekers from all over the world. Facilitators with skills to share. Ideas from the worlds of spirituality, psychology and healing. Creative projects to engage with. Locals, volunteers, longer-term staff gathering in different configurations. Creating community. I reckoned guests were drawn back by three main components: one-third the courses on offer, one-third the ambience/food and one-third the nurturing connections with others.

I trusted that, in some way, I was contributing to a bigger picture, that what we offered staff and guests might extend ripples of humanity into the wider world. I enjoyed creating systems, clearing clutter, looking at how the background administration could flow smoothly – helping to spin the evolution of Chrysalis. Witnessing the arrival of the fax machine, computers, email, the internet, mobile phones, websites, the simplicity of our black-and-white printed programme becoming almost obsolete in the latter years.

I fell in love (twice), had burnout (twice), became a Hare Krishna (briefly), wrote programme copy (copious), had a sabbatical (USA), attended counselling (essential), wondered about the meaning of life (ongoing), wrote a cookbook (still handy), did workshops (varied), got married (once), ran a craft shop (deeply satisfying), explored the Enneagram (number one), walked the lanes (still do), helped plan the building's expansion (noisy) and all the while being beside Ann Maria.

She was a witness, a guide, a mover, a touchstone. As vulnerable as I was sometimes. A strong and determined force. A tender, empathetic friend. Juggling different roles. Pioneering new courses. Co-creating deep healing for many.

These were my fruitful years. Full of creativity. I needed a cocoon when I arrived, safety to explore inner tangles. I had the privilege of twenty years a-growing . . . and counting. Still a learner in life, still seeking and deeply grateful for the wild and wonderful journey at Chrysalis.

# The Sharing

### Edwina Gateley

We told our stories – That's all.

We sat and listened to each other

and heard the journeys of each soul.

We sat in silence

entering each one's pain and

sharing each one's joy.

We heard love's longing

and the lonely reaching-out

for love and affirmation.

We heard of dreams

shattered

and visions fled.

Of hopes and laughter

turned stale and dark.

*We felt the pain of isolation and*

*the bitterness of death.*


*But in each brave and lonely story*

*God's gentle life broke through*

*and we heard music in the darkness*

*and smelt flowers in the void.*


*We felt the budding of creation*

*in the searching of each soul*

*and discerned the beauty of God's hand*

*in each muddy, twisted path.*


*And God's voice sang in each story.*

*God's life sprang from each death.*

*Our sharing became one story*

*of a simple lonely search*

*for life and hope and oneness*

*in a world which sobs for love.*

*And we knew that in our sharing*

*God's voice with mighty breath*

*was saying love each other and*

*take each other's hand.*


*For you are one though many*

*and in each of you I live.*

*So listen to my story*

*and share my pain and death.*

*Oh, listen to my story*

*and rise and live with me.*

(A poem I read at the end of the survivors' workshops in Chrysalis.)
Reproduced with kind permission of Edwina Gateley.

# PETER

*The time for the healing of wounds has come.*

Nelson Mandela

When Peter came into my life, I faced a dilemma. It was almost like being torn between two lovers. If I chose our relationship, I knew it would mean sacrificing my Catholicism, which was a foundation stone in my life. Choosing Peter was challenging. In the eyes of the Church, he was still married. I had to overcome many doubts to allow myself to be with him. It caused a lot of inner turmoil because my life was very connected to the Church and its activities.

My mind whirled at times with this inner conflict. *Is it more life-affirming to go with love and this man? Or would my life be richer if I committed to God and my religious beliefs and shut the door on our relationship?* Peter was a humanist, and even though he was very supportive, he didn't really understand my struggle.

If it was today's world, the whole issue of marriage probably wouldn't have even arisen. We probably could have lived together. It sounds old-fashioned now, but the eighties was still an era where living with someone, especially a person who was technically married to someone else, was frowned upon. It was a time when people were more judgemental. I probably had more difficulty than most because my upbringing was so conservative.

My Aunt Nora's eyebrows certainly raised when she discovered Peter was married. It didn't matter to her that he was separated because she strongly believed marriage was for life. Her sentiments were: *Your poor mother would turn in her grave if she thought you were with a married man.* That was the society I lived in. There was always a distinct chill when the subject of Peter came up in Aunt Nora's company.

At the same time, my vision of the world was broadening. My faith and religious beliefs were largely inherited without much personal consideration or choice. For a long time, my faith was what I was brought up with. Taizé, with its ecumenical vision, welcomed people of different religions and opened me up to new possibilities. India also gave me a whole new perspective of spirituality, opening another door to the world of Eastern wisdom and spirituality. These new insights were liberating. During the early years of Chrysalis, I was exposed to many spiritual traditions, as I searched to find a new path for my life.

I moved away from Roman Catholicism in almost imperceptible degrees. It was a gradual process. There was never a time when I said, 'I'm no longer a practising Roman Catholic.' That never happened. It was a gradual easing away from structures and confines of Catholicism as I explored other forms of spirituality. I felt drawn to another form of meditation and devotion. In the end my conscience allowed me to side with love. But I did feel that I had to resign my role as minister of the Eucharist in my parish community.

Peter was incredibly supportive in the early days of Chrysalis. We had a sense of a shared mission as we worked well together to begin with. But even then, it was apparent that we argued incessantly. We both brought emotional baggage from our past, and we never seemed to be able to fulfil each other's needs.

That familiar fear of mine – abandonment and loss – shadowed me in this as in every relationship. It was almost like anticipatory grief, an overwhelming dread of what life would be like without Peter. Despite the constant arguing, we still needed each other and wanted to be together. We ignored all the warning signs, and we decided to get married in 1990. Peter engaged a lawyer in the Dominican Republic and got what was called an 'overseas divorce'.

As there was no legal recognition of divorce in Ireland, we had to marry in the United States. I was an American citizen and could marry there without any legal issues. We booked the ecumenical church in the United Nations in New York, and we sent out invitations to a nearby restaurant. It was an intimate affair, my friend Marian Petty was the only person to fly over from Ireland.

Days before the wedding, I remember beginning to feel the first stirrings of panic. We were staying with my friend Judy Barnard in New Jersey, who by now was married to George Pizzo. I was having doubts about our whole relationship. *Do I really want to marry Peter? And what is the point in getting married when neither the Church nor State in Ireland will recognise it?* Peter and I had these tremendous arguments, and it made me very anxious about going forward with the wedding. I remember walking with Marian through the Metropolitan Museum of Art in New York, one of the world's finest art museums. I was so stressed about the wedding that I got sick on the museum's stone floors.

Only a day or two before the wedding, Peter was in the living room talking to George, and I was in the kitchen with Judy. She was talking about the wedding and the dress she was wearing. My mind was all over the place, and I couldn't keep it in any longer.

'I don't think I can go through with it.'

'Go through with what?'

'The wedding.'

'Oh my God!' Judy's eyes widened, and her mouth dropped. 'You mean you're *NOT* going to get married?'

I was certain by now. 'No. It doesn't feel right.'

I basically got cold feet, and the wedding was called off. To be honest, I don't remember Peter's reaction. Maybe he was as relieved as I was; perhaps he was bewildered by me. I do remember feeling awful for Marian because she had come all the way from Ennis, County Clare, for a wedding that never happened. She was very understanding under the circumstances.

For some reason the aborted wedding wasn't enough of a red flag to deter us from trying again. Peter and I decided to get married the following year. I was in the United States studying group dynamics at Iona College, in upstate New York, and Peter flew over to join me.

We got married on a glorious midsummer's day, on 26 July 1991. Peter looked handsome in white trousers and a white shirt, and I wore a pretty dress in pastel pink. I expected a cold legal process with a couple of quick signatures in the civic offices. Instead it turned out to be an extraordinarily warm, meaningful and beautiful ceremony presided over by the mayor of New Rochelle. Most of my classmates from Iona College were the guests.

Jesuit priest, Jim Dolan, a friend of Myles O'Reilly, blessed our marriage in the college campus church. American-born, he worked with the renowned priest and psychotherapist, Tony de Mello, in Sadhana in India. Jim was known as a radical thinker in the Catholic Church. He was also a compassionate and kind man, who hosted many retreats in Chrysalis in the years afterwards.

Peter and I honeymooned on the west coast of America with the late Lou Atha. Lou, a larger-than-life figure, was also a friend of Myles. When he was a student, he spent a summer painting her house in America, and they remained lifelong friends. Lou lived in the coastal city of Torrance in California and had a holiday home on Catalina Island. I was lucky enough to spend a lot of time with her, and she lived life to the full before dying at age ninety-two in 2018.

Throughout the nineties, Chrysalis was growing and getting more established. Some of the most cutting-edge facilitators from around the world were now hosting workshops at the centre. Life was very busy professionally. I did a lot of training and facilitated many groups. The centre was all-consuming at times, with long hours and full weekends. I even fell into a mother-figure role for some of our more vulnerable staff, which at times was draining. My life was totally absorbed with Chrysalis; there always seemed to be more projects, but I had endless energy to tackle them. In hindsight, my busyness was an avoidance. It helped distract me from the real issue, which was sorting out my personal life. Married life was challenging, and Peter and I were struggling as a couple.

I decided to take six months off in February 1994 to attend a therapist training programme in codependency at the Caron Foundation, in Wernersville, Pennsylvania. The training was intensive with emphasis on dealing with family dysfunction and in-depth personal therapy. Peter started further training in counselling too. He studied addiction counselling with the Aiséirí Addiction Treatment Centre in Cahir, County Tipperary, before joining me at Caron for his placement.

When I returned to Ireland, I started a codependency programme in Chrysalis. After Peter qualified as an addiction therapist, he began to work with me on those workshops and eventually took over the programme entirely. Throughout our marriage, Peter and I were flying back and forth to the United States training in new and ever-expanding fields of therapy.

After codependency training at the Caron Foundation, I studied for a certificate in experiential techniques. Peter was doing other placements and training. Our courses overlapped in Caron at times. I remember both of us lived on campus at one stage, but we were going through another rough patch and we weren't living together. We went into therapy, of course, as we always did. We were still trying to figure things out and find a way forward together, but the cracks in our relationship were becoming unbearable.

As a therapist I felt conflicted working on clients' relationship issues when my own personal relationship was in difficulty. It wasn't from any lack of commitment to working on our relationship; we always seemed to be in therapy. Of course, it's not realistic to expect every therapist to have their lives fully functioning and perfect. Yet there were many times when I thought, *Good God, how can I be in such a supportive role to others when my own marriage is falling apart?* I felt troubled by this disconnection and thought of the Bible quote: *Physician heal thyself.*

I loved Peter, but it drove me crazy when we argued. Everything became a debate, and we both argued our side. Inevitably, though, Peter would fly off the handle. His temper was volatile, and I couldn't deal with big explosive scenes. When I was growing up, I rarely saw any expressions of anger. There was only polite adult discussion around me, and Uncle Jimmy never raised his voice in his life. As an only child, I never even experienced the everyday rough and tumble that goes on between brothers and sisters. I was raised to be polite, accommodating and nurturing. I never had a role model for a healthy expression of anger.

Even though Peter came from a family of sixteen, he never had a role model for a healthy expression of anger either. In troubled relationships, anger usually provokes an instinctual fight-or-flight response. People typically fight back or shut down, and neither one is good for communication. Peter would fight. He usually flew off the handle when he got angry. And I would shut down and withdraw; I simply didn't know how else to respond. This was the dynamic between us.

Peter was different from any man I met before. He was very outspoken, very candid. He would just say things as they were and would let fly during a confrontation with anyone. We had different coping strategies; it was hard to find common ground, even in how we argued.

We attended all sorts of therapy to try and reconcile our situation, but nothing seemed to ease the strain between us. It sometimes felt that counselling was merely bandaging over wounds that refused to heal. While Peter was in America, he heard of a highly recommended workshop called Imago Relationship Therapy. His own therapist said he and his wife had found it the most helpful therapy they had ever done. According to Imago theory, when we're attracted to a potential love partner, we pick the perfect person to help us work through our wounds from childhood. Peter rang me in Ireland.

'Let's give it a go, Ann Maria. It's a four-day residential workshop,' he said. 'It sounds like it could be just the kind of help that we need.'

Peter felt the Imago workshop was the most meaningful and significant relationship therapy he had ever done.

'Oh my God, this is brilliant,' he said, halfway through. 'This will work really well with my clients.'

I remember fixing him with a cold stare, anger simmering within me. 'We are supposed to be here for us, not your clients,' I said. It was striking to me that we couldn't even be on the same page while in the company of a renowned relationship counsellor.

It was a very well-presented course, and we felt a glimmer of hope that we were making progress as a couple. We were referred to a therapist in Dublin who was trained in Imago therapy. However, Peter felt disappointed by this therapist's approach. We wanted things to improve between us, but the old patterns of behaviour resumed, and it was incredibly challenging.

My attitude to our relationship experienced a critical groundshift after an episode in the American Embassy. Peter was planning to go to America to study again, and he needed an extended visa. To cut through the red tape and paperwork, he made a visa application as the husband of an American citizen.

We sent in all the paperwork that the US Department of Immigration demanded, including our marriage certificate. Then we received a call asking us to attend an interview at the embassy in Ballsbridge. I remember that day, queuing outside and then being called to stand at a Perspex glass partition. The woman behind the screen was polite, dispassionate and cold. She had a file of Peter's documents in front of her.

'Sir, I'm returning your passport. Your application for a visa is denied.'

Peter was taken aback.

'You have all the paperwork there, absolutely everything you asked for.'

'Sir, your application for a visa is denied. There is nothing further I can do except return your passport.'

'But why has the visa application been denied?' I asked, fearing Peter would erupt.

She flicked through the pages of the file. 'You're not legally married,' she said simply.

I was stunned and couldn't quite grasp what she was saying. 'But you have a copy of our marriage certificate. We were married in New York!'

She pulled out a single-page document from the file and glanced over it. 'We've taken legal opinion on the divorce. As your husband was not legally domiciled in the Dominican Republic, the country in which he received his divorce, the divorce cannot be recognised. As a result, neither can your marriage certificate.'

It was irrelevant, apparently, that the same paperwork was accepted in New York when our marriage licence was issued. The US Department of Immigration declared our marriage null and void. I remember just looking at Peter in shock when we were outside of the embassy.

'Good God, we're going through all of this angst and therapy, and we're not even married?' I said.

That was the beginning of the end. It offered an easy way out. Emotionally it was messy, but legally, at least, it was straightforward as we didn't have to get a divorce. We had some good times together, but the memories were scarred by bitter arguments, disappointment, heartache and loneliness. The negative dynamic between us was difficult to break out of. Neither of us was able to sustain a mature relationship and give emotionally to the other.

In ways, I was living a double life as I tried to avoid my personal difficulties encroaching on my professional life in Chrysalis. I was often despondent and distressed about the state of my marriage, sometimes only barely holding things together. We were spending more and more time apart.

Then one night Peter called me from the United States to say he was coming home. I was sitting in the kitchen on my own, and I knew I wasn't willing to give it another go. I was too tired to try again. That was the first time in our relationship that I didn't meet him at the airport. He ended up staying with a friend, and later he got his own place in Dublin. On so many occasions, we said, 'Let's try again. We can work this out.' I took a firm stance for the first time and said, 'No more.' I guess I knew by then the relationship was over.

There was no big drama, no welter of resentment and acrimony, no big final parting scene; our relationship fizzled out by the end of 1998. It is still hard for me to pinpoint precisely what went wrong. It was a complicated relationship, so there was a combination of many things involved. We were each too wounded in our own ways to enable us to meet each other's needs. We didn't have the communication skills for a balanced, healthy, mature relationship.

In the following years, Peter and I met on several occasions. We talked openly about our life together, which was healing and allowed us to finally cut the ties, acknowledge our differences and disappointments and move on. Thankfully, we remain friends to this day.

Even today I am struggling to put words on it. You can look back and dissect everything and say, 'This happened, and that happened.' We tried hard to resolve our differences with therapy. We did our best to keep going, but in the end, we couldn't find a compatible way to live harmoniously and had to accept our lives would be better apart.

# Radiance Sutra 70

## Lorin Roche

*Sting of a wasp,*
*Rip of a nail,*
*A razor's slice,*
*The needle's plunge.*
*A piercing word,*
*A stab of betrayal,*
*The boundary crossed,*
*A trust broken.*
*In this lacerating moment,*
*Pain is all you know.*
*Life is tattooing scripture into your flesh,*
*Scribing incandescence in your nerves.*
*Right here,*
*In this single searing point*
*Of intolerable concentration,*
*Wound becomes portal.*
*Brokenness surrenders to*
*Crystalline brilliance of Being.*

*Reproduced with the kind permission of Lorin Roche.*

# THE MONK

―̄§―̄

*If we could see that everything, even tragedy is a gift in disguise,*
*we would then find the best way to nourish the soul.*

Elisabeth Kübler-Ross, MD

As the first golden fingers of dawn filtered through the bamboo shades, I gazed at his profile in silhouette beside me. I could see the full sweep of his thick lashes, the slope of his long, broad nose and his full, sensuous lips. Even in sleep, I could see the smile that seemed to permanently tug at the corners of his mouth.

I loved everything about him, from his golden-brown skin to his dazzling smile, and especially the sparkle of his brown eyes. He made me laugh, really laugh. He saw the joy in everything, and he brought out the fun side in me. We loved to meditate together, to play together, to pray together. We were even the same age. He was the perfect man for me except that he was a Buddhist monk.

To protect this man's identity, I shall call him Kumar. He was a meditation master and spiritual teacher who entered a temple in South West Asia when he was thirteen years old. I met Kumar at a retreat in India.

He had never been intimate with a woman, but from the start, there was electricity, an attraction, that neither of us could deny. Both of us had a lot of resistance to an intimate relationship, so to begin with, it was a tortured love affair. There are only four transgressions that result in expulsion from most Buddhist monastic communities: theft, murder, falsely claiming divine powers and sex. Neither of us wanted him to break his vows of celibacy. However, the attraction between us was overwhelming, and eventually we surrendered to it. I was very much in love with him, and he was in love with me. It was a heady passion, but we also had a deeply spiritual connection.

I met with Kumar when he travelled to facilitate retreats, often in exotic locations. Afterwards he would remove his saffron robes and dress in so-called 'civvies'. We would holiday together, sometimes for weeks, looking like any normal couple. He brought such a sweetness to ordinary life that the relationship was transformative. Kumar's love of life was infectious; he was gentle, kind and wise and was the most incredibly sensitive lover. It was a very nurturing and loving relationship.

I believed that he would give up being a monk for me. I was convinced that he would relinquish his vows, disrobe, and we would set up a life together. We both knew that he could still teach meditation as a layperson. I hasten to add that he never promised that he was going to leave the monastic life. That was some fantasy or self-deception that I created all by myself. But I really didn't think that our lives could be any other way. I thought that we would be together forever.

The secrecy in which we conducted our relationship was a significant strain. I didn't like living a double life, deceiving people and having to cover up my sudden disappearances and trips abroad. I had to be secretive to protect him and his position, but I thought it would be worth it. It was only a matter of the right timing, and he would leave and live with me. It took two years before I understood that he wasn't going to give up his role as a Buddhist monk.

I had a friend in Ireland who was in a long-term relationship with a priest. I knew the heartache she was going through, and I knew I couldn't bear a life like that. I was torn. I didn't want to give him up but I couldn't live with the secrecy and the despair, both of us yearning for the next time that we could be together. The love that brought me so much joy to begin with became a source of pain and angst when he refused to choose me. When we split up near the end of 2000, my heart was broken, really broken. The ground was pulled out from beneath my feet. That sense of abandonment hit me again, and terrible loneliness enveloped me. The death of my Aunt Nora that year, my last close family member, accentuated that pain.

I fell into a dark depression. I was so bereft that I lost all faith in spirit and a higher power. There was no spiritual consolation to cling to, no merciful God I could turn to. It was a spiritual, existential and psychological crisis. I felt a deep sense that life was meaningless. *What is the point in living?* There was only desolation and a crushing sense of abandonment as I went through what I can only describe as my dark night of the soul. The darkness was so severe I feared that I might be committed to a psychiatric hospital. I couldn't eat or sleep. The sense of despair weighed so heavily upon me that even having a shower or brushing my teeth was beyond me most days. There was no colour left in the world for me, only bottomless pain and isolation. I really feared losing control, being so overwhelmed that I could no longer function; I feared the worst, remembering my mother's awful struggles.

I saw a therapist; I took homoeopathic remedies for depression; I got acupuncture; I went for craniosacral therapy, a gentle form of bodywork on the head and spine to alleviate stress. I was going for all sorts of energy work, anything to centre me and hold me together. But my world became smaller and I feared I was going deeper and deeper into a pit of depression. I was terrified that I wouldn't be able to pull myself out of it. I met up with my friend and well-known psychiatrist, Dr Michael Corry. I remember his stark advice: 'Put your seat belt on and prepare for the journey, Ann Maria. The only way out of this is to go through it.'

I contacted Peter during this time because I was so concerned that I would end up in a psychiatric hospital. He reassured me of his support and said he would not allow it to happen. I know psychiatric hospitals have their place, but from what I had witnessed with my mother, I knew it wasn't an option for me. My underlying fear was that I would crack up completely and become like my mother, unable to function at all. I was very close to it. It was the first time that I truly understood how my mother must have felt when she made that last journey to Dún Laoghaire pier. For the first time in my life, I was frightened by the depth of my hopelessness and despair. Nothing was giving me relief.

I couldn't continue to live like this, so I searched for some kind of residential healing centre as an alternative to a psychiatric hospital. My search brought me to a residential facility in Edenderry, in

County Offaly, called Kedron. This therapeutic residential centre was run by Dr Jim O'Donoghue, a well-known psychotherapist. I signed myself in for their thirteen-week programme. Everyone in Kedron was dealing with crises of various forms. The remarkable thing was that nearly all the patients were members of religious congregations. Some had returned from the missions, totally burnt out and disillusioned, in need of a new direction. Only three of us were laypeople. We were all in the same boat, however, suffering from chronic depression and various life crises. The facility provided one-to-one therapy, group work and art therapy and slowly the black fog that had descended on my life began to lift again.

Gradually something shifted, and my spirituality, which had been submerged by a weight of anger and pain, also broke the surface again. There were a few synchronistic events, small messages, which seemed to come to me from the spirit world. They were little things: a butterfly landing on my arm, a chance encounter, an email, a gift or a phone call at exactly the right minute. It was enough to encourage me to keep going, to put one foot in front of the other. I started praying and meditating again. I handed my life back into the hands of a higher power and sought help and healing for my life.

When I emerged after three months, I was better than I had been. I felt some fingers of early morning light permeating the darkness. There were glimpses that the dawn was coming, but there was no miraculous cure. The dark night of the soul seemed to be here to stay. Sometimes I tried to outrun it by travelling to far and distant places, but the blackness followed, like my personal luggage. I distracted myself with work and projects and busyness. I wore a happy, smiley face and tried to pretend it away. But this undercurrent of depression was there a lot of the time.

I went to a good therapist, which was a great support. Being more honest about my feelings to friends and not always concealing my inner truth helped too. Isolation is a factor in depression, but it was a big step to accept what was happening in my life. I felt ashamed and also fearful because of my mother's condition. There was an element of thinking, *What do I have to be depressed about, when so many other people have worse problems?* But I stopped trying to pretend my feelings away anymore. Mindfulness was a life tool that helped me enormously too.

On reflection, depression followed me even before my relationship with Kumar ended and before I went to Kedron. There was inner grief there, lying just below the surface, that never healed. Sometimes it was low-level depression that didn't significantly affect my life. However, that cloud became a perfect storm when my abandonment issues came to the fore, usually after a failed love relationship. Feelings of bleakness were also accentuated by the long winters in Ireland, when my energy levels fell noticeably lower. Hormonal and menopausal issues came into play around this time too. Scattered throughout my journals, I've found evidence of continuing depression: *All I want to do is go to bed and keep this a secret. I worry will I be plagued by this feeling of disconnection from people and entering this empty void. All I know is I have these self-defeating thoughts. I've low energy. My life seems meaningless and empty. There's a dark cloud of depression around me.*

I was dipping in and out of that darkness for a long time, and there was no magical cure. I did everything to support myself through this difficult dark time.

My intuition guided me to explore my creativity by going to acting school for the first time. For years I didn't have the confidence to join even a local drama group. I had a fear of being visible, of being judged and rejected. At college I secretly yearned to join the drama society, but it was many years later before I had the self-assurance to explore acting. After leaving Kedron, I felt the fear and did it anyway. I was committed to taking a step into the world of acting. I went to San Francisco to join an intensive acting course at the American Conservatory Theatre's summer training congress. I came to acting late in life but I really loved it. I finally discovered a side to my creativity that had been buried for decades; it gave me a new lease of life. The following year I signed up for the one-year performance course of evening classes at the Gaiety School of Acting.

Afterwards I landed a year-long leading role in the interactive dinner theatre show, *Joey and Maria's Comedy Wedding*. I was a paid actor in a show that had started in Boston and went on to play in New York, Las Vegas and all around the United States. Our production opened in September 2003 in the Gresham Royal Marine Hotel in Dún Laoghaire and toured to other Irish hotels. Three nights a week I performed as the mother of the bride, one of a troupe of fifteen actors in the show. The audience sat down to dinner as the 'guests' at our big American wedding reception and watched the show unfold. Each night, as part of the theatre, the actors 'worked the tables' as they called it, interacting with the guests.

'Oh honey, it's so great to see you!' I'd say, flinging my arms around a member of the audience. 'We weren't sure if you were out of rehab yet!' A lot of each show was improvisational, and it was terrific fun.

I performed in other theatre productions including *The Crucible* and *The Vagina Monologues*. I was also involved with Dublin Playback Theatre for several years. Playback is a collaboration between performers and the audience, where someone from the audience tells a story from their life, chooses actors to play the different roles and then watches as their story is immediately recreated. It's a creative and improvisational form of theatre. I really enjoyed those years as an actor. Tapping into my creative resources was life-giving and renewing.

Despite my best efforts, by the time I reached my fiftieth birthday in July 2004, I was still suffering from ongoing depression. My journal notes around this time: *It seems like this empty void is hovering in the background of my life.* At first, I decided that I wasn't going to make a fuss about this significant birthday. I had a lot of reservations about celebrating at all. Then I felt a growing defiance. *Good God, I've got here. I've managed to reach this milestone! Surely that's worth celebrating.* After that, I just went for it. *Go big or go home*, I thought. I raised a marquee on the grounds of Chrysalis and I invited people from all around the country and from overseas.

The cast and crew from *Joey and Maria's Comedy Wedding* led a huge synchronised version of the Los del Rio hit 'Macarena'. I recall hundreds of people doing all the hand movements and hip thrusts. There was a piper, a harpist and a DJ, and we danced until the sun came up. It turned out to be *an event*. I always loved any excuse for a party and for dancing. I was so glad that despite my earlier reservations, I had held a fiftieth party to remember.

I decided to mark that milestone year with a significant journey too. Myles O'Reilly held a study group in Gonzaga College where we worked on a book, *The Undefended Self*. Written by Susan Thesenga, it contained exercises to explore spiritual concepts and help the readers to break through conflicts and crises. My birthday gift to myself was to stay at the author's retreat centre, Sevenoaks, in the United States. Located in the Blue Ridge Mountains in the state of Virginia, Sevenoaks was a serene and beautiful place.

As I was getting ready to leave Sevenoaks, Susan asked if I'd be interested in going to Brazil for an ayahuasca healing retreat. I had heard of ayahuasca, a medicinal plant drink. A sacred and ceremonial brew, it is used for religious purposes by ancient Amazonian tribes and by some spiritual communities in Brazil.

Ayahuasca has powerful hallucinogenic properties that lead to altered states of consciousness, and under US law it was considered an illegal substance. So Susan had to be discreet about holding this retreat. It wasn't advertised; she just personally invited people. I told Susan that I would think about it.

Ayahuasca was, and still is, used as an alternative therapy for a range of psychological and mental health issues, so I didn't think long about it. As soon as I got back to Ireland, I rang Susan and told her I was in. This retreat wasn't decided on a whim to experience a hallucinogenic trip. I was hoping ayahuasca could lift me from the depression that had dogged me for several years.

A group of twelve of us met in São Paulo, in southeast Brazil. We boarded a bus and drove for hours to a very remote and isolated place up in the hills. We stayed in a collection of small, thatched houses in the rain forest, surrounded by lush tropical trees and foliage. I remember waking to all these unfamiliar sounds, the squawks of macaws, whistles of tamarin monkeys, the croaks of tree frogs and the background thrum of crickets and cicadas. Exotic birds with colourful plumage fluttered around the gardens.

Traditionally, experienced healers, like a shaman or curandero, lead ayahuasca ceremonies. In our case, Susan, who had learnt from the shamans, boiled up the brew from the leaves of the *Psychotria viridis* shrub and the stalks of the *Banisteriopsis caapi* vine.

I was apprehensive as some ayahuasca 'trips' cause distressing hallucinations. For some people there's also a purging aspect to ayahuasca, and they suffer unpleasant side effects such as vomiting and diarrhoea. Others experience hallucinations, out-of-body experiences and euphoria. Ayahuasca translates as 'vine of the soul' but is often referred to as 'the key to the universe'. I was willing to risk the adverse side effects in the hope it might shift that black cloud following me.

In my journal I wrote: *I pray for healing of my loneliness and depression. The terrible darkness of the last three years has been hell. The loneliness of my spirit has brought me such pain that I wanted to die. I pray now that God will fill that darkness with light.*

For some time I had suspected part of my depression was not linked to my own personal issues. During training in codependency in the Caron Foundation in Pennsylvania, we invited clients to go through their family tree to examine the issues in past generations. It was uncanny to see the patterns of addiction, mental illness and dysfunction that came down through the ages. Disease and addiction are not the only illnesses that are passed on through our DNA.

Research is showing that the destructive effects of trauma are also passed down from generation to generation. Scientists in the emerging field of study called epigenetics have shown that people whose ancestors survived periods of starvation in Sweden and the Netherlands displayed the effects of famine for at least three generations. I certainly believe the source of my depression was intergenerational and existed before I was born. This 'inherited trauma' theory made a lot of sense to me. During healing explorations, especially in holotropic or intense breathwork, I reached places of emotional pain and fear that I didn't relate to in my lifetime.

My mother, due to her previous miscarriages, was very fearful when she was pregnant with me. It's known that anxious mothers can raise the cortisol levels in amniotic fluid, which means these high-stress hormones are absorbed by the foetus. I firmly believe that my mother's fears were transferred to me in the womb, and that I was born imprinted with her trauma. I feel there's a malaise that has been with me since the beginning of my life.

Similarly my mother may have inherited her depression from her own mother. My maternal grandmother was sent to an asylum after one of her children died. Generations of women in my family may have unconsciously inherited and carried traumas and destructive patterns of behaviour down our ancestral line. That's why I relate to the wisdom of a statement that's often attributed to women's health doctor Christiane Northrup: *Every woman who heals herself helps heal all the women who came before her, and all those who come after her.*

By the time I reached Brazil, I suspected that I was carrying trauma from my ancestral line. Even though I was nervous, I hoped that this ancient form of medicine, this vision quest, might help on my healing journey. I noted in my journal: *For this Brazilian journey, my intention is to know God within the depth of my being and to develop my intuition, to experience truth, to experience peace.*

We drank the ayahuasca brew as part of a formal ceremony with ancient rituals involving chanting and singing. Two guitar players in the room accompanied the singing. The brew itself tasted pretty awful, bitter, oily and earthy. Then, within thirty minutes of taking my first sip, I began to enter an altered state of consciousness.

What happened to me after that was the most expansive feeling of God-spirit I have ever known. My heart opened to union and bliss. Words still fail me. I felt outside my body. I felt that I was pure love and God was love, and I was one with God. I also experienced a deep connection with Mary, as the divine cosmic mother. I was filled with wonder and awe.

My journal read: *Today was an experience of initiation. My heart opened, I felt a deep inner connection with the Divine Cosmic Mother. A tremendous awareness of her beauty inside of me; her peace. I don't have words to describe the feeling of expansiveness, this knowing of her presence. My body took shape, my head vibrated. I felt powerful energy coming into me. I opened to receive the power and force. I was in union and bliss.*

We took part in an ayahuasca ceremony daily. Some people

experienced side effects like vomiting, paranoia, panic and nightmarish visions. I felt blessed because I only experienced profound euphoria and beauty. During one ceremony, I heard a song about light. I felt everyone was singing about the Christ light, and this Christ light was within me. I had a tremendous love and feeling of the mother, the Divine Mother. And then I received these words: *You are my beloved. You are my beloved child.* That was the message: *You are my beloved. You are my beloved child.*

On other days I had very visual experiences of incredible light and colours of blue and gold, shimmering and swirling around me. Some people would say, 'Well, she was high on ayahuasca.' But to me it seemed that ayahuasca broke down physical barriers and brought me on a very profound journey inside space and outside time. There was a sense of well-being, enlightenment and a realm of kaleidoscopic beauty that I've never experienced before.

I wrote afterwards: *I'm so grateful to God for this experience. It has been like an initiation. From this day forward in my life. May I be a channel of love and peace and healing in the world.*

After Brazil, I was still exploring my spirituality and seeking clarity about my life's purpose.

Ever since I first visited India, I considered the idea of following a guru or 'one who is enlightened'. Adherents of Indian spirituality choose a guru to guide them on a path of spiritual awakening or self-realisation. For years I resisted following a guru. At some level I was probably afraid of losing my autonomy and independence. I often wondered if having a guru would help my spiritual evolvement. I remember posing this question to a Zen teacher from America.

'Well, all any guru can do is point the way but ultimately, you have to travel the road and find your own inner guru,' he said.

This made perfect sense to me. Also, it seemed that following a guru's guidance involved some loss of individual autonomy and critical thinking. I had been attending Sister Vandana's retreats for some years and I really trusted and admired her as a teacher. I finally decided to take the step and ask her to be my guru.

I wrote to her in Jeevan-Dhara Ashram in Jaiharikhal, India, and set out to visit her in September 2005. After the long-haul flight to Delhi and a day-long journey overland, I finally arrived at the bus station nearest the remote village where she lived. I didn't know it was the monsoon season. I was in the hectic bus terminal, drenched to the skin, clutching my rucksack and feeling exhausted and conspicuous. A Western woman travelling unaccompanied was an unusual sight in the foothills of the Himalayas.

Chaos was all around me: sleeping bodies huddled in groups, children begging, vendors yelling about their wares. The noise was deafening. I tried to enquire about the bus from a ticket seller, but her English was poor. *Buses are cancelled . . . Roads blocked . . . landslide . . . monsoon . . .*

I felt like crying. A stranger approached, saying that he overheard that I was trying to get to Jaiharikhal. He said he was travelling to the village by jeep and he had one seat left in his vehicle. Feeling both relief and suspicion, I followed him outside. I could see smiling faces peer from the darkness of the back of his jeep. The men extended hands, calloused hands, to help me climb on board.

The next six hours were spent stopping and starting on the dirt track through the mountains. The men chatted among themselves, and in conversational lapses, the car filled with the sound of the rain drumming on the canvas roof. The smell of the diesel fumes made me feel nauseous, and I had to shift in my seat to avoid leaks of dripping rain. The driver negotiated giant potholes, crossed steep crevices and gushing waterfalls and crept along the edge of sheer cliff faces. My stomach somersaulted when I saw a sheer drop into vast nothingness on one side of the dirt track. I knew that one slip of the wheels in the mud and it would be all over for us.

We came to a sudden halt and there was much excitement and shouting. The men clambered out of the jeep into the teeming rain. Working as a team, they removed rocks and rubble from a landslide blocking the track. They heaved aside boulders, rocks big enough to crush a jeep. Now I was worried about rockfalls too. *Is this my end? Will I die in this remote place?* I started praying. *Jesus, Mary and Joseph, protect me.* I repeated the mantra *Om shanti, om shanti* (peace for all humankind), anything to distract me from impending doom. I started bargaining with God. By the time we finally arrived at Jaiharikhal village, I was shattered.

At the village I enquired about the ashram. It was still a mile away and could only be reached by foot. A young local presented himself as my guide and, heaving my rucksack onto his head, he beckoned. I followed, feet dragging. My arrival at the ashram caused colossal confusion. People gathered around me, shrugging and gesticulating until I finally understood that Mataji (Mother) Vandana was not in Jaiharikhal. Nor was she in her other ashram in Rishikesh. She had left on pilgrimage. She had gone to a place called . . . *Bihar?*

Consulting my Lonely Planet guide, I discovered that Bihar was eight hundred miles across the far side of the country, with virtually no bus or rail connections. The guide helpfully added that it wasn't safe for 'solo travellers' and the word 'bandits' jumped off the page. I had made this massive trek, risking life and limb to ask Vandana to be my guru only to find she was in another part of the world. So that was my answer. I abandoned the idea of following a guru.

The Dublin Playback Theatre Company received an Arts Council grant to attend an international theatre conference, in São Paulo, Brazil, in August 2007. Group members Helen Blackhurst, her husband, Slavek Kwi, and I went to the five-day conference. Afterwards, Helen and Slavek decided to go to the Amazon River to record sounds from nature. But I planned to visit a well-known medium in the healing world called John of God. I first heard about this spiritual healer from a man in Chrysalis. His wife, who had a cancer diagnosis, had gone to see John of God in Brazil. She subsequently died, but her husband believed that she left John of God feeling prepared for her death. Healing doesn't always appear in the way we pray for, so my curiosity was piqued.

After the conference I took the ninety-minute flight from São Paulo to Brasilia and from there took a van that travelled two hours to the remote village of Abadiânia. It was a dusty town of 15,000 inhabitants, with a few shops and businesses. John of God's 'spiritual hospital' was on a hillside on the outskirts of the town. There was nothing imposing or grand about the Casa de Dom Inácio de Loyola (House of Saint Ignatius of Loyola) or 'the casa' as it was simply known. It had the appearance of a cluster of whitewashed single-storey school buildings surrounded by a fence. Within the compound was a serene garden area with benches and a panoramic view of rolling green hills. The casa was called after Saint Ignatius, founder of the Jesuit order, because he was one of the many spirits that John of God incorporated into his body during trances.

John of God, or João de Deus, in Portuguese, was born into poverty in 1942 as João Teixeira de Faria. At age sixteen he claimed the spirit of King Solomon entered his body, and he performed his first healing. For years João wandered Brazil offering healings. In the late seventies he built the casa on the hill where he became known as John of God. His fame as a spiritual healer grew after Hollywood actor Shirley MacLaine claimed she was healed of stomach cancer after 'spiritual surgery' at the casa in 1991.

I only spent five or six days at the casa on my first visit. A lot of that time I was in the 'current' room, an intrinsic part of the work in the casa. A place for prayer and meditation, the current room was filled with lines of people dressed in white, sitting in plastic chairs. The 'entities' or spirits requested that everyone wore white clothing to the casa. Eyes were closed, arms and legs uncrossed to allow the energy to run freely for healing.

During those few days at the casa, I met people who told me they were healed. One of them was a young man, Matthew Ireland, from the state of Vermont in the United States. He was suffering from stage four inoperable brain cancer, and his doctors advised him there was nothing more they could do for him. Yet, after spending time at the casa, his tumour disappeared. He was cured. I talked with this man, and he was a level-headed, rational person, a very ordinary man. His life totally changed after the healing. He devoted his life to the casa as one of many volunteers working there, and he got married to a Brazilian woman.

On Fridays, when the morning 'current' finished, John of God met people on the lawn where he would pose for photographs. He was heavyset, with dark hair, sallow skin and blue eyes, but my immediate impression was of a man who looked exhausted. Grey and haggard looking, it seemed his work as a trance medium had claimed a toll on his health.

It's hard to put words on what happened to me in Brazil. I was fascinated by the energy of healing there and by John of God's mysterious work. The visit was an uplifting one, where I experienced deep tranquillity and a spiritual awakening.

I thought the place was extraordinary. I left feeling awestruck and feeling that there was something profound and palpable happening there.

# Coming Home

KAVERI PATEL

I can't do this anymore,
dance this dance where my heart
is armoured, an oyster shell
clammed shut against the soft
meat of what really matters.

I want to know how it is for you,
how the pearl inside is forming
from the irritation of life –
layer upon layer of courage
surrounding the suffering
with warm presence.

Let there be time and space
to show you your pearl
having sat with my own,
cupping my heart in my hands
so I may know yours.

*Reproduced with the kind permission of Kaveri Patel.*

# CANCER

*Any treatment that attends only to the symptoms is not good therapy.*
*The best treatment is one that balances the whole and does not create other disorders.*

Ancient Ayurvedic text from the Charaka Samhita

The sky was overcast and steely grey but the day felt even darker for me. We stood, Lucille and I, staring at one another outside Saint Vincent's University Hospital. It was February 2008 and I had just been diagnosed with cancer.

The previous months had been busy. Combining my love of travel and the spiritual, I started the business of guiding groups on international tours, which I called Sacred Journeys. I brought a group to Turkey in October, where we meditated and visited the House of the Virgin Mary and the Basilica of Saint John at Ephesus. This was followed by two twelve-day pilgrimages to the temples of Chiang Mai in northern Thailand during December and January.

When I returned to Ireland in the new year, I went for a mammogram, one of the regular health screenings offered to the over-fifties. I wasn't unduly alarmed when the Breast Check clinic on Merrion Road called me back for further assessment. When I was called for another follow-up appointment, however, I started to feel apprehensive.

Yet, when the consultant surgeon, Denis Evoy, told me they had found a tumour in my left breast, it was like a meteor strike, a huge body blow. I couldn't believe it. I was still reeling from the news when he started flicking through his diary for available surgery slots. There was a carousel of confusion turning around and around in my head.

The thing that struck me at that moment was that I was about to leave on another Sacred Journey trip, which, for the first time, was to John of God in Brazil. I needed time to reflect on how to proceed with healing this tumour.

'I'm not ready for surgery,' I said.

I'm not sure where I found the strength to say the words but I remember Dr Evoy looking up, perplexed.

'I'm going to Brazil, and I'm going to explore other methods of healing.'

He must have thought I was deranged when he heard that, but I was adamant.

'I need seven weeks, and then I'll decide about the surgery.'

It seemed like providence that I was about to return to the casa where I could heal under the auspices of John of God. At the back of my mind too was an inspirational book by the American author and motivational speaker, Brandon Bays. She wrote a book, *The Journey*, which was an account of how she healed herself from cancer in seven weeks with diet, visualisations and meditations.

Having spent twenty years in the field of mind–body healing, I wasn't about to allow a surgeon to go to work without trying to heal myself. When it comes to cancer, all orthodox medicine does is cut, burn and poison. It cuts out the tumour, radiates the area and then floods the veins with chemotherapy, a poison. I felt conflicted about allopathic or science-based Western medicine. I wanted to treat my illness from a broader, holistic view. I'd grown to understand that illness is not something to be treated in isolation; to me, the disease is often a symptom of other underlying problems.

Going to Brazil was a chance to activate my body's natural defences to work against the cancer cells. I just needed to step back and be able to participate in my own treatment, not merely be controlled by the medical profession. John of God's healing powers were just a few days away, and I focused on that.

Lucille had, thankfully, accompanied me that day. As we stood in the cold and wind outside the breast clinic afterwards, she said what so many other people repeated later: 'You don't drink. You don't smoke. You're a vegetarian, so very clean eating. Of all the people to get cancer, how did it happen to you?'

It was clear to me that emotional and psychological triggers contributed to my illness. To my mind, the cancer was stress-related. The immune system is damaged by stress, and exactly a year earlier, I had been floored by the failure of another relationship.

My relationship with Eamon Wolfe was an intense, whirlwind romance. Although it lasted for only six months, we spent a lot of time together. We met in Chrysalis at the end of 2006, just before I was due to lead a Sacred Journey pilgrimage to Thailand. It turned out Eamon was going to Thailand at the same time. It seemed providential to be able to spend this time together. Surrounded by Chiang Mai's lush mountains and ancient temples, we had an idyllic time in Thailand.

Shortly after, we went to Turkey where he had a magnificent *gulet*, a traditional Turkish wooden schooner, moored near Bodrum. We sailed along the Gulf of Gokova in the Aegean Sea anchoring in beautiful coves, swimming in turquoise waters and eating in small fishing villages. It was such a fluid and easy trip as Eamon spoke fluent Turkish, albeit with a Dublin accent. It was a truly magical time. The only dark cloud over the relationship was his acrimonious divorce, which seemed to involve many solicitors' meetings and rancorous demands.

Eamon was someone on a committed spiritual path. He was a truly kind person, and I loved how he looked after me. I've been an independent person from the time I was a child. I've always had to rely on myself and spend a lot of time on my own. However, Eamon took the initiative when booking flights, plotting routes and picking restaurants. He brought me to places he knew I'd enjoy, and he thought about my well-being and needs. It was lovely to relinquish the reins and let someone else take over organising the minutiae of life. I loved the feeling of being cared for. And certainly, with Eamon, there was a lot of that. I fell deeply in love with him. He was a sensitive, affectionate, caring man with a free spirit; he loved music, attending live concerts, riding his Harley Davison motorcycle, and he loved sailing. His passion and his love of life opened me up to the infinite possibilities of a shared life together.

I used to joke sometimes and say: 'You're really not my type, Eamon.' And he would say, 'Well, you're not my type either.' And we'd laugh together. We had a lot of fun and lightness.

Then one night, after roaring up on his motorbike to take me to a concert, he dropped a bombshell.

'I don't know how to tell you this Ann Maria, but I've been talking with my wife again,' he said, tears welling in his dark eyes. 'It sounds crazy, I know, but we're considering giving our marriage another go.'

He was distraught telling me this, and he was clearly conflicted about reconciling. However, he was still talking about going back to his wife. Instead of shouting, screaming or throwing something at him, I went into counsellor mode, listening to his struggles and the dilemma he faced and shelving my needs. My heart was breaking, but I hold marriage very sacred.

'If you want to reconcile with your wife, I'm not going to put up a fight,' I said. His marriage broke up afterwards, but I supported him in his decision to go back to his wife.

During the aftermath of our break-up, I felt angry, bitter and resentful. He presented himself as in the final stages of a divorce. If there was even an inkling that his marriage could be revived, I felt he should never have started seeing me.

However, I also recognise a pattern in my life where I seem to fall in love with unavailable men, and when the relationship ends, I'm unable to deal with the fallout.

We are never as vulnerable as when we love and connect deeply with someone. The heart opens towards a whole new world of possibilities. An intimate relationship allows us to journey into the unknown with the other. It can be a wonderful adventure, but it can also be a painful experience. I never wanted a man in my life just for the sake of having a man. I was longing for a deep connection, for a partner, a companion, to accompany me in life's journey. I enjoyed this with Andrew for four years, so I knew that soulmate connection is possible.

This is not about blaming anyone; rather, it is about highlighting a relationship that meant a lot to me. I found it difficult to deal with the aftermath of the relationship. I didn't look after myself very well. I was feeling hurt and depressed the year before my diagnosis. I believe that stress was a contributory factor to my cancer diagnosis

I was determined to restore my health and to avoid the surgery. Before leaving for Brazil, I embarked on a holistic health and wellness programme through nutrition, herbs, meditation and visualisation. It was a quest to heal myself outside of orthodox medicine.

As scheduled, I led a group on a Sacred Journey to Brazil for two weeks in early March 2008. For me it seemed like it was far more than a coincidence that this trip was arranged to depart almost immediately after my cancer diagnosis.

Early each morning I led the group from the pousada (guesthouse) to the casa, where we joined another thousand people from around the world. Money never changed hands for healing sessions at the casa. John of God prescribed herbs and passionflower pills, which were sold at a nominal cost. However, the casa also had shops selling the requisite white clothes as well as jewellery, healing crystals, videos, biographies, photographs and other souvenirs. Donations were also welcomed. However, all healing work was free at the casa. John of God was always clear that the spirits or 'entities' were the ones performing the healings.

'I do not cure anybody,' he said. 'God heals, and in his infinite goodness, permits the entities to heal and console my brothers. I am merely an instrument in God's divine hands.'

It was claimed that up to forty different spirit doctors and saints were 'incorporated' into John of God's body at different times. When the spirits flowed through him, his eyes rolled back, and he had the appearance of being in a trance. The spirits included Saint Francis Xavier, Saint Francis of Assisi and a German doctor called Oswaldo Cruz. You always knew when Saint Ignatius took over because John of God sat up very erect and bore an expression that was full of love and compassion.

The queues were long, and the air was hot and humid when the day came for my healing. I remember John of God's face perspiring, his hair flopping onto his face by the time it was my turn to appear before him. He placed his hands on my shoulders, and a powerful surge of energy went through my body. It was like an electrical pulse surging through me. The physical reaction took me by surprise, and I lost my balance. One of the casa's aides caught me before I fell. I remember the bones in my legs felt like jelly. They helped me into a wheelchair and brought me to the recovery room, where I slept for two hours. I woke up hopeful that I was going to go home healed of the tumour.

Most of the 'surgeries' were non-invasive or invisible; they were described as 'psychic' or 'etheric' surgeries conducted by the spirits' supernatural powers. The psychic operations took place in a room off the 'current' room where groups of us sat and meditated in the hope of a cure. There was an air of incredible emotional release in there, and many were openly crying.

Only people who specifically requested John of God's physical surgeries were considered for those treatments. He carried out physical surgeries with no anaesthesia and seemingly, no pain. It's hard to describe what happened, even though I saw it so many times. Aides, carrying trays of surgical instruments and stainless-steel kidney trays, accompanied John of God for these surgeries. The patients were usually standing, lined up by the wall. I saw John of God take gauze-tipped steel forceps, dip them in holy water, and force the forceps up the patients' nostrils and twist them violently. He'd pull out a bloody swab and blood usually trickled down the patients' faces. Often I flinched at the sight of him scraping people's eyeballs with a knife and then wipe a viscous substance from the blade onto the patients' shirts. At other times, he sliced people with surgical scalpels across the chest. The lack of pain was explained by the fact that people received 'spiritual anaesthetic'.

On another day during that trip, John of God appeared in the current room. He came down the centre aisle and placed his hand on my head as he passed. Again I felt a huge surge of energy run through me like a shockwave. By the time I left Brazil, I felt confident I was cured. My journal of the time reads: *I'm trusting that the cancer has been removed. Will have a scan on my return and thoughts of surgery in Saint Vincent's are diminishing, but we'll cross that bridge when I need to. For now, I'm trusting that this cancer is going out of my body.*

I believed I was going to be healed and was willing myself a miraculous cure. At the same time, memories of Andrew were weighing on my mind. Andrew and I were so positive about his healing, but within a year, he was dead. If I survived this, I vowed that things were going to change. For nearly two decades now, my life had revolved around Chrysalis. I needed to concentrate on my health in the immediate future.

I continued seeking complementary treatments in Brazil. I attended a doctor in orthomolecular medicine, a form of alternative medicine through nutritional supplementation. Dr Marcos Sandoval had no English, and I didn't speak much Portuguese. After a three-way conversation through a translator, he prescribed me a collection of supplements to take.

As soon as I got back to Ireland, I sought confirmation that the tumour was gone. A medical centre in Clane, County Kildare offered thermography, a radiation-free technique for detecting tumours by infrared. When the clinician couldn't confirm the presence of a tumour, I left confident that I had been healed in Brazil.

The following week, I attended Saint Vincent's for an ultrasound. I was sure that the tumour was gone or at least had dramatically shrunk. When the doctor said that the tumour was still there, as large as life, I was devastated. I was in complete denial. *No, it can't be still there!* I remember hoisting myself up to see the screen and saying, 'Show me! I need to see it myself.' I could hardly believe the evidence before my eyes. I was so disappointed. After everything I had gone through in the last seven weeks, the doctor in Saint Vincent's was telling me the tumour hadn't budged. I was deflated, totally disillusioned, sad and angry. The doctor said I needed the surgery sooner rather than later, but I still wasn't ready.

If I was going the orthodox route, I wanted to be a hundred per cent behind it and not go in half-heartedly. Dr Donn Brennan, one of the first Western medical doctors to train in India in Maharishi's Vedic Approach to health, influenced me to change my mind about the surgery.

'Look on this cancer tumour as a bold child that managed to get into your house and is trying to take over,' he explained. 'The child has to be reprimanded and taken out of your house, or you don't know what damage he will do while he's there. It doesn't belong there.'

He explained it to me in terms a child could understand, but maybe that's what I needed because something finally clicked with me. He gave me the courage to say, 'Okay, I'll do the surgery.' I made it clear, however, that I would not have chemotherapy. Right from the start, I said I'd never be treated with that type of cancer treatment. The memories of Andrew's body emaciated by chemotherapy haunted me.

I made a date for surgery, but later that week, astrologer Andrew Smith told me the timing wasn't auspicious. I called the oncology nurse to reschedule. Deferring the surgery for another week and perhaps avoiding a negative outcome made sense to me. I needed to feel everything was in alignment for the procedure. The deferral also reflected my fear of conventional medicine. I had seen what had happened to Andrew in the space of a year, and I was scared. I'd lie in bed grappling with the knowledge of this disease in my system and thinking about the impending surgery. I also wondered what message this cancer was sending me about my relationship with my life. And what changes did I need to make in my future?

I had breast-conserving surgery where they removed the tumour. During the five or six weeks of recovery time afterwards, I used castor oil poultices and herbal packs for the wound. I went to a healer twice a week and pulled in every resource to keep myself well. Myles arranged a circle of prayer for me, with friends coming together in prayerful solidarity. He performed the Sacrament of the Sick, a laying on of hands and anointing with oil. That evening brought me a deep peace of mind. For years I grappled with feelings of loneliness, but looking around the circle of friends, I felt such consolation, love and support.

After I recovered, the radiotherapy treatment began. The radiotherapy sessions were Monday to Friday for five weeks. Despite my self-care regime, the treatment sapped every ounce of energy from me. The daily car journeys for radiation made the fatigue worse. I remember one day holding a basket of groceries in a supermarket and feeling crushed by a wave of exhaustion. I put the basket down in the aisle and left the shop. I couldn't muster up the strength to go on.

By the time the radiation treatment finished in July, I felt washed-out, weak and sick. I felt my whole approach to life had to change. I knew I needed to shift my focus and to enter a new phase in my life.

My priority now was my wellness and health, and I gradually grew to realise that I didn't want the responsibility of Chrysalis anymore. The fire, which had burnt inside me, went out. The centre had been transformed from a passion to a burden in the face of my diagnosis.

I resigned from the board of Chrysalis and broke the news of my decision to sell the property. I owned the property and Chrysalis was a charity with a separate legal existence. However, I never expected Chrysalis to leave the Old Rectory. I gave the directors the first option to purchase, and a year to begin buying me out. The centre had been my life, my baby, but it had grown into an internationally recognised holistic centre, which was nearly twenty years old. Chrysalis and I were now travelling on different paths, and I knew it could run independently of me. I said, 'My work here is done.' It was time for other people to take the reins.

Within days of finishing my cancer treatments, I left the country to lead my second Healing Journey tour to Brazil that year. Being in the casa and the current room offered me a place to meditate and recover, but what Brazil really offered me was a place to rest. Abadiânia was a sleepy town, and the climate was wonderful. After the body shock of cancer, I felt like sleeping all the time. I was about to lead many more Sacred Journeys to Brazil, and I knew I wanted to spend a lot more time in Abadiânia. My tour groups stayed in a lovely pousada called Irmao Sol, a short walk from the casa. I approached the pousada's owner, Martin, a kind man who lavished care and attention on all his guests.

'Martin, are there any auctioneers or estate agents in Abadiânia?'

'No, selling is by word of mouth. Why?'

'I feel I'm going to be spending a lot more time here. Do you know of any places for sale?'

That day I was introduced to a lady called Gizella, who was a caretaker for several houses in the town. I hopped into her car, and she brought me down a quiet little avenue, a short stroll from the centre of the town. The house was in a very secluded position.

'It's owned by an English woman who wants to sell.'

The minute I walked through the door, I knew I didn't need to look at anywhere else. It was the most beautiful two-bedroom house, bright and spacious, with lovely artwork on the walls, tiled floors and the most magnificent views over the valley. The exotic garden was filled with trees laden with oranges, mangoes and avocados. This was the house of my dreams.

It all happened quickly. By the time I held my third Healing Journey tour of that year, the house was mine. I never saw an estate agent, a solicitor or a surveyor in the entire process. That's the way things happened in Abadiânia. Everything happened in fast-forward in the town, as if there was a heightened energy there. The house was as perfect as its name, Casa Nirvana. I spent hours lying on a hammock on the veranda. The only sounds I heard were the birds singing and the soft, warm breezes rustling through the trees.

In between sleeping a lot, I was exploring ways to rebuild a healthy immune system and found myself riveted by Dr Oscar Carl Simonton's book, *Getting Well Again*. As a young specialist in radiology and oncology, Simonton was mystified why patients with similar diagnoses and treatments had such different outcomes. He observed that people who had a more positive attitude often lived longer and had fewer side effects. A pioneer in the field of psycho-oncology, this doctor found evidence that many cancer patients experienced high stress or trauma in the years preceding the onset of the disease. The timescale fitted with my traumatic break-up with Eamon.

Dr Simonton emphasised the importance of meditation, mental imagery and complementary treatments to help treat cancer. I liked his methods. It gave people more of a sense of control over their illness and allowed patients to actively participate in the healing process. He believed that attitudes, lifestyle choices, spiritual and psychological perspectives could dramatically affect the course of the disease and overall well-being. In November 2008, I flew to the Simonton Center in Malibu in the United States to attend his programme.

I was fortunate to attend at that time because Dr Simonton died suddenly only months later. His programme incorporated psychotherapy, visualisations of healing and even sessions where we faced our mortality and prepared for death. We were told to visualise our white blood cells fighting cancer cells and winning. We were asked questions like: *Is there anyone in your life you need to forgive? Are there unresolved issues in your life? Are there toxic relationships in your life?* I knew that resolving emotional distress had to be a priority in my healing journey. I felt a burning resentment towards Eamon that I needed to address. Doctor Simonton believed that we needed to investigate every aspect of our lives to successfully heal cancer.

'Look, everybody in this room has cancer,' he said. 'This is a time to re-evaluate your life. What changes do you want to make? Look at everything in your life and ask: "Does this give me deep joy and fulfilment?" and if it doesn't, let it go.'

That was one of his key phrases: *Does this give you deep joy and fulfilment?* It was like a mantra that I have brought with me ever since. I certainly knew Chrysalis wasn't bringing me joy and fulfilment anymore and looked forward to shedding the responsibility of the business.

After completing the Simonton programme, I continued my healing journey by going to Hippocrates Health Institute in West Palm Beach, Florida. Their three-week detox programme took place over Christmas and into the new year 2009. Their Life Transformation programme featured a raw vegan diet, lectures, psychotherapy and treatments such as colonics and massage, all designed to improve overall health. I was introduced to the benefits of wheatgrass and to a wholly organic and raw plant food diet. Meals consisting of fruits, vegetables, nuts and seeds were prepared with methods like juicing, blending, dehydrating, soaking and sprouting.

I felt so good after my stay that I stayed on a raw plant food diet for a further eighteen months. After Hippocrates, I had arranged to bring my young godson, Eoin Byrne, to the Disney World resort. A friend, Patricia Crimin, and her daughter, Siobhán, travelled with him, and the four of us had a wonderful, fun time together. My energy soared for the first time since the radiation treatment. I felt alive again.

I was due to lead another Spiritual Journey tour to Brazil in early March, so rather than face the winter in Ireland, I went to Abadiânia. For the next few weeks, I lay in my hammock and let the world go by. I was learning that just as cancer affects your physical health, it affects your emotional health too. It certainly made existing feelings seem more intense. Loneliness was always an issue for me, and that certainly raised its head again. Cancer often makes people feel distant from others. There's an element of thinking that no one else really understands what you're going through except the other people in the cancer wards. I had supportive people around me, and I received so many cards, emails and encouraging messages. The circle of prayer that Myles organised gave me great solace during a time of fear and uncertainty.

But serious illness like cancer brings a lot of *thinking time*. There are extended periods when you feel too ill to do anything but lie down and rest. And there are those dark hours in the middle of the night when you lie awake pondering your fate. It can be an isolating time regardless of your circumstances. Dealing with cancer is a lonely time. No matter who is there for support, I knew, ultimately, I had to make this cancer journey alone.

# Goodbyes

AUTHOR DISPUTED

After a while you learn the subtle difference between
holding a hand and chaining a soul;
and you learn that love doesn't always mean
learning and company doesn't always mean security.

And you begin to learn
that kisses aren't contracts
and presents aren't promises
and you begin to accept defeats
with the grace of an adult
and not the grief of a child.
And you learn to build
all your roads on today because
tomorrow's ground is too uncertain
and plans have a way of falling
down in mid-flight.

*After a while you learn that even
sunshine burns if you ask for
too much.
So plant your own soil
instead of waiting for someone to
bring you flowers.
And you learn that you really
can endure;
that you really are strong
that you really do have worth
and you learn and you learn
with every goodbye you learn.*

# ENDINGS

*Forgiveness alone can switch us from fear to love,*
*Pain to peace, past to present and despair to freedom.*

Fr Jim Cogley

The Chrysalis brochure was among a pile of post waiting for me when I got back from Brazil. I had been away from Ireland for nearly a year by the time I returned in May 2009. But it was the programme for Chrysalis that interested me most, and I scanned over it eagerly.

These brochures were vast, detailing the next hundred or so workshops scheduled for the coming months in the centre. I opened it and spread it out fully, scouring both sides, back and forth. Nothing. My heart sank with disappointment. There was no mention of a fundraising event to purchase the Old Rectory. It was now a year after announcing my intention to sell, and there was no sign of the directors making a move to buy the place. The words of Dr Simonton were ringing in my ears: *Does this give me deep joy and fulfilment?* I needed to free myself up and simplify my life.

The sun blazed in a clear, blue sky on the twentieth anniversary of Chrysalis, 25 June. I could hardly believe that twenty years had already passed since the centre opened. It was also the day that Claire, the manager, and Mags, a director, read to me a formal letter stating that the charity was 'withdrawing its interest in purchasing the Old Rectory'. The charity said it wasn't in a position to make me an offer. I was taken aback and disappointed with this news. It certainly dampened any sense of celebration after twenty years. The three of us went to the sanctuary, lit a candle and prayed for a positive outcome. I was still convinced a miracle would happen so I could move on, and Chrysalis could remain in the Old Rectory.

From the early days of Chrysalis, I felt uneasy about the prospect of charging fees for spiritual work. I decided to set up the centre and its activities as a charity. I invited people, whom I considered to be competent and honourable individuals, to become trustees of the charity. They were all friends, people whom I liked, admired and trusted. So that's how the centre came under the auspices of an educational charity. I was the executive director, and the other directors met for the annual general meetings, but they were not involved in the day-to-day running of the centre.

I continued to own the house, and the charity leased the property from me for a nominal rent. In the event of anything happening to me, I bequeathed the house to the charity in my will. I was on a small salary, and like every other facilitator, I was paid for my workshops at Chrysalis.

When the five-year lease for Chrysalis came up for renewal for the first time in 1994, my solicitor, Pearse Mehigan, advised me not to renew. The directors and I attended a meeting with Pearse, where he explained that if the charity occupied the property for more than five years, it became entitled to long-term tenancy rights.

'A typical commercial lease, for that reason, lasts for four years and nine months,' he said. 'Otherwise, the tenant holds long-term rights to the property. My advice, Ann Maria, is not to renew the lease.' The directors looked indignant: *Ann Maria's interests would always be foremost in our minds . . . If she ever wanted to sell, we would never stand in her way . . . We understand fully that it is her property . . . Her needs would be paramount.*

Everyone said all the right things. But I remember clearly what Pearse said in reply: 'That's all right now, but in the future, some latchiko might get on the board who mightn't have Ann Maria's interest at heart. As her solicitor, I'm advising her not to renew.'

I remember him saying this because it was the first time I ever heard the term 'latchiko'. Apparently, it's an Irish slang word for a thoroughly unpleasant person. I was committed to the work of the charity and never foresaw a future where I would want to sell, so against his legal advice, I renewed the lease. Pearse advised the directors that this was a gentleman's agreement, but he warned me that the agreement would not stand up in court. The directors assured me that they were appalled at any suggestion that they might exert their tenant's rights over the property in the future.

Over the years, Chrysalis continued to prosper and grow, and I oversaw a total of five building developments including a chalet, two hermitages and a coach house, all of which I personally funded. The centre was my vision and fulfilled my hopes to be of service in the world.

However, my cancer diagnosis changed my perspective on everything. I no longer wanted to be responsible for owning a big house or running the charity. At some level, I felt I had outgrown the centre, or it had outgrown me. I needed to simplify my life and focus on my health. I wanted a place where I could retreat to, a home of my own, but most of my funds were already invested in the centre.

Initially I was delighted because the charity expressed interest in buying the property. I held off going public with the sale so the board could get the finance together. I never thought for one moment that Chrysalis would cease operating there. Running a successful fundraiser was an option because the charity had the goodwill and support of over ten thousand people on their mailing list. It was eminently achievable. Obviously, it would have been unethical for me to organise the fundraiser so the charity could buy me out. But I even referred them to a person who had extensive experience in running a charity and in fundraising in the hope that it might inspire action. I believed in the maxim: *If there's a will there's a way.*

By the time I came back from Brazil in 2009, I had an idea of how I'd like to live going forward. I wanted to spend more time in Brazil and to move to a home by the sea in Greystones. I had friends who lived in Greystones, and I enjoyed the community feel of the town. I also liked the Happy Pear vegetarian cafe and admired the founding twins, David and Stephen Flynn.

In September 2009 the directors came back with an offer to buy me out over twenty years. My accountant described the offer as an insult. I didn't see it as an insult at first, but the proposal wouldn't have provided me with funds to buy my own house. The twenty-year proposal also came at a time when I was recovering from a critical illness, and I didn't know what the future held for me. The offer turned me, effectively, into a banker, and the charity would pay a mortgage to me over twenty years. The more I thought about the offer, the more incensed I felt. *Do they think my brain is affected by this illness?* Sadly, things were going downhill between the charity and me.

I remember the shock when soon after, I received an email from the new manager of the centre informing me they would no longer include my programmes in the Chrysalis brochure. I organised the Spiritual Journey tours independently from Chrysalis and paid to advertise the trips in their brochure. Their email also stated that they would no longer be using my services as a facilitator in mindfulness meditation. I felt a knife going through my heart that day. It was awfully hard to take. It felt like I was being ostracised and being punished for wanting to sell the property.

There was an air of animosity towards me. I realised the staff were living with uncertainty and may have felt their jobs were at risk. Yet I didn't feel it was unreasonable to release myself from the place and move on with my life.

I wrote an email requesting mediation, an intervention often used in a marriage break-up. The directors' reply was brusque. *We don't feel it's the right time for mediation.* My hands were tied. I was powerless because I had resigned as a director in 2009, and no longer had a say in running the place.

This massive rift felt profoundly painful. One of the staff at Chrysalis described it as like an acrimonious divorce. The people whom I considered my family and whom I entrusted with my vision had become an implacable force against me. It seemed like a Gethsemane moment, a place of great mental agony and spiritual suffering. I felt betrayed, abandoned and a massive sense of loss. They were all long-standing friends and confidantes; one of them was my best friend, and her son was my godchild. The severing of all these relationships was agonising. The hardest part for me was the estrangement from *my tribe*; so many good friends who were like family to me. I felt devastated. My health and a desire to start afresh were my priorities, but there were two sides, both with rights. All the values, loyalty, integrity and spirituality of Chrysalis seemed to disappear in the face of this dilemma. The fact that this debacle dragged on for years made it even worse.

I started on a two-year teacher training programme in mindfulness-based stress reduction around this time. I'm so grateful that I did because I never anticipated just how essential mindfulness would prove to be in the years ahead.

I returned from Brazil in 2011 to take final vacant possession of the Old Rectory. What had unfolded in the meantime was a long, drawn-out and expensive business arrangement. When we finally reached an exit date, I paid a sizeable amount of money to the charity. I also had to repay grant money from the Wicklow Enterprise Board, which had funded an extension at the Old Rectory. The whole thing was a costly and stressful nightmare.

Just before the charity left, I spent a day in the Old Rectory library with my accountant Gerry Daly. We sat opposite the charity's accountant Pat Kelly and the centre's manager, Claire Harrison. We had to go through a list of property in the house and divide who owned what. It really did feel like a divorce.

After that I wandered the grounds and felt the imponderable silence and stillness of the place. All that remained were ghostly memories of the laughter, tears and healing that once resounded through the Old Rectory. It was heart-breaking that Chrysalis was no longer in its home. I always believed that it would be there long after I was gone, as a legacy of sorts. I'm not wearing rose-tinted glasses when I say Chrysalis was an extraordinary place. Its loss was a huge bereavement during those stressful years.

The charity relocated to the former Ardenode Country House Hotel, in Ballymore-Eustace, County Kildare for six months or so. The charity brought out a new programme, and they ran workshops. But they never really found a new full-time home for Chrysalis. It wound up as a company and deregistered as a charity in recent years. They emailed an eloquent notice of closure, decorated with butterflies, to all former course participants. The notice talked about Chrysalis being the first holistic centre in Ireland, but they airbrushed my name from its history. It was a fresh source of sadness and regret for me that the old wounds remained.

The whole debacle has taken me years to work through emotionally. My biggest disappointment was that the values and ethos upon which I founded the centre seemed to dissolve in the face of the legal issues between us.

In hindsight I realise the directors by their actions and business-like communications were simply looking after the interests of the charity. Any fallout affecting me was an unfortunate side issue. My heart was filled with resentment and bitterness towards them, a sense of betrayal burned deeply inside me. I felt wronged, misunderstood and ostracised. Eventually I recognised their actions were not intended to hurt or offend me. During that difficult time, one of the directors resigned from the board and remains a loyal and trusted friend.

Since I believe there exists a connection between unresolved emotions and cancer, I needed to employ my best efforts to heal those emotional scars. I turned to the Mindfulness Metta practice of compassion, a practice that entails working with 'difficult persons or situations' by sending loving kindness and good wishes to them. It became part of my daily meditation in an attempt to deal with and heal my negativity.

Marcus Garvey, a Jamaican activist, wrote in the 1940s, 'We are going to free ourselves from mental slavery. While others can free the body only we can free the mind.' The journey to healing and letting go was long. Owning my tendency to dwell on the past and harbour hurts has been an ongoing process. The transformation began by releasing negative traits and feelings towards those I felt had wronged me. It led to forgiveness. I can't honestly say the wounds are totally healed, but I was heartened to learn that reconciliation does not always follow forgiveness. Mixing business and my personal life and expecting the same in return was my downfall. Since I recognised that these people were focused on what was best for the business, there has been some softening in my heart. Sadly the valued friendships I once cherished will never be the same again. I can now live comfortably with this, however.

To quote from Mark Nepo's *The Book of Awakening*, 'Compassion in practice does not require us to give up the truth of what we feel or the truth of our reality. Nor does it allow us to minimize the humanity of those who hurt us. Rather we are asked to know ourselves enough that we can open to the truth of others even when their truth or their inability to live up to their truth has hurt us.'

The Old Rectory was free of all encumbrances by 2011, but by now the world was in recession. I had been spending a lot of time in Brazil, living in a sort of a cocoon there. I didn't realise just how bad things were. The charity moved out only months after the European Troika arrived into Ireland and imposed drastic austerity measures on the country. The economy was in free fall.

I walked around the rooms, my footsteps echoing through the empty house, thinking, *what am I going to do with this place?* I didn't want to leave it idle. I moved into the larger two-bedroom hermitage called Nirvana in the gardens of the Old Rectory. Cosy and comfortable, it offered a spacious home in a secluded part of the grounds. Eventually, I formed a limited company and opened the Old Rectory as a venue where facilitators hosted groups for weekend workshops. Yoga and meditation groups, hill-walking clubs, creative writing circles and artists' groups used the venue. The Dublin Buddhist Centre was among the many organisations that held regular retreats there. I returned to teaching mindfulness meditation, which was where my heart lay. I also trained as a wedding celebrant, and the house became an intimate venue for small weddings.

The truth of it is, I didn't want to have the responsibility of running the place, but I didn't feel I had a choice. Trying to run a business while accommodating estate agents' viewings at the same time was a delicate balancing act. Most facilitators plan at least six months or even a year in advance, so it was complicated taking bookings. But this went on for years. It was a time of trust, patience and perseverance. Fortunately, during this time, I had the support of Andrea Crowe, who came to work at the Old Rectory. She was an angel, always preparing the place with vases of flowers before each viewing.

I could never understand why the Old Rectory wasn't selling because there was a lot of interest. My hopes soared and crashed repeatedly. I was convinced that the right person would buy the house, someone with a vision for a new project in a beautiful place.

'Any luck with the sale, Ann Maria?' people would inquire.

'Oh yes, I met a lovely Buddhist Lama who's from Tibet, and his community are based in Canada, and they're looking for a retreat centre in Ireland. He loves the Old Rectory and the surroundings. He says he and the other monks have to do their divination before he can confirm, but I think this is the one!'

I received an email soon afterwards telling me the divination wasn't favourable, and I was heartbroken. But soon after came another promising viewing.

'Any news with the house?'

'Yes, there's a group from an addiction centre. They came down with their psychologist and a team of people. They're very keen. I think this definitely could be the one!'

But that didn't come to anything either. Then there was a couple from England who wanted to start a vegan boutique guesthouse, but the husband thought there was too much maintenance for him. A man from the north of Ireland was interested in opening a glamping business, but he faded out of the picture. The people behind the Irish Vipassana Trust in Shankill in Dublin were looking for a venue, but they decided the place wasn't big enough. A friend, Dr Michael Corry, who's no longer living, talked to a syndicate of people who were interested in setting up a healing centre there, and that fell through too.

Every time there was a viewing due, I would sit on a bench underneath a beautiful tree in the grounds and pray. *If these people are the right owners, may the sale happen easily and effortlessly. And may it all be blessed for the greater good of all.* I wanted the right owners for the Old Rectory; that was important. It was a place of spirituality from its inception in the early 1700s. My journal documented my hopes that: *The new steward of this place will inherit the legacy of strong healing energy here. I hope the right people will come bringing their energy, their vision, their commitment to the next phase. I trust in Spirit that has supported me and continues to, wherever I go.* I kept saying to myself all the time, *the right people are out there, and Spirit will bring them.* That hope kept me going for years.

Meanwhile, I was travelling over and back to Brazil, guiding several Sacred Journey tours a year. The town of Abadiânia was a quiet place, and one of the few social events of the week was movie night in the local juice bar, Frutti's. Everyone met up on Frutti's veranda on Sunday evenings to watch the movie on their outdoor screen. One night in December 2011, they showed a documentary about Leonard Cohen, featuring excerpts from a Dublin concert I had attended with Eamon. Despite my earlier grief over our break-up, we had remained friends. I sent him a message to tell him I'd been watching our concert in Brazil.

Later we had a long conversation on Skype. He revealed that one of the regrets in his life was not being with me and asked me if we might get back together again. Naturally I felt cautious, but I remember calling my eighty-year-old friend, Maura, to tell her this news. She responded, 'Well if love calls, don't shut the door on it.'

In January 2012 Eamon came to Brazil and joined my Sacred Journey tour group at the casa. When we talked, I was frank about how the break-up had affected me. I told him how I felt very let down, disappointed and resentful towards him. We had lengthy discussions into the early hours, and many tears were shed. As time went on, we realised that something fundamental had changed between us. In the intervening years, we had both moved on, and it became clear to both of us we had reached the end of the road. Although we didn't end up together, Eamon is still in my life as a friend, and I know he still cares for me. Unfortunately, though, there was no happy-ever-after ending.

The spiritual connection with John of God and the casa began to end for me around this time too. I started to hear rumours, vague accusations from unnamed sources. No one had spoken out and levelled explicit accusations at John of God. It was all speculative but worrying. My discreet enquiries were met with a wall of denial. I was told the rumours were wild fabrications and vicious falsehoods. My suspicions grew when I discovered two internationally well-established casa guides disappeared without a trace and deleted their websites.

I was conflicted. I recalled the clerical child abuse scandals in Ireland. It made me uncomfortable remembering how priests had continued abusing for decades because of a culture of silence, disbelief and respect for spiritual authority. *Is this what's going on in Abadiânia?* My conscience wouldn't allow me to lead another group to Brazil until the rumours were addressed. But there appeared to be no appetite at the casa to discuss these scandalous accusations at all. People visibly recoiled when the subject was broached. I regarded João as a gifted trance healer. For years I had faith in him. I witnessed healings at the casa and received healing in my own life. I needed to give him the benefit of the doubt. However, the rumours tainted my trust in him and in my work there.

I could not continue to bring people to the casa if these allegations were true. After a number of sleepless nights, I began a discernment process, and guidance came clearly: *Your time in Brazil is over.* It was too late to cancel my next scheduled group, which was the last pilgrimage I accompanied at the casa. I immediately removed all advertising and cancelled all future Sacred Journeys. I found a buyer for my house and within a very short time the sale was completed. Spirit was assisting me to leave Brazil easily, and I did so with a heavy heart

John of God continued in Abadiânia until the Me-Too movement reached Brazil in 2018. Then he was charged with multiple sex abuse allegations. He was found guilty of the rape of four women in December 2019 and was sent to prison for nineteen years. Others at Casa de Dom Inácio continue to offer the healing work of the spirits today but to far smaller numbers of people.

I know abusers can be status figures in a community; it just never occurred to me that João was one. It took time to reconcile myself to my blind-sightedness. From my therapeutic work with survivors of sexual abuse, I had seen the horror and hurt many felt when allegations of sexual abuse were made against members of the clergy. This breach of trust caused a deep wound for many people. In time I was able to forgive my ignorance. I was comforted by the guidance and support from spirit that led me to quickly break ties with the place.

It's still a source of confusion for me, but I witnessed many healings, and I believe there was spiritual energy at work at the casa. I think a dichotomy existed between the medium and the man in John of God. There was an authenticity to John of God the medium, and I feel he did have healing abilities. However, he failed to address his shadow side, the human failings of the man born as João Teixeira de Faria.

João became famous, very fast, with celebrities like Oprah Winfrey paying homage to him at the casa. He let his ego take over, forgetting he was just a channel of the spirits' healing powers. His moral compass was lost, and his dark side began to eclipse the light of the gifted healer. John of God abused his spiritual authority as a healer and hurt many women, which was a great sadness for me and others who spent time in Brazil. The only consolation I have is that I was guided to end the tours and leave the casa many years earlier.

Meanwhile the failure to sell my house in Ireland continued to be a source of bewilderment to me. I even invited a shaman to clear any negative energy on the land at the Old Rectory in case it was holding me there. It seemed I was so connected to the place that it wouldn't let me go.

It wasn't until the end of 2015 that I finally accepted an offer on the house. The purchasers were an Irish family, returning from Britain, and the husband's parents were going to live in one of the hermitages. The estate agent received confirmation that the funds were in place to proceed with the sale. Still, she took no chances and contacted the buyers again weeks after the sale was agreed. Her message to the purchasers was emphatic: *Ann Maria is closing her business on the strength of this offer. I need to know that your intention is serious and that you are proceeding with this sale.* When they reassured her that they were committed to the purchase, I went ahead and cancelled all the future bookings in the Old Rectory.

Afterwards I sent out invitations to friends and the many people who loved the centre to join me in a night called A Farewell to the Old Rectory. The Playback Theatre came, and people shared their memories of the place. It was a way of honouring the place that had been an essential part of my life for twenty-eight years. It was also a letting go of what once was. It was closure.

The completion of the sale was due to take place during Easter week of 2016. I contacted different charities to take the furniture, keeping some pieces for the new home I planned to buy in

Greystones. The beds were due to go to Sister Consilio in the Cuan Mhuire addiction centre in Athy, County Kildare. A charity from Dublin was coming to collect the bedclothes. All twenty-two beds were stripped. Andrea and I spent ages rolling up all the duvets and tying them in neat bundles before the charity was due to collect them.

I awoke the morning the charities were to arrive and saw snow on the Velux window over my bed. No one could get through the roads to collect the last of the contents, but I was ready to go. The place was almost cleared.

It was then that I got the phone call from the solicitor to tell me that the purchasers had pulled out. The collapse of the sale blindsided me. I was shocked, devastated really. I had already unshackled myself emotionally from the place and said my goodbyes. The house was practically stripped. It was a shell of a place with all the contents in boxes and crates. I'm not sure how my heart held out after that phone call. There were no apologies, no excuses, just no sale. Physically, I couldn't move for ages from the shock.

In retrospect I remembered my solicitor saying that he was chasing their solicitors for the contracts, but I was busy clearing the house. I knew there were always delays in sales, so I didn't see it as a red flag. A few days earlier, the estate agent had also phoned me.

'I've been calling your purchaser, but he's not returning my calls. Have you heard anything?'

'No. Should we be worried?'

'No. No, I don't think so.'

I had to put space between myself and the Old Rectory after that news. I spent that Easter at Holy Hill Hermitage, a retreat centre in County Sligo where I cried a torrent of tears. *What am I going to do now?* Even while I tried to recover from the shock, someone else called to say they heard the sale had fallen through, and they were interested in the place. That was the way it was. As soon as I despaired, another glimmer of hope appeared.

I picked myself up and reopened the Old Rectory again. It was only through the grace of a snowfall that I still had the bedding left. I remember Catherine, the wife of our gardener, Pat, kindly arriving down to help me remake all twenty-two beds. That was such a blessing because I was also suffering from a yoga injury for months by then and was limping badly. I sent an email out to all the facilitators to tell them that the sale didn't go through: *If anyone wants to run a workshop or a retreat, I am reopening.*

But I felt like a shadow of myself. I thought, *How can I ever start again?* I read an inspirational quote: *The courage of living is to believe, to love, to start again.* So, that's what I did. I took a deep breath, and I started again.

# Let Your God Love You

### Edwina Gateley

*Be silent.*

*Be still.*

*Alone.*

*Empty*

*Before your God.*

*Say nothing.*

*Ask nothing.*

*Be silent.*

*Be still.*

*Let your God look upon you.*

*That is all.*

*God knows.*

*God understands.*

*God loves you*

*With an enormous love,*

*And only wants*

*To look upon you*

*With that love.*

*Quiet.*

*Still.*

*Be.*

*Let your God –*

*Love you.*

*Reproduced with the kind permission of Edwina Gateley.*

# THE RECURRENCE

*The soul chooses, voluntarily,
to undertake the experience in order to heal.*

Gary Zukav

The fact that he didn't return my smile, as he usually did, should have been the giveaway. Dr Goodwin McDonnell, a lean man, formed a steeple with his fingers. His expression was sombre, but I still never expected what came next. It was midsummer 2016 and that yoga injury to my right leg hadn't healed, but I wasn't concerned. It was a torn ligament; a muscle injury at most.

'I've bad news, Ann Maria,' he said. 'The MRI results have shown up a tumour on your hip, at the top of your femur.'

All the oxygen seemed to leave the air at that moment. The doctor's words were like some terrible echo from a dark past almost forgotten. *A tumour? Dear God, could this really be happening again?*

Dr Goodwin is a homoeopath, osteopath and a general practitioner in Dublin. I've known him for more than twenty years. He's a kind man who has been a supportive presence in my life, often during times of depression. He says I have seasonal affective disorder, which explains my low energy and mood levels during the winter in Ireland. He prescribes homoeopathic remedies and recommends that I go to the sun in the winter. Back in December 2015, I had followed his advice and travelled to Lanzarote in the Canary Islands. One morning on the island, I used a strap to increase movement and extend my yoga stretch. Suddenly I felt a jolt in my leg; it was nothing major. I hadn't used a strap before, so I thought I'd overdone the stretch. I came home in January still feeling pain in the leg, but I was too busy to do much about it. I had to get ready to vacate the house in advance of the sale closure date at Easter. I have a good tolerance for pain, so I limped along and worked through it.

'It's just a yoga injury. It only hurts when I put pressure on it,' I said when people enquired about the limp.

Even after attending a chiropractor and a physiotherapist, I felt no improvement. Then the sale of the house fell through, and I had to get the Old Rectory up and running again. By the time July arrived, I was limping badly.

'For God's sake, Ann Maria, would you ever go and see a doctor?' said Lucille.

I was referred for an X-ray and then an MRI, and now Goodwin was telling me this torn ligament was actually a cancerous tumour. Even in the haze of shock that followed, I could see Goodwin was upset.

'You're well over the five-year milestone now,' he said, shaking his head. 'I felt sure you were over it.'

Goodwin had spoken before of this magical five-year criterion. Once a person reaches that milestone without a cancer recurrence, he or she is supposed to be clear. I'd reached that milestone in 2013, a full three years earlier. I remember coming out of Goodwin's surgery and calling Lucille, voice quavering with shock, still not quite believing the news. Saying the words out loud, 'The cancer is back,' made it real and more frightening.

Harriet and her husband, Martin Andrews, came from their home in County Louth as soon as they heard the news. Our lives had remained intertwined since the days Harriet and I lived in Fauna Cottage all those years ago. She and her husband had even investigated the possibility of buying the Old Rectory years earlier. But the recession happened, and they followed work opportunities, first to Australia and then to Ethiopia, where a few years earlier, they adopted their three beautiful children. Our lives stayed connected even when they lived abroad, and I travelled to visit them in both countries.

As well as my concerns over the cancer recurrence, I was anxious about the diary of events in the Old Rectory. My biggest booking of the year was due to happen while I was in the hospital having surgery. A group from England planned to host a week-long self-development programme called The Hoffman Process in the house. I had already booked a chef to cater for the group, but I was meant to be on-site to do everything else. It was a relief when Martin came to the rescue and offered to step in and help. The couple stayed overnight in the Old Rectory, as they had on many occasions before.

I don't know why it was, but when I woke up the next morning, my first thought was, *I wonder would Harriet and Martin buy the place?* I hobbled over from Nirvana hermitage to the Old Rectory. Harriet was still there, but Martin had already left for an appointment in Dublin. There was no preamble; I was too excited.

'Would you be interested in buying the house?' I said.

Harriet was momentarily thrown.

'Martin and I were only saying last night how much we love it here,' she admitted. 'We were reminiscing about being here when the children were small and how special it is in our memories.'

There was an extraordinary convergence of my needs and their irrepressible love for the Old Rectory. It felt like it was the hand of God intervening in our lives. All along, I couldn't understand why the place wasn't selling and why the Old Rectory wasn't relinquishing its grip on me. I felt there was something bigger going on but kept believing the universe would manifest the right buyer. After so many disappointments in the past, everything aligned just when I needed it most. I thought of the words that I'd written all those years ago. My hopes were that: *The new steward of this place will inherit the legacy of strong healing energy here. I hope the right people will come bringing their energy, their vision, their commitment to the next phase. I trust in Spirit, which has supported me and continues to, wherever I go.*

I thought, *Who could be better to take over the Old Rectory than Harriet and Martin and their family?* For the first time in years, I felt confident the place would release me. I had found the Old Rectory the right people to inherit its healing and spiritual legacy. I felt a sense of urgency when I rang Martin that Thursday morning.

'I'm going into hospital on Monday,' I said. 'I don't think I'll ever be able to run this place again. If you're really interested in buying, will you put an offer together?'

Everything was happening extremely fast. My doctor asked me to check my health insurance to see if I was covered for the Beacon Hospital. He hoped to refer me to the best oncologist he knew. Fortunately my insurance did cover me, and I ended up in the capable hands of Dr Jenny Westrup, an American and the director of oncology at the hospital.

Further scans showed that the tumour was at the top of the femur where it met the hip bone and that it had also spread to my lower back and spine. I remember Harriet sitting with me in the hospital when I felt extremely low, reassuring me that she would look after me when the end came. I had surgery to remove the tumour, and due to its location, I also required a half-hip replacement.

To recover from the operation, I went to Caritas, a convalescent nursing home on Merrion Road in Dublin. Within a few days, I was able to hobble around on a crutch. From there, I was taken by ambulance every day to the Beacon Hospital for radiotherapy.

Post-surgery I met with the oncologist to discuss the cancer recurrence. Harriet or Lucille came with me, as I couldn't always absorb all the medical information myself. Jenny is not only smart and talented, she also happens to be a beautiful, willowy blonde. But her lovely appearance belies the brutal nature of the disease she battles.

'You have stage four breast cancer which has metastasised to your bone, Ann Maria,' she said. 'This means that the cancer has progressed to an advanced stage that isn't curable.'

To hear those words spoken aloud felt excruciating. It meant recovery was no longer an option, and I had to live side-by-side with this disease from now on. The fear cut through me like a knife. I managed to clear my throat and break through the heavy silence hanging in the room.

'In your clinical experience, what is the prognosis for somebody with stage four cancer? How long do I have, Jenny?'

Her expression was pained.

'Probably two years.'

Even now I feel a bit emotional thinking back to that moment.

My life started to retreat from me, and a fresh torrent of tears was unleashed. I'd been given a death sentence; there was a two-year reprieve but a death sentence nonetheless. After another shocked silence, Jenny suddenly spoke again and qualified what she said.

'Well, you know, depending on how you respond to treatment, it could be four years or longer.'

At that, I looked up and rallied somewhat. There was a glimmer of hope; another deferral of the death sentence.

'Okay, I'm going for four years or longer.'

My immediate priority was to put the sale of the rectory behind me. Harriet and Martin and their family were living in Castlebellingham in County Louth, in a renovated cottage that belonged to one of Harriet's ancestors. The first person to view their cottage bought it. Through the eyes of faith, it was another sign that their decision to buy the Old Rectory was providential. Selling the Old Rectory wasn't easy because there were a lot of legal issues to iron out. However, we managed to come to a financial arrangement, and the Old Rectory is now Harriet and Martin's family home. It freed me from looking after the old house and grounds, and I have a lifetime interest in the hermitage, Nirvana.

In a way, the Old Rectory got its way. It never let me go because I still live in Nirvana on the grounds. After being told that I probably had two years to live, I didn't want the upheaval of moving again. Anyway, after selling the Old Rectory to Harriet and Martin, I got to enjoy the place to the full, without the burden of maintaining and looking after it. Instead I concentrated on other things. A terminal cancer prognosis has a way of focusing you on what you want out of life.

Facing death has made me sit up and value life more deeply. It certainly has been a springboard to living at a deeper level of consciousness. At the same time, there has not been a calm sense of acceptance of this life-limiting disease. My terminal prognosis hasn't come with a spiritual voyage to a more conscious and nobler life. The truth is I have been damn angry at times, furious that I only have a short time to live.

Before this I felt sure that cancer was a thing of the past. In hindsight, however, the recurrence shouldn't have been such a shock. After all, I was very stressed in the years before it. Unable to sell the Old Rectory, it was like living in a marriage that I didn't want to be in. There were so many disappointments when it came to selling the place that I was quite stressed and depressed a lot of the time. We know that emotional and psychological issues can trigger illness. All that stress may have provided fertile soil conditions for cancer to grow again.

One of the first things I had to do after the prognosis was to get my affairs in order. I remade my will and made the arrangements for my death. Once those practicalities were sorted, I thought about what I wanted to do with the remainder of my life.

*Do I need to correct the way I'm living? Are there people I need to forgive and hurts that I need to let go? Do I need to be more forgiving to myself and what self-recriminations and regrets do I need to lay to rest? Who do I want to spend time with? Where do I want to invest my energies?*

A terminal prognosis certainly sharpened up my sense of purpose in life. It made me more resolute, determined to free myself from issues that no longer mattered.

My mindfulness practice became a cornerstone in my life, bringing me into the present moment. It helped me see everything that was life-enhancing, and it stopped me deep-diving into negativity and despondency over the imminent end of days.

One of the first things I did after the prognosis was to make a wish list of what I wanted to do with the rest of my life. Some people refer to it as a 'bucket list' – as in a list of things you want to do before you kick the bucket. But Jenny prefers to use the more lyrical term wish list.

I knew that if I only had two years left, I didn't want to spend them being a patient, waiting to die. I was determined to live my life to the full. By the autumn of 2016, my treatments were over, and I felt a rare sense of freedom and joyfulness. I had a new focus and a renewed desire to enjoy all that life had to offer. Ticking off all the items on my wish list became my motivation to live into the future.

# *Excerpt from* Anam Cara

JOHN O'DONOHUE

*A glimpse at the face of your death can bring immense freedom to your life. It can make you aware of the urgency of the time you have here. The waste of time is one of the greatest areas of loss in life. So many people are, as Patrick Kavanagh put it, preparing for life rather than living it. You only get one chance.*

*You have one journey through life; you cannot repeat even one moment or retrace one footstep. It seems that we are meant to inhabit and live everything that comes towards us. In the underside of life, there is the presence of our death.*

*If you really live your life to the full, death will never have power over you. It will never seem like a destructive, negative event. It can become, for you, the moment of release into the deepest treasures of your own nature, your full entry into the temple of your soul.*

*If you are able to let go of things, you learn to die spiritually in little ways during your life. When you learn to let go*

## Carried on Spirit Wings

*of things, a greater generosity, openness and breath comes into your life. Imagine that multiplied a thousand times at the moment of your death. That release can bring you to a completely new divine belonging.*

From Anam Cara: Spiritual Wisdom from the Celtic World.
by John O'Donohue copyright © 2008.
Published by Transworld Ireland 2008.
Reproduced by permission of Penguin Books Ltd.

# THE WISH LIST

---※---

*Carpe diem! (seize the day).*
*Rejoice while you are alive.*
*Enjoy the day, live life to the fullest.*
*Make the most of what you have.*
*It is later than you think.*

HORACE

'Dolphins to starboard!' cried the captain, and everyone craned their necks as he veered and brought the rigid inflatable boat to a halt. My crewmates unzipped their windcheaters, adjusted their snorkels and began diving overboard. Leaving my crutch behind, I followed, landing with a splash into the sapphire waters of the Indian Ocean. The sea was colder, and its swell felt larger and stronger than I expected. The others were already fast approaching the tell-tale fins and flukes of the bottlenose dolphins circling nearby. I struck out in the same direction, throwing one arm over the other. I was never the best of swimmers, so it was half a minute before I realised, I wasn't getting any closer. My right leg, the one which had been operated upon, felt like a useless appendage in the water.

'Move your legs!' shouted the captain.

The current was working against me, and even though I was pulling hard, I was treading water rather than advancing. The others were now gathered, bobbing around in the water with the dolphins

'Move your legs!' the captain yelled again. 'Move your legs!'

I remember him barking those instructions as I flailed in the ocean, frustrated and practically in tears. I wanted to shout back, *I'm moving my legs as much as they'll move, you idiot!* but I was already swallowing too much saltwater.

Swimming with dolphins was one of the items at the top of my wish list. It felt fortuitous when I received an email from a travel agent offering encounters with the remarkable creatures in Mozambique. Going to Mozambique also offered an opportunity to spend time across the border in South Africa. I knew I could catch up with my cousin Dominic from Inchicore, now living in exclusive Camps Bay in Cape Town.

I think I had a vague notion that the dolphins would swim up to me, that we'd make eye contact and we'd have this beautiful connection. Research has proved that swimming with dolphins is an effective therapy for mild to moderate depression. But I never considered the practicalities of trying to swim with wild dolphins in the ocean while still recovering from hip surgery. Every time we went to see the dolphins, we had to wade into the sea in life vests and clamber on board the boat. I didn't anticipate the problems of getting in and out of a giant, inflatable rubber dinghy with a crutch and a lame leg. Most people seemed to vault into the vessel, but for me, without the power in my legs, it was more of an undignified scramble.

There were times that week when the dolphins were tantalisingly close but still out of reach for me. However, I did succeed in having one close encounter. The dolphin and I made eye contact, and it was thrilling, but then he just flipped over, and with a flick of his tail, he was gone. The others had multiple encounters, so I was certainly reminded of my physical limitations during that trip.

Despite a dearth of dolphin encounters, it was a wonderful trip with a whole programme of rejuvenating events like dance and movement every evening. The facilitator was a beautiful South African woman called Shakti Malan, a teacher of tantra with a doctorate in social anthropology. She had a magnificent silvering mane of curls and a vibrant smile. Like me, she also had secondaries from breast cancer. But Shakti was bubbling with life and enthusiasm with lots of plans for the future. When I heard less than a year later that she had died, it was a real shock. It was hard to believe that her exuberance and her joie de vivre could be extinguished so brutally. Moreover it was a sobering reminder of my mortality and the insidiousness of this disease we shared. If anything it provided a sense of urgency to complete the items on my wish list. Shakti was a reminder that my time was limited, and this disease was unpredictable.

Harriet and I were due to start a two-year spiritual development course called the Sacred Art of Living and Dying. But after I learnt I had bone cancer, I reconsidered. *If my time is limited, I'm not spending it studying and producing essays.* I rang the organisers to cancel my participation in the course. However, the programme leaders were keen for me to continue despite my circumstances. 'Look, we would love to have you on the course,' they said. 'Just participate to the level that you're comfortable.'

Several of the modules were to be hosted over weekends in Our Lady's Hospice in Harold's Cross in Dublin, but the remainder of the programme was an online course. It was manageable. All the participants were split up into groups called Céile Dé, or companions of God, to work through the modules. My Céile Dé group consists of four other women, all health care staff and therapists. I was the only person with an illness. The amazing thing is that even after the course ended, this group has continued to meet. When I was in Lanzarote, the group came out and stayed with me. We've evolved into a supportive network of soul friends, who talk at a deep level about what's going on in our lives. They have been a great support in recent years.

My wish list also included spending more quality time with certain friends. I went to Wernersville, Pennsylvania, to spend time with my friend Barbara Leinbach, a facilitator who I met in the Caron Foundation. She facilitated workshops in Chrysalis and loved being in Ireland, but she was now in her eighties and no longer travelling.

When I arrived to see her, she was about to move into the Highlands, an exclusive retirement community in Pennsylvania. I was astonished at the beauty of the place, located within a hundred acres of rolling hills and forest. But Barbara is a woman who believes in the Spanish concept of *mañana*. She's a procrastinator. We met the admissions manager the week before she was due to move in, and the woman wore a stern expression.

'Barbara, I want to make it clear that we still need all these documents before we can allow you to move in. We also need a copy of your car keys, a copy of your power of attorney, full names and addresses of your next of kin . . .'

The list went on and on. Barbara and I spent the full week tackling everything on the list, and we still had a fun time together.

There were other friends with whom I pledged to spend quality time. My college friend Marian and I enjoyed the electric atmosphere of the Theatre District in New York. I flew to see my other college friend, Mary Kate, while she was in Florida. After that I took advantage of the location to return to Hippocrates to attend a one-week programme for cancer patients. Barry Ahern invited me to join him and his wife, Nuala, in Kamares in Greece, where we had a special time together. Rosaleen Scully and I enjoyed a visit to a health spa. Dave Kenna, who had shared many times with me in Brazil, visited me in Lanzarote. My godchild Andrea Fewer and I spent a weekend together. Olive Dunlop invited me to her home in Turkey, while Noreen and I went away to a resort, and Harriet and I revisited Lourdes and Taizé.

One essential item on my wish list was to reconnect with my godson, Eoin. I became estranged from Eoin's mother, Mags Mooney, one of the directors on the board of Chrysalis during that whole legal debacle. As a result, I hadn't spent quality time with Eoin since I took him to Disney World in Florida in 2009.

On reflection I could have stayed in touch; Mags would never have stopped me seeing Eoin. I just felt seeing him would have been too awkward between his mother and me. I always sent him a birthday present, but one of my regrets was not having more contact with him. I lost so many critical years. Eoin was an intriguing child, drawn to meditation from a young age.

I finally reunited with him in the summer of 2017. He was now in his late teenage years, but he was still interested in Buddhism and meditation. We drove to Cunnamore Pier in West Cork and took the four-minute ferry to Heir Island, an unspoilt, tranquil haven. We joined a kayaking and mindfulness week at Hehir Island

Sailing School in the company of my friend Brendan McCann. The following summer, Eoin and I went to Plum Village, a well-known Buddhist monastery in the Dordogne, in south-west France, where we had another wonderful week together.

After leaving Plum Village, I ticked off another item on my wish list by returning to Taizé for the first time in nearly thirty years. Sister Diane had left by now to lead the order of the Sisters of Saint Andrew in Belgium. However, I was reunited with Tessa, a permanent whom I worked alongside in 1984. She had since become a sister of Saint Andrew. Tessa remembered spending time in Fauna Cottage on the last holiday she had before entering the convent. We looked at the way our lives diverged over the years, but neither of us had regrets.

Taizé had grown a lot bigger than I remembered it. I was also astonished to see security guards, barricades and security bollards. I couldn't recall any security in Taizé when I was there in the eighties. However, I discovered the liturgies and the chants remained the same as did the sense of peace in Taizé. It was wonderfully nostalgic to reconnect with a place that had played such a significant role in my youth.

Lucille and I took the opportunity to spend more time together by taking part in a four-month arts project with Andrea Scott's Floating World Theatre group. Every participant produced a scene based on an incident in our lives, and the cast collaborated to perform it as part of a show called *Life Memos*. I told the story of my journey to reach Sister Vandana's ashram as part of my contribution to the project. We performed the *Life Memos* show before a full house in the Mill Theatre, Dundrum, in Dublin in June 2018.

One of the highlights of my wish list was to return to India for the first time in more than twenty years. I realised this dream when I landed in Mumbai in November 2019. I spent the next seven weeks in meditation, contemplation and basking in the spiritual and mystical atmosphere of the subcontinent.

The first stop on my itinerary was Govardhan Ayurveda hospital, nestled in the beautiful mountain range, Sahyadri. My Ayurvedic doctor was honest as he sat before me. 'We cannot treat your cancer,' he said. 'But what we can do is boost your immune system.'

I spent the next two weeks enjoying exquisite oil treatments where two masseurs and four gentle hands worked on me for hours at a time. I was prescribed herbs, supplements and a diet of vegetarian food that was specially tailored to suit my *dosha*, or metabolic type. Everything was done out of *seva*, or loving service. Every treatment was provided with respect, dignity and care, and I left feeling renewed and refreshed.

After that I flew to Tamil Nadu, South India, to visit Father Korko Moses. Korko is a saffron-clad Jesuit priest who also assumes the name Swami Sharanananda. He lives a simple, monastic life in an ashram near the town of Dindigul. He came to Chrysalis on many occasions as a spiritual guide, teaching contemplative practices of meditation and yoga. A very influential teacher, he is inspired by both Christian and Eastern religious traditions, so his teachings are like those of Sister Vandana. After two heavenly weeks in Govardhan, the very basic and rustic facilities at Korko's ashram, Dhyanavanam, brought me back down to earth with a bang. However, it was wonderful to spend time with Korko again.

My journey continued into the mountains where I stayed in Bodhi Zendo monastery, two kilometres uphill from the village of Kodaikanal. The spiritual practice at the monastery is an interesting amalgamation of Roman Catholic Christian, Japanese Zen Buddhist, and Indian Hindu traditions. Surrounded by jungle hills, it was one of the most tranquil and pleasant places I've ever stayed.

I returned to Govardhan Eco Village for a Mystic Healing Therapy retreat with a Spanish group led by Javier de Salas, whom I've known for several years. Afterwards, I travelled south again to the golden beaches of Alleppey, Kerala, where I walked the beaches, gazed into the rolling waves of the Indian Ocean and relaxed. I was at peace.

At the end of seven weeks in India, I felt glowing, vibrant and alive. I lived an almost mystical dream, experiencing a strong Divine presence and guidance during those wonderful weeks. I never dreamt that this soothing calm was a preparation for the storm I was to face soon after my return to Ireland.

# *Happiness*

### Venerable Lama Gendun Rinpoche

*Happiness cannot be found*

*through great effort and willpower,*

*but is already here, right now,*

*in relaxation and letting go.*

*Don't strain yourself, there is nothing to do.*

*Whatever arises in the mind*

*has no importance at all,*

*because it has no reality whatsoever.*

*Don't become attached to it. Don't pass judgement.*

*Let the game happen on its own,*

*emerging and falling back – without changing anything –*

*and all will vanish and begin anew, without end.*

*Only our searching for happiness prevents us from seeing it.*

*It is like a rainbow which you run after without ever catching it.*

*Although it does not exist, it has always been there*

*and accompanies you every instant.*

*Don't believe in the reality of good and bad experiences;*

*they are like rainbows.*

*Wanting to grasp the ungraspable you exhaust yourself in vain.*

*As soon as you relax this grasping,*

*there is space – open, inviting and comfortable.*

*So make use of it. Everything is already yours.*

*Search no more,*

*Don't go into the inextricable jungle*

*looking for the elephant who is already quietly at home.*

*Nothing to do,*

*nothing to force,*

*nothing to want*

*and everything happens by itself.*

# MINDFULNESS

*Mindfulness is a lifetime's journey along a path that ultimately leads nowhere only to who you are.*

JON KABAT-ZINN

'We have the results of your scan, Ann Maria, and there's no easy way to say this, but we've discovered multiple spots on your liver.'

My oncologist, Jenny Westrup, paused, waiting for the ominous words to sink in. I felt my chest tighten and glanced at Lucille, perhaps expecting her to object in my place. I turned back to Jenny, almost indignant.

'That can't be!' I exclaimed. 'I feel great. For goodness' sake, look at me!'

And I did feel great. My energy levels were high and free-flowing. I came back from India to attend a family wedding and surprised cousins from England who hadn't seen me in a long time. 'You look terrific!' many of them remarked, visibly surprised. I think some people who hear that I have stage four cancer expect me to look ghostly, be missing my hair and eyebrows and wearing a tell-tale headscarf.

Jenny's diagnosis came as a terrible blow, arriving as it did days after a routine scan and less than a week after the wedding. Lucille came to the appointment, not because I had any concerns but because she always asks the questions I forget to ask. The very next day, I planned to escape the Irish winter and fly to Lanzarote for three months. Now Jenny was talking about 'multiple spots' on my liver.

I didn't look or feel sick. There was a huge discrepancy between

Jenny's revelation that the cancer had spread to my liver and how I felt at the end of November 2019. I couldn't understand it because I had no symptoms at all. On reflection, it seemed like India had been a journey to prepare me for this blow.

'We need to start doing something about this now,' said Jenny.

My heart sank at this news.

'But I'm going away tomorrow!'

Everything was planned. I had rented my usual little house on the island, and friends had booked to come out and stay. I had even bought the flights home for my three-monthly Zometa infusion, a drug that prevents bone fractures in cancer patients. They were my only treatments since I'd finished the radiotherapy for the cancer in my femur, lower back and spine in 2016. Jenny described Zometa as a kind of vitamin complex for bones.

She shook her head and sighed.

'I wouldn't advise you to travel. We need to make a start treating your liver. You don't want the spots to get bigger or to multiply further. I'm recommending a medication called Xeloda.'

'Is that a form of chemotherapy?'

'Yes, it is, a very effective form.'

'You know that I don't want chemotherapy.'

'Look, chemotherapy has changed in the last twenty years, Ann Maria. We get excellent results from it. It's particularly good at targeting metastatic breast cancer, and you don't even need to come into the hospital. It is taken in pill form.'

I was still very reluctant to accept any chemotherapy. I closed my eyes, took a deep breath, and centred myself. Then I decided.

'I need a little more time.'

I decided to go to Lanzarote as planned. I already had arranged to meet my friends, Dr Anthony Sharkey, his wife Lisa Markham and their daughter, Bella, on the island. I organised a consultation with an oncologist in the Canaries for a second opinion. It felt like I was killing two birds with one stone. Jenny had said if I found a consultant there, I could have the Zometa bone infusion treatment in the Canaries without any need to return to Ireland.

Anthony is a holistically oriented medical doctor. With his broad-based approach to healing, it seemed like providence that he could be there to meet the Spanish oncologist, Adolfo Murias. Anthony and I took a commuter flight to the neighbouring island of Gran Canaria to attend the consultation in University Hospital San Roque in Las Palmas. The hospital provided a translator as we had little Spanish, and Dr Murias didn't speak English. The consultant surprised me by recommending a hormone-based therapy rather than the chemotherapy that Jenny was urging me to have. At one stage, Dr Murias even phoned his daughter, an oncologist in the UK, who agreed with his recommendation. I felt totally conflicted by now.

When I got home, Anthony suggested getting a third opinion with an American oncologist, Dr Dana Flavin, who was a keynote speaker at a medical conference he had attended. Dr Flavin, who integrates synthetic and natural treatments for cancer, agreed to an online video consultation from her base in Germany.

'Xeloda gets excellent results, so some of my patients are on it,' she said. 'In my opinion, the dosage your doctor is recommending seems high. However, if you go ahead, I can give you a list of supplements which will counteract a lot of the adverse side effects.'

I felt conflicted about accepting chemotherapy, but I had to do something. It was a case of weighing up the risks versus the potential benefits. I took a leap of faith and agreed to try the chemotherapy drug, Xeloda. I figured that I had to place my trust in somebody, and Dr Westrup had been my doctor for the past two years. Dr Flavin's belief that the right supplements could counteract the worst of the side effects settled the debate.

Christmas in Lanzarote was cancelled and my friend Marian, who was supposed to join me in the sun, came to stay with me in Donard instead. Early in 2020, however, I started feeling ill. I rang the oncology nurse at the hospital to say that I had nausea and diarrhoea. She reassured me that it was a side effect of the medication, but she offered the option of returning to the hospital.

'Do you think you need to come in?'

'No,' I said. The last thing I wanted was to be hospitalised.

Two days passed, and the symptoms were worse, so I rang the nurse again.

'Do you have a temperature?'

Neither Harriet nor I had a thermometer between us, so she went to a neighbour to borrow one. My temperature was high, so the nurse advised me to come straight into the Beacon Hospital. By now, on top of vomiting and diarrhoea, I had developed painful mouth sores, peeling skin and was experiencing burning sensations all around my body. The soles of my feet felt scorched, making it painful to walk. By the time I reached the Beacon, I was very unwell, and they put me into isolation because they feared I had a virus. They attached me to a drip to hydrate me and had to feed me intravenously. I remember little of the next ten days. When I started to have difficulty breathing, they discovered a clot on my lung.

I do recall waking with fright to see Myles standing over me, as he gave me the Sacrament of the Anointing of the Sick. 'Oh, Myles!' I said, happy to see him, but never suspecting for a moment that I was critically ill. I spent a month and a few days recovering in hospital. After I left isolation, I was walking the corridor for exercise when a nurse stopped me.

'Oh, Ann Maria, you're looking so much better now!'

I looked at her blankly.

'I was looking after you when you were in isolation,' she said.

'Thank you, but I'm sorry, I don't remember much after I was admitted.'

'The yoga? You don't remember?'

I hadn't a clue what she was talking about.

'The time you had the clot, and you weren't breathing properly?'

I had been told about the clot, but I didn't recall anything about it. The nurse was wide-eyed that I didn't remember.

'I told you that we needed to give you oxygen, and you insisted that you didn't need it. You sat up in the bed and said, "I know a yoga position that will help me breathe." You stuck out your tongue and made strange noises, and you said it was called the lion's roar!'

The lion's roar is not the most dignified pose, so it's not for the self-conscious. You start on all fours, tongue pointing down from your mouth, your eyeballs raised to the ceiling. Then you take a deep breath and make a loud sound on exhalation. She told me I did this in the bed when she was trying to put me on oxygen. We were both laughing by the end of her story, but I had no memory of the event at all.

While I was in the hospital, I was prodded and poked; more blood tests were taken and more scans were done. Then suddenly the medical team descended on me with a new file and another bombshell.

'Ann Maria, we have a bit of bad news,' the doctor said. 'We've discovered a tumour on your brain.'

I gasped in disbelief. *So not only do I have multiple 'spots' on my liver, but now there's cancer in my head?* I was reeling. Suddenly the focus swung away from the liver, and all attention switched to my brain. *Breathe, Ann Maria, just breathe,* I reminded myself over and over.

Harriet accompanied me as I attended a consultation with Jenny. Lucille joined us on Zoom from France and Anthony was also online from Wicklow. There were five of us in the room for more than an hour, but Anthony, with his medical knowledge, posed most of the questions. Jenny answered all his concerns with frankness and clarity, and for the first time, it dawned on me that I was pretty sick. A grape-sized tumour was located in the occipital lobe in my brain, an area which controls eyesight. The location was of less importance than the tumour's propensity to spread. Jenny recommended a very high dosage of radiotherapy to my brain to stop that happening.

'What if I decide not to have radiotherapy?' I asked.

'If it's not treated aggressively, you could be dead within six months,' Jenny replied.

The bad news seemed to fly around like shrapnel in an explosion. My stomach was a ball of anxiety, and my mind was a whirl of confusion. Harriet had to go away to meditate after the consultation.

'What do I do, Harriet?' I asked when she returned.

'Well, you don't have much choice, Ann Maria. Do you want to be alive in six months?'

I didn't need to think about that.

'You're right. I don't have a choice,' I said. 'I'm not ready to go yet.'

The liver issue, which had been such a priority in November, was shelved so the medical team could tackle the brain tumour. Once the radiotherapy was completed, the focus switched back to my liver. I felt drained and exhausted, but I was resolute when Jenny suggested going back on Xeloda.

'I'm not taking chemotherapy again.'

'We can give you a smaller dose this time.'

'It's not an option. I'm not doing that to my body again.'

She switched me to the hormone-based therapy that the Spanish oncologist and his daughter advised me to take.

The start of 2020 was challenging. I felt a bit like an emergency forest fire for a while – as the firefighters were busy extinguishing one blaze, another one broke out somewhere else. But I survived it, and I've been managing my health well ever since.

While I was in the hospital, I met with the palliative care team. People think of palliative care as a way to comfort the dying. But doctors now offer palliative care to all cancer patients as soon as the disease is diagnosed. Doctors recognise the emotional and mental toll of a critical illness these days, so they work towards alleviating those symptoms too.

Cancer certainly afforded me a clear insight into the benefits of mindfulness. My mindfulness training and meditation practices sustained me throughout a tumultuous time. I reminded myself to breathe deeply and remain in the present moment, and I remembered Jon Kabat-Zinn's wise words: *You can't stop the waves, but you can learn to surf.* In my prayers, I handed my life to God in trust. Mindfulness also helped me through radiation treatment. Before the radiographers could begin targeting my brain tumour, they had to make a mask or mould of my head. The day I was due for the fitting, the nurse came to my bed with a tranquilliser.

'You need to take this before we bring you down.'

I shook my head.

'No, thank you. I won't need tranquillisers.'

The nurse rang radiotherapy to tell them that their patient was refusing sedation. The reply came back: 'She needs to take it.'

I didn't budge. I didn't need this medication.

'Tell them I've been meditating for over twenty years. I will relax and remain still for the procedure. I'll be fine.'

And I was fine. I went in there and lay down, and I just kept deep breathing like it was one long meditation session. I've used meditation to get through multiple CAT scans, PET scans and MRIs. I never expected my meditation practice to help me so much in the hospital situation, but it has given me great inner strength to cope with endless medical procedures.

Most of all, mindfulness helps me curb the stress response to all the bad news. Mindfulness-based instructor Karen Ryders says: *Breath is with us all the time. It can be used as a tool, like an anchor, to bring stability to the body and mind when we deliberately choose to become aware of it. We can tune in to it at any moment during everyday life.*

Without mindfulness, I don't know how I could have coped with the stark news of cancer gatecrashing into my life again and again. It has been an essential life tool while navigating my way through these rough waters.

By bringing awareness to my breathing, I can exert some control over how I feel. I'm also reminded of the quote: *Between stimulus and response, there lies a space.* In that space is our power to choose our response. I'm learning that to remain in that space or in the moment can sometimes be the solution to what seem like life's most intractable problems.

# DEATH

*May death come gently towards you.*
*Leaving you time to make your way*
*Through the cold embrace of fear*
*To the place of inner tranquility.*°

JOHN O'DONOHUE

There is no handbook when facing the end of your life. Although I've experienced many bereavements, I've only been present at the passing of my father's life as a young child and later, at my husband's passing. Holding Andrew's hand until he drew his last breath was a profound experience. The radiance about him as he surrendered to death felt very natural, and I sensed the merging of his spirit with the Divine. It was peaceful, as I hope it will be for me.

I don't pretend to know any universal truths about life and death. I'm not a philosopher. However, the gentle dissolution of the spirit or soul into another realm is part of my belief system. I don't see death as an absolute but as a transformation or process. I believe death is when the soul, or spirit or consciousness leaves the body and merges with the Source of God. Witnessing Andrew's death certainly gives me hope that death is not the end.

A lot of evidence suggests the existence of an afterlife. Psychiatrist Elisabeth Kübler-Ross wrote a collection of essays, *On Life After*

---
° *'For the Dying' from* Benedictus: A Book of Blessings *by John O'Donohue, reprinted with permission from the John O'Donohue Legacy Partnership.*

*Death*, based on her studies of more than twenty thousand people who had near-death experiences. All the stories indicate that there's another journey ahead. Anita Moorjani's book *Dying to be Me* gives a graphic account of what happened during her near-death experience.

Across cultures and throughout the ages, near-death experiences appear to be universal phenomena with similar characteristics. People report a process of detachment from their bodies, feelings of levitation and an ability to watch people in the room. They say they feel drawn to a warm, serene and welcoming light where they see loved ones who have gone before. People whose lives are snatched back from lifelessness relate such similar accounts that they are difficult to discount.

Although I believe death is not the end, it is still a huge jolt to face your own death. I'm not going to make a terminal diagnosis sound easy. There are days when I feel I'm living on a razor's edge, going through so many emotions, and other days when I feel acceptance and peace.

There's also a dichotomy to living with a life-limiting illness. Do I regard myself as living, or am I dying? I've been living in these parallel universes since the diagnosis of metastasised breast cancer in 2016. In reality we're all in the process of dying, but I never internalised that reality until the clock started ticking down on my mortality.

In April 2019 Russ and Emer's son, Eoin, phoned to ask if I would be celebrant for his marriage to Orla. The date was set for 9 August. I'd known Eoin since childhood and felt honoured to be invited to take part in the couple's special day. But my fear soon kicked in. *How will I be in August? Will I have enough energy for the event?* They wanted a simple, no-fuss wedding, with a ceremony that reflected their own values and beliefs. I agreed to do it provided Eoin found someone to co-celebrate with me; this was my safety net. If, when the time came, I wasn't well enough, at least someone else could carry the day. Eoin asked his neighbour Fr Turlough Baxter, who agreed to take part, and we all met to plan the day.

The wedding took place in a marquee in the quaint village of

Killashee, County Longford. The couple were surrounded by their families and friends and it was a beautiful occasion. I really enjoyed the day and danced into the early hours. Next day my voice was gone and I got a chest infection. But it was worth every minute.

A year ago my friend Noreen started planning her daughter's wedding in Spain due to take place this year. I was delighted to be included in the wedding plans, but at the same time, my internal dialogue was, *Well, there's no point in me booking anything yet because I might not be alive.* Of course, that's not something I said out loud, not wishing to dampen Noreen's joy and anticipation. As it happens, the wedding was cancelled due to the Covid-19 lockdown, but I don't make long-term plans. I see the future in three-month modules that coincide with my scheduled Zometa transfusions. There is an inevitable loneliness in this. I no longer take it for granted I'll be a part of anyone's future plans.

One of my most immediate concerns, after receiving a prognosis of two years, was: *Will I be ready?* I had a sense of urgency about the practical, personal and spiritual matters to attend to. I needed to put to rights, put in order, revise, amend, rectify and tidy up many aspects of my life. It helped to be able to attend the Forum on the End of Life organised by the Irish Hospice Foundation in Dublin Castle in 2017. Each of the speakers gave guidance on the practical aspects of facing death. They distributed a twenty-six-page booklet called *Think Ahead*, which was invaluable in organising my affairs. The booklet prompts the reader to record all their preferences in the event of an emergency, serious illness or death. Most people make a will, but the *Think Ahead* booklet goes further. In the event of one's future inability to communicate, it allows individuals to record their own advanced health care decisions. It was reassuring to work through the pages and outline my wishes on treatment before I die and my preferences after I die.

Of course, everything may not happen as I would like it, but at least no one will be put into a position where they have to second-guess my wishes. It allowed me to fill in an advance health care directive, about the type and extent of medical or surgical treatment I want if I'm unable to make that decision in the future.

The booklet also lays out options for funeral preferences.

Do you want burial or cremation? Have you preferred funeral arrangements, readings or music? There is legal information to register your enduring power of attorney if you have one. It really helped me to look after some of the practicalities of end of life. It's all filled out, and my friend Harriet knows where to find it.

The forum also discussed end-of-life pain management. It was reassuring to hear from doctors that the medical goal is to avoid pain, not just control it. It means that people can die in a dignified and compassionate manner.

People might find it hard to believe, but the End of Life Forum wasn't a morbid, dark or depressing day. It was all about creating an awareness of death with the view to helping people make the most of their lives. It allowed me to reflect on what I wanted towards the end of life and particularly, my end-of-life care.

Going to the forum was a liberating experience in a lot of ways. After birth, the most significant event everyone will experience is death. Yet few talk about it. Today, end of life tends to be a sanitised experience overseen by the medical profession and the undertaker. People are naturally 'death-phobic' and can be fearful of discussing the subject. I'm comfortable talking about my death, but it's not something many other people are comfortable doing. It was refreshing to hear death discussed in a transparent, practical and communal way. We're all going to die, so it's good to get a few guidelines, to gain greater awareness of what to expect, so we can approach the end with more understanding.

Most life-limiting illnesses require patients to navigate through a minefield of complex and intimidating treatments. The Simonton Center has a useful maxim to use when facing decisions: *I always do the best I can with the information and understanding I have at the time.* I use this mantra when it comes to making choices about my health. I've discovered that I know more than I realise about my body. We all have intuition and instinct for what's right for us. If I trusted my instinct, I could have avoided a month in hospital recovering from an adverse reaction to chemotherapy. Doctors know how to treat the disease, but I believe we often know what's best for our own bodies.

That's not a criticism of my oncologist, Jenny Westrup. She is an incredible woman. When we meet, she greets me with 'namaste'. I mean, what consultant in Ireland greets their patient with 'namaste', or *I bow to the Divine in you?* While Jenny has given me some difficult news over the years, I've been extremely fortunate to have found an oncologist with deep compassion and heart.

Ultimately, however, I am responsible for the physical care of my body. Some people are happy to hand themselves over to the care of their doctors, and that's their prerogative. I choose to be my own health manager. I do that by *trying to do the best I can with the information I have and the understanding I have at the time.* However, it's easy to be overwhelmed by all the medical and clinical treatments. For me it has been essential to engage with other forms of therapy that put me first and not my diagnosis. As a result I've developed a holistic health care support team that includes an acupuncturist, a reiki therapist, a homoeopath, a craniosacral therapist and a psychologist.

I met clinical psychologist Dr Ursula Bates as part of a six-week programme when she worked as the head of psychology services at Our Lady's Hospice. I've found our sessions extremely helpful and supportive.

However, it is my friends who have been my greatest support throughout my life. My primary support person is Lucille. She accompanies me to most of my consultant meetings. I don't give advice to people with cancer, but if I were to recommend one thing, it is that patients don't go alone to the consultations. There is so much information to absorb, and Lucille is a highly effective listener. Afterwards we have a cup of tea and chat. It means I can ask, 'What did she say about this?' and 'What did she mean by that?' Two heads are better than one. I always have somebody with me. If I want to actively participate in my wellness, I must have all the information.

Looking after my physical wellness is vital, but it was equally crucial after the prognosis to prepare myself spiritually. With death on the horizon, the search for meaning, purpose and hope takes on greater urgency. To contemplate on dying 'well' or having a 'good' death, I spent the month of June 2017 in Dzogchen Beara, a Tibetan Retreat centre on the Beara Peninsula in County Cork.

The centre's panoramic view overlooking the Atlantic Ocean is a reminder of one of the essential doctrines of Buddhism: the impermanence of life. A blanket of thick fog sometimes covers the place in the early mornings. When the mist burns off, the sun reveals the swooping gulls and the glittering white peaks of the waves. Yet within hours, the skies and sea can turn dark navy blue, and soon the centre is whipped by wind and heavy rain.

Rigpa senior instructor and spiritual care educator Christine Whiteside accompanied me during my retreat. I spent time contemplating parts of the *Tibetan Book of Living and Dying*, a manual of Buddhist wisdom that is both inspiring and comforting. The Dalai Lama wrote the foreword, which includes a pleasant analogy for death: *I tend to think of death as being like a change of your clothes when they are old and worn out, rather than some final end.*

I learnt and practised a guided visualisation called Phowa, which is sometimes described as the practice of conscious dying. It is about preparing spiritually for death and involves visualising light or the image of your soul ascending out of the body with ease. Phowa meditation can be used even if you're not in the last stages of life. This practice helped me to see death in a new way: a letting go of the ego, breathing into surrender and opening to transcendence. It reminds me of the energy and radiance I experienced around Andrew on his deathbed many years ago.

I also spent time practising Metta loving-kindness meditation, a way of cultivating compassion, benevolence and connection towards others and oneself. In essence Metta is about expressing good wishes for the well-being and happiness of others, including people who have harmed or hurt us. It involves repeating phrases such as: *May you be well. May you be happy. May you be at peace. May you be free from pain. May your life be filled with happiness, health and well-being. May you be at ease.* I also used an ancient forgiveness process with four simple phrases: *I forgive you. Please forgive me. Thank you. I love you.* I immersed myself in these phrases.

I continue to use Metta in my daily life and I've experienced a softening in my heart and a breaking down of barriers, especially towards people with whom I've had difficulties. I believe this practice subsequently supported me to repair and heal certain fractured relationships. I made a list of people with whom I wanted to reconcile, and when the time was right, I met them. I acknowledged my mistakes and sought forgiveness and extended forgiveness to them. It was humbling and healing. Some people remain on my list, but I trust I'll get around to meeting them before the end.

The retreat was not without challenges. I sometimes went through deep-rooted sadness, anger and rage. Some days I was flooded by emotions; at times, it was really tough and exhausting. Yet, after spending a month in Dzogchen Beara, I felt less fear. I felt lighter and I had a greater acceptance of my death. I also felt a renewed sense of freedom, hope and peacefulness. I decided: *If I've two years left, I am going to live them to the very best and enjoy them to the full.* I embarked on my bucket list, or wish list, with people to see, places to go and adventures to experience.

It is natural for grief to arise towards the end of life. There is a sense of loss for the unlived life, and for me, the regret was that I didn't have a life partner to share my journey. Grief is part of the process of letting go of a dream, a natural reaction when life hasn't worked out as we hoped. It is as inevitable as the tide ebbing and flowing because we all face regrets, losses, disappointments before we adjust to the loss and accept the life we have. It seems that grief and loss have been my karmic theme imprinted since childhood. But if it is true that we only grieve what we have truly loved, then I know I have experienced great heights of love and passion in my life.

While reflecting on her long life, eighty-five-year-old Nadine Stair wrote a beautiful poem, 'If I Had My Life to Live Over'. Ultimately she urges her readers to fully embrace life while they can. If I could talk to the younger me, I realise my advice would be similar. I would say, 'Ann Maria, lighten up, make more time for fun, play and picnics.' I'd also say, 'Stop worrying about getting it *right* and worrying about making the *right* decision.' I would urge her to take even more risks: 'Be more fearless, be more courageous. Forget about what others think about you. Speak your truth.' I would advise her to focus more on the present than on future plans. I would also encourage her to laugh more and smile more, and not to wait too long to follow her passion for acting and dancing. I would ask her to reiterate the mantra from the Simonton programme: *Does this give you deep joy and fulfilment?*

Above all I'd remind her that developing a loving, nurturing and conscious relationship with herself is the best foundation for all other relationships, and that true healing requires exploring the depths of our wounds. I'd advise her to never believe she has absolute control over her life because Spirit, God, Karma, epigenetics and many universal laws combine to weave our destinies. Most importantly, I would tell the younger Ann Maria to lean in to the story of her life, to accept what arises and be at peace with what is.

Facing a life-limiting illness changed both everything and nothing. I always knew I was going to die, but until I got a terminal diagnosis, death was a distant rumour, something far into the future. After the diagnosis, and as the inevitability of death gets closer, I am straddling two universes of being alive and realising I'm dying. I'm obviously a work in progress because I'm still here, still earthbound. I'm a little bit surprised that I'm still alive, but here I am, still showing up! Some of the vitality and energy I once took for granted has ebbed away, but I've been well, and I am grateful for my wellness and my life at the moment.

I've heard some people describe cancer as 'a blessing' but I'd never go that far! However, sometimes it takes coming to terms with your own mortality to make you happier, more appreciative and more likely to live life to the full. I feel the last few years have been a precious gift. The Buddhist teacher Jack Kornfield says: *At the end of life our questions are very simple: Did I live fully? Did I love well?* A terminal prognosis has allowed me to live with enhanced purpose and meaning, to live and love more fully. Writing this book reminded me of all that I have to be grateful for; the wonderful people I've met and all the beautiful places I've visited. Some people have no final conversations and no chance to prepare. Not everyone is given the opportunity I've been given to review my life, to make amends, to spend time with friends, to experience the world on another level.

John O'Donohue writes about living 'like a river flows, carried by the surprise of its own unfolding'. Lately I am surprised how my life is unfolding. I feel aware of being in the flow and of experiencing a new sense of freedom in my second lease of life. I live with a greater intensity than I've ever lived before. Being faced with my mortality has heightened my perceptions of everything around me. I'm more aware of the extraordinary beauty of nature. I notice rainbows more often. I find myself gazing in wonder at children playing. I watch a squirrel springing from bough to bough. The sound of birdsong stops me in my tracks. I'm experiencing everything differently, more deeply. I'm living more urgently, loving more fiercely. I'm savouring all the elements of life around me.

*The Tibetan Book of Living and Dying* includes these words of wisdom: *When we finally know we are dying, and all other sentient beings are dying with us, we start to have a burning, almost heartbreaking sense of the fragility and preciousness of each moment and each being, and from this can grow a deep, clear, limitless compassion for all beings.* These words resonate with me at a deep level.

I don't pretend to know any universal truths or have any penetrating insights into the afterlife. I trust I will be led down a path of healing into wholeness and fullness, which I have been trying to achieve in this lifetime. I believe death is the final stage of my growth, a journey of my original essence to the Source of God within me.

This belief comes from knowing that a Universal Spirit or God has guided me throughout my life. I feel I've been carried on spirit wings all my life. I trust this guiding presence will continue to show me the way forward.

In the end I pray for the courage and wisdom, to surrender and let go. There's no handbook for dying, but I believe that we all come to a momentary merging of two worlds, where we have to let go and make a leap into the unknown. It's frightening but freeing at the same time. All I can do is trust that my essence, my spirit or soul will be carried one last time on spirit wings into a new awakening.

# If I Had My Life to Live Over

Author Disputed

If I had my life to live over again,

I'd dare to make more mistakes next time.

I'd relax.

I'd limber up.

I'd be sillier than I've been this trip.

I would take fewer things seriously.

I would take more chances,

I would eat more ice cream and less beans.

I would, perhaps, have more actual troubles

but fewer imaginary ones.

You see, I'm one of those people who was sensible and sane,

hour after hour,

day after day.

*Oh, I've had my moments.*

*If I had to do it over again,*

*I'd have more of them.*

*In fact, I'd try to have nothing else – just moments,*

*one after another, instead of living so many years ahead of each day.*

*I've been one of those persons who never goes anywhere without*

*a thermometer, a hot-water bottle, a raincoat, and a parachute.*

*If I could do it again, I would travel lighter than I have.*

*If I had to live my life over,*

*I would start barefoot earlier in the spring*

*and stay that way later in the fall.*

*I would go to more dances,*

*I would ride more merry-go-rounds,*

*I would pick more daisies.*

# ACKNOWLEDGEMENTS

―――⸜―――

I wish to thank Harriet and Lucille for your love and your supportive presence in my life for many years. You finally persuaded me to write my life story after I procrastinated for so long. The cocooning months during the Covid-19 lockdown allowed me the opportunity to seize the moment.

Harriet, you are an example of someone who gracefully surrenders everything to God and finds all of life's details are automatically taken care of.

Lucille, I could not have wished for a more reflective and insightful companion along the way. You have been there at every turn with ideas, assistance and with words of encouragement and support.

I wish to express heartfelt gratitude to Derek, Patricia, Brendan, Iris and Geraldine for so openly sharing your personal stories. I was privileged to journey with you and to witness your resilience and strength in the face of huge adversity.

Thank you, Peter, for your generous and honest contribution to the book, and for all your support in the early days of Chrysalis.

Thank you, Claire, for sharing your experiences with my readers. Our paths in West Wicklow were destined to meet. Your boundless energy and creativity over two decades allowed Chrysalis to be the sacred space it was for so many fellow pilgrims. Your support for me, personally, and for my vision, was immeasurable.

There was no blueprint for a place like Chrysalis in the Ireland of the eighties and nineties. It took countless people to trust in its vision and to bring their gifts to bear on its unfolding beauty. Whatever part you played in the story of Chrysalis, howsoever small or large, it made a difference.

To Kathryn Rogers, my co-author and editor: I'm very grateful for your professionalism and patience in co-creating this book. You took the jigsaw of my life events, journals and dissertations and pieced them together to shape my story.

I'm appreciative of Emily Doyle's tireless creativity in producing the front cover. I love it!

Thank you, Mary Kate, for your life long friendship and assistance with copyright research.

Gratitude to the best travel companion ever, David Kenna. Your equanimity in selecting our final photos was inspiring. I wish to acknowledge your contribution on our many journeys together.

Thank you, Olive Dunlop, for your lasting friendship and thank you also to those who visited and cared for me in Lanzarote.

Thank you to Chenile Keogh, Robert Doran and all the helpful team at Kazoo Independent Publishing Services.

To my friend Greg, you promised to shred my journals after my death. Instead, you meticulously proofread the drafts of the book. You are now off the hook! To Lisa, my *Playback* friend, thank you for your reflective feedback and nurturing meals during the lockdown. Thank you to Lani O'Hanlon for taking the time to read a draft of the book and for your helpful feedback and suggestions.

To Peter Sheridan, thank you for being a source of support and encouragement in my short-lived acting career and for agreeing to launch my book.

I want to express deep gratitude to my medical team. To my GP, Dr Goodwin McDonnell, you have been an uplifting and compassionate support in my life for over twenty years.

To my oncologist, Dr Jennifer Westrup, who greets me with the Indian blessing, namaste, you have walked with me on this tough cancer journey with remarkable kindness and heart.

Thank you, Dr Anthony Sharkey, for your friendship, your research and advice on complementary and holistic treatments. I have really appreciated your wisdom, treatments and support.

Thanks to my cousin, Dr Patrick Lavin, USA, who was always at the end of the phone with helpful medical advice.

Also, I wish to send grateful thanks to the many alternative complementary therapists and energy healers who nurture my body and spirit when I need it most.

A special thank you to Tom Grace, for your care in recent months.

To my Anam Cairde companions, your listening presence so often blessed and soothed my wounded soul.

I also want to particularly thank the medicine women of my Céile Dé: Martina, Karen, Mary and Maire. You cannot know how much our time together meant to me.

Gracias to Patsy and Michael O'Brien, Lanzarote, who descended like angels of light into my life during my recent stay on the island.

Thank you also to Terrie Loughlin and her team who interviewed me in Lanzarote for the launch and to Fionnuala Gill for her beautiful musical contribution.

Certain people have breathed and walked with me on my life's journey, and your hidden faces are ever present between the lines of my unfolding story.

I have immense gratitude for the many friends who have been holding me in prayer since my cancer diagnosis; I have indeed been carried on the wings of your prayers.

Om shanti, shanti.
Peace and blessings to all my readers.

*Ann Maria,*
*January 2021.*

# AUTHOR BIOGRAPHY

Ann Maria Dunne was born in the United States, to Irish parents, and grew up in Dublin. After the untimely death of her husband, Andrew Dunne, Ann Maria began a search for meaning in her life. She founded Ireland's first holistic retreat centre, Chrysalis, in County Wicklow.

Ann Maria has a law degree, trained in spiritual direction, psychotherapy, group dynamics, neuro-linguistic programming, cosmic energy healing, and acting, and she is a qualified mindfulness teacher.

Ann Maria was diagnosed with breast cancer in 2008, which recurred in 2016. She continues to live a full and active life in Donard, County Wicklow, Ireland.